Italian and Italian American Studies
Stanislao G. Pugliese
Hofstra University
Series Editor

This publishing initiative seeks to bring the latest scholarship in Italian and Italian American history, literature, cinema, and cultural studies to a large audience of specialists, general readers, and students. I&IAS will feature works on modern Italy (Renaissance to the present) and Italian American culture and society by established scholars as well as new voices in the academy. This endeavor will help to shape the evolving fields of Italian and Italian American Studies by reemphasizing the connection between the two. The following editorial board consists of esteemed senior scholars who act as advisors to the series editor.

REBECCA WEST
University of Chicago

JOSEPHINE GATTUSO HENDIN
New York University

FRED GARDAPHÉ
Queens College, CUNY

PHILIP V. CANNISTRARO†
Queens College and the Graduate School, CUNY

ALESSANDRO PORTELLI
Università di Roma "La Sapienza"

Queer Italia: Same-Sex Desire in Italian Literature and Film
  edited by Gary P. Cestaro, July 2004
Frank Sinatra: History, Identity, and Italian American Culture
  edited by Stanislao G. Pugliese, October 2004
The Legacy of Primo Levi
  edited by Stanislao G. Pugliese, December 2004
Italian Colonialism
  edited by Ruth Ben-Ghiat and Mia Fuller, July 2005
Mussolini's Rome: Rebuilding the Eternal City
  Borden W. Painter Jr., July 2005
Representing Sacco and Vanzetti
  edited by Jerome H. Delamater and Mary Anne Trasciatti, September 2005
Carlo Tresca: Portrait of a Rebel
  Nunzio Pernicone, October 2005
Italy in the Age of Pinocchio: Children and Danger in the Liberal Era
  Carl Ipsen, April 2006
The Empire of Stereotypes: Germaine de Staël and the Idea of Italy
  Robert Casillo, May 2006
Race and the Nation in Liberal Italy, 1861–1911: Meridionalism, Empire, and Diaspora
  Aliza S. Wong, October 2006
Women in Italy, 1945–1960: An Interdisciplinary Study
  edited by Penelope Morris, October 2006
Debating Divorce in Italy: Marriage and the Making of Modern Italians, 1860–1974
  Mark Seymour, December 2006

A New Guide to Italian Cinema
    Carlo Celli and Marga Cottino-Jones, January 2007
Human Nature in Rural Tuscany: An Early Modern History
    Gregory Hanlon, March 2007
The Missing Italian Nuremberg: Cultural Amnesia and Postwar Politics
    Michele Battini, September 2007
Assassinations and Murder in Modern Italy: Transformations in Society and Culture
    edited by Stephen Gundle and Lucia Rinaldi, October 2007
Piero Gobetti and the Politics of Liberal Revolution
    James Martin, December 2008
Primo Levi and Humanism after Auschwitz: Posthumanist Reflections
    Jonathan Druker, June 2009
Oral History, Oral Culture, and Italian Americans
    edited by Luisa Del Giudice, November 2009
Italy's Divided Memory
    John Foot, January 2010
Women, Desire, and Power in Italian Cinema
    Marga Cottino-Jone, March 2010
The Failure of Italian Nationhood: The Geopolitics of a Troubled Identity
    Manlio Graziano, September 2010
Women and the Great War: Femininity under Fire in Italy
    Allison Scardino Belzer, October 2010
Italian Jews from Emancipation to the Racial Laws
    Cristina M. Bettin, November 2010
Anti-Italianism: Essays on a Prejudice
    edited by William J. Connell and Fred Gardaphé, January 2011
Murder and Media in the New Rome: The Fadda Affair
    Thomas Simpson, January 2011
Mohamed Fekini and the Fight to Free Libya
    Angelo Del Boca; translated by Antony Shugaar, January 2011
City and Nation in the Italian Unification: The National Festivals of Dante Alighieri
    Mahnaz Yousefzadeh, April 2011
The Legacy of the Italian Resistance
    Philip Cooke, May 2011
New Reflections on Primo Levi: Before and After Auschwitz
    edited by Risa Sodi and Millicent Marcus, July 2011
Italy on the Pacific: San Francisco's Italian Americans
    Sebastian Fichera, December 2011
Memory and Massacre: Revisiting Sant'Anna di Stazzema
    Paolo Pezzino, translated by Noor Giovanni Mazhar, February 2012
In the Society of Fascists: Acclamation, Acquiescence, and Agency in Mussolini's Italy
    edited by Giulia Albanese and Roberta Pergher, September 2012
Carlo Levi's Visual Poetics: The Painter as Writer
    Giovanna Faleschini Lerner, October 2012

Carlo Levi's Visual Poetics

Carlo Levi's Visual Poetics

The Painter as Writer

Giovanna Faleschini Lerner

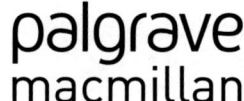

CARLO LEVI'S VISUAL POETICS
Copyright © Giovanna Faleschini Lerner, 2012.

All rights reserved.

An earlier version of the Introduction was published as "Carlo Levi's New Humanism" in *Annali d'italianistica* 26 (2008): 283–97 and is hereby published by permission of *Annali d'italianistica*.

Some parts of Chapter 1 appeared in "Francesco Rosi's Cristo si è fermato a Eboli: Toward a Cinema of Painting," *Italica* 86.2 (2009): 272–92, and are hereby included by permission of Indiana University—*Italica*.

An earlier version of Chapter 2 was published as "Carlo Levi's L'Orologio: A Revolution in Words and Images," in *Creative Interventions: The Role of the Intellectual in Contemporary Italian Culture*, eds. Eugenio Bolongaro, Rita Gagliano, and Mark Epstein (Newcastle upon Tyne, UK: Cambridge Scholars Publishing, 2009) 63–91, and is hereby published with the permission of Cambridge Scholars Publishing.

First published in 2012 by PALGRAVE MACMILLAN® in the United States—a division of St. Martin's Press LLC, 175 Fifth Avenue, New York, NY 10010.

Where this book is distributed in the UK, Europe and the rest of the world, this is by Palgrave Macmillan, a division of Macmillan Publishers Limited, registered in England, company number 785998, of Houndmills, Basingstoke, Hampshire RG21 6XS.

Palgrave Macmillan is the global academic imprint of the above companies and has companies and representatives throughout the world.

Palgrave® and Macmillan® are registered trademarks in the United States, the United Kingdom, Europe and other countries.

ISBN: 978-0-230-39064-5

Library of Congress Cataloging-in-Publication Data

Lerner, Giovanna Faleschini, 1972–
  Carlo Levi's visual poetics : the painter as writer / Giovanna Faleschini Lerner.
    p. cm. — (Italian and Italian American studies)
  ISBN 978-0-230-39064-5 (hardback)
  1. Levi, Carlo, 1902–1975—Criticism and interpretation. I. Title.

PQ4827.E93Z69 2012
858'.91409—dc23   2012013262

A catalogue record of the book is available from the British Library.

Design by Scribe Inc.

First edition: October 2012

10 9 8 7 6 5 4 3 2 1

Printed in the United States of America.

Per Miriam e Daniele

Contents

List of Illustrations	xi
Acknowledgments	xiii
Preface: Carlo Levi's Visual Poetics: The Painter as Writer	xv
Introduction: Carlo Levi's New Humanism	1
1 The Magic of Painting in *Cristo si è fermato a Eboli*	21
2 *L'Orologio*: The Challenge of Time	53
3 Portraits of the South in *Le parole sono pietre* and *Tutto il miele è finito*	85
4 *Quaderno a cancelli*: The Space of Memory	125
Notes	153
Works Cited	171
Index	183

Illustrations

Cover image	"Portrait of Carlo Levi," Library of Congress, Prints and Photographs Division, Carl Van Vechten Collection, LC-USZ62-131771	
Figure 1	Carlo Levi, *Grassano come Gerusalemme* (1935)	29
Figure 2	Carlo Levi, *Il ritratto della madre* (1930)	31
Figure 3	Carlo Levi, *L'eroe cinese* (1932)	32
Figure 4	Carlo Levi, *Giulia la Santarcangelese (Ritratto di Giulia Venere)* (1935)	40
Figure 5	Carlo Levi, *La Santarcangelese* (1936)	42
Figure 6	Carlo Levi, *Ritratto del dottore* (1936)	43
Figure 7	Carlo Levi, *Ritratto di Rocco Scotellaro* (1952)	93
Figure 8	Carlo Levi, *Lamento per Rocco Scotellaro* (1953)	95
Figure 9	Carlo Levi, *Le parole sono pietre* (1955)	102
Figure 10	Carlo Levi, *Ritratto di Danilo Dolci* (1956)	103
Figure 11	Carlo Levi, *La porta del sud* (1953)	105
Figure 12	Carlo Levi, *Lucania '61* (1961)	120
Figure 13	Mario Carbone, Lucanian woman on a donkey (1961)	121
Figure 14	Mario Carbone, Lucanian woman with two children (1961)	122
Figure 15	Carlo Levi, *Narciso* (May 8, 1973)	140
Figure 16	Carlo Levi, *Gli Amanti* (1973)	142
Figure 17	Carlo Levi, *Perdita della madre* (February 21, 1973)	146
Figure 18	Carlo Levi, *Perdita dell'immortalità* (March 19, 1973)	147

Acknowledgments

This book could have never come to completion without the support of many people and institutions over the course of several years. At the University of Pennsylvania, Penny Marcus believed in this project before anyone else and encouraged me to pursue it with passion and rigor. Victoria Kirkham, Kevin Brownlee, Stefano Cracolici, and Fabio Finotti were scrupulous and insightful readers.

Many friends and colleagues listened patiently as I sorted out my thoughts, and carefully read drafts of chapters and sections in various stages. Among them, I owe thanks to Meg Greenberg, Georgina Torello and Riccardo Boglione, Fabiana Cecchini, and Deborah Amberson. Paola Bonifazio, Silvia Carlorosi, and Nicoletta Marini-Maio were particularly influential in shaping the direction of my analysis in Chapter 3; Eugenio Bolongaro, Mark Epstein, and Rita Gagliano offered useful advice on Chapter 4, and Valeria Castelli helped me with the very last revisions to this chapter. Elena Past read everything multiple times and always made it better. I owe her more than I can begin to say.

I am grateful to my friends and colleagues at Franklin & Marshall for modeling the difficult balance between teaching and scholarship. Thanks to Alan Caniglia and Kim Armstrong, who, as chairs of the Italian Department at different moments, always made sure I had enough time to think and write. Thanks to Anna Maria Bertini-Jones, Daniela Ciceri, and Gianluca Rizzo for presenting wonderful examples of collegiality. Angela Jeannet always offered words of encouragement. Particular thanks go to Genevieve Abravanel, Kabi Hartman, and Emily Huber for providing me with the discipline to get things done; to Gretchen Meyers for our *sacrosanti* Wednesday lunches; to Carrie Landfried and Jon Stone for accepting my invitation. Thanks for their generous friendship (and help with child care) to Tama Goodman and Matt Hoffman, Maria Mitchell and Guillaume de Syon, Lisa and Rafe Knox, Maya Greenshpan and Marco Di Giulio. As always, thank you to Kathy and Jim Spencer and Joel Eigen, on whose friendship and support I know I can always count.

A Salvatori summer research grant from the Center for Italian Studies at the University of Pennsylvania in 2001, followed by a departmental research award in 2003, allowed me to conduct research in Matera and Aliano as well as at the Archivio Centrale dello Stato, the Biblioteca Nazionale Centrale in Rome, where the staff was extremely helpful, and at the Fondazione Carlo Levi, where the indefatigable Dr. Antonella Lavorgna was an endless source of information, references, and advice. Thanks to faculty research funds from Franklin & Marshall, I later completed archival research at the Centro di ricerca sulla tradizione manoscritta di autori moderni e contemporanei at the University of Pavia, at the library and museum in Alassio, and in the Archivio di Stato in Turin. Funds from the Committee on Grants allowed me to hire an excellent research assistant, Gina Mangravite, who carefully checked every page reference and translation in the manuscript. I also owe huge thanks to the provost, Ann Steiner, to Alan Caniglia, and to Dean Michael Billig for providing the funds necessary for the illustrations in the book.

For her help in navigating the complexities of copyright laws, I must thank Lexi Kadlec at the Artist Rights Society in New York. Thank you to Ms. Marta Ragozzino and Ms. Pina De Leo at the Soprintendenza per i Beni Storici, Artistici ed Etnoantropologici della Basilicata for providing various images and to Roberto Carbone of the Archivio Mario Carbone for generously allowing to reproduce Mario Carbone's photos. I am also grateful to Donato Sperduto and Daniela Bartalesi-Graf for their practical suggestions.

Gregory Pell, who first suggested that I discuss my project with Stanislao Pugliese at Palgrave Macmillan, deserves more recognition than I can give him here. At Palgrave, thank you to Stan Pugliese, who believed in and encouraged this project through an exacting and extremely helpful review process, to the wonderfully patient and supportive editor Brigitte Shull, and to her assistants, Jo Roberts and Maia Woolner.

Finally, I must thank my grandmother, Silvia Albini, and my parents, Renzo and Graziella Faleschini, for believing in the life of the mind; my siblings, Diego, Donata, and Giulio Paolo, for putting up with me; my in-laws, Gwen and Irv Lerner, for being there every time I needed them. Thank you to Miriam and Daniele, who kept everything in perspective. And, as always, thank you to Scott, without whom none of this would have happened.

Preface

Carlo Levi's Visual Poetics: The Painter as Writer

> Levi era soprattutto pittore, e lo era anche quando scriveva e quando parlava ... Cominciò a scrivere *Cristo s'è fermato a Eboli* a matita come se disegnasse, con un tratto ampio e agile, arrestandosi di tanto in tanto per porre mano ai pennelli, e riprendendo più avanti la matita come se lo scrivere e il dipingere fossero parti dello stesso discorso ininterrotto.
>
> *Levi was above all a painter, and he remained one even when he wrote or spoke ... He began writing* Christ Stopped at Eboli *with a pencil, as though he were drawing, with broad and light gestures, and he stopped once in a while to pick up the paint brush, later taking the pencil again, as though writing and painting were part of the same uninterrupted discourse.*
>
> —Manlio Cancogni

It has become almost commonplace, among Carlo Levi's scholars, to maintain that Levi was essentially a painter and that he remained such even as a writer. Manlio Cancogni's observation that "Levi era soprattutto pittore, e lo era anche quando scriveva e quando parlava" ["Levi was above all a painter, and he remained one even when he wrote or spoke"][1] is often quoted in this regard. This book constitutes an attempt to understand what this claim means. This is not, therefore, a book about Levi's painting but an examination of the relationship between visual and verbal forms of representation *in his writing*. What does it mean for a painter, I ask, to remain a visual artist when engaged in another form of artistic expression? How does the intersection of literature and painting play out in Levi's texts? What are the stylistic consequences of this intersection? In which ways does the dialogue between verbal and visual forms of representation emerge in Levi's literary work?

The question of word/image relations has been the object of intellectual inquiry for centuries. In the first recorded example of interart comparison, Simonides of Ceos is reported as stating that painting is "mute poetry" and poetry is a "speaking picture." By underscoring the deficiency of painting in comparison to poetry, his claim establishes a hierarchical relationship between them and makes manifest the competitive nature of the relationship between visual and linguistic semiotic systems. Such antagonism is so fundamental that it is always present, according to W. J. T. Mitchell, "in the fabric of signs that a culture weaves around itself" (Mitchell, *Iconology* 43). The entire history of Western culture, Mitchell maintains, could be rewritten as the story of a struggle for dominance between pictorial and linguistic signs (43). This question remains particularly pertinent to postmodern culture, as Mitchell has argued persuasively in *Picture Theory*. Mitchell describes the increasing concern with the role of images as a "visual turn" in critical theory. This visual (or pictorial) turn is "not a return to naïve mimesis, copy or correspondence theories of representation, or a renewed metaphysics of pictorial 'presence': it is rather a postlinguistic, postsemiotic rediscovery of the picture as a complex interplay between visuality, apparatus, institutions, discourse, bodies, and figurality" (16). In interart criticism, therefore, it is necessary to move beyond the simple comparison between systems of representation, in order to engage its ethical, ideological, and political implications.

What are, then, the ideological, as well as aesthetic, implications of the interplay of iconic and verbal systems of signification in Levi's work as a writer? Where does he stand in regard to the rivalry between word and image? In seeking an answer to these questions, I examine Levi's most significant narrative texts and essays. My study includes the "philosophical poem" *Paura della libertà* (*Fear of Freedom*, 1946), the memoir *Cristo si è fermato a Eboli* (*Christ Stopped at Eboli*, 1945), the novel *L'Orologio* (*The Watch*, 1950), the two travel exposés, *Le parole sono pietre* (*Words Are Stones*, 1955) and *Tutto il miele è finito* ("All the honey is gone," 1964), and, lastly, the "zibaldone" *Quaderno a cancelli* ("Notebook with bars," 1979). Through close readings of these texts, I propose a new interpretive key to Levi's writings, arguing that the nexus of visual and verbal expression is at the core of his "visual poetics." Levi's painterly vocation manifests itself in his writing through a visual use of language characterized by an impulse toward ekphrasis, both in its strict sense of verbal representation of a work of art and as a broader principle that emphasizes vision and spatiality over temporality. The visual drive of Levi's writing introduces a productive tension between description and narration that is characteristic of his whole literary corpus. I suggest that, through this visual poetics, Levi articulates the relationship between verbal and visual modes of representation as a complex dialogue, whose terms are constantly redefined and renegotiated in his writings. The complexity of the interaction between word and image, moreover, foregrounds Levi's interest in the issue of representation itself, with its important corollaries regarding power and influence. Levi's concern with the question of authority and power grounds his visual poetics in an ongoing reflection on the ethics of representation, which he explores in the essays *Paura della libertà* and "Paura della pittura" (1942) as well as in other philosophical and political writings. For the humanist Levi, aesthetic choices are never devoid of ideological and ethical implications, for art is inevitably *engagé*, and the artist bears a burden of responsibility toward both his audience and the subjects of his representation.

Levi's cultural project is based on a profound ethical commitment to the Other, which takes artistic form precisely in the interplay between word and image that he establishes in his texts. By adopting ekphrasis as the dominant trope of his literary production he opens the language of literature to its Other, the pictorial sign. In *Cristo si è fermato a Eboli*, the dialogic quality that his writing assumes by constantly interacting with painting expresses on the level of style a political and cultural project that would make it possible for North and South, historic progression and mythical time, to achieve the national unity that the Risorgimento failed to accomplish. In *L'Orologio*, Levi's visual poetics institutes a productive dialogue between the temporal dimension of the verbal narrative and the spatial quality of the image, which subverts traditional forms of narration and operates, on the level of form, the social revolution that historically the Italian Resistance movement was unable to achieve. In his travel accounts, Levi pushes to the limits the descriptive qualities inherent in the genre of travel writing by recreating in language landscape scenes or verbal portraits of the peoples he encounters. Finally, *Quaderno a cancelli* records the author's intimate dialogue with the self-as-other, which takes place both in writing and through the visual media of drawing and painting. The dialogue between painting and writing that can be identified as a constant formal and substantive thread in Levi's writings fulfills his need for a coherence between all aspects of his intellectual activity—a need that, in turn, derives from his humanistic cultural philosophy.

Titled "Carlo Levi's New Humanism," the introductory chapter aims to contextualize Levi's intellectual project through a reading of his major theoretical texts, *Paura della libertà* and "Paura della pittura," as well as other philosophical essays. Although humanism is the guiding ideal of all his cultural activity, Levi avoids giving a clear definition of the concept, which he shapes and develops in ongoing dialogue with the great European intellectuals of his time. Influenced by Piero Gobetti's humanistic rejection of positivist determinism, Levi's thinking is close to Jean-Paul Sartre's engaged existentialism but also shares Martin Heidegger's faith in the power of art and language. In this chapter, I argue that through the dialogic inclusiveness of his philosophical approach, Levi is able to accommodate the contradictions and paradoxes of these positions and create an original definition of humanism. Essential in the development of Levi's humanist philosophy is the mediation of Giambattista Vico's organic thought and a concern for the Other that anticipates—and can be illuminated by—Emmanuel Levinas's "humanism of the Other."

Levi explicitly traces his fascination with otherness back to his discovery of southern Italian culture during his political confinement in Lucania in 1935–36. In *Cristo si è fermato a Eboli* Levi reconstructs his encounter with another world, locked in the eternal repetition of its cyclical traditions, whose ahistoricity and immobility contrasts with the progressive mentality of his native Turin. As I show in Chapter 1, "The Magic of Painting in *Cristo si è fermato a Eboli*" in the face of this diversity, Levi rejects the position of "un conquistatore o un nemico o un visitatore incomprensivo" ["an enemy, a conqueror, or a visitor devoid of understanding"] and instead recognizes in the agrarian civilization of the South a critical position from which to judge modernity (*Cristo* 4, 4). In order to break through to the mythical mentality of Lucanian peasants, Levi must recognize the limitations of Enlightenment thought and adopt another approach—a "magic key," as he writes, that would allow him to open the door to a world in which everything hides a magic aspect. In this chapter, I show how Levi uses his painting as the magic key that allows him to overcome the restrictions of rationalism and embrace cultural difference. Painting is, thus, instrumental to Levi's epistemological approach to Lucania. But the desire to know and represent the Other, whether in visual or verbal forms, also raises, for Levi, the problem of power—a problem he confronts explicitly in describing the act of violence he resorts to in order to persuade his housekeeper to pose for a portrait. The episode illustrates the conundrum of representation for Levi as an engaged, northern intellectual who wants to give voice to the southern peasants. By depicting them in words and images, Levi gives recognition to their civilization and empowers them as actors in the historical process, from which they have been traditionally excluded. At the same time, he necessarily imposes upon them a form, fixes the flux of their experiences in an image of his own making, and thus exercises a type of authority over their lives. The challenge implicit in Levi's painting and writing about Lucania finds its stylistic equivalent in his visual poetics. His visual style in fact introduces an element of dialogic instability into his narration, which shifts constantly between the spatial quality of the image and the development of a narrative temporality. Levi's writing thus reflects the paradox of representing the peasants' cultural resistance to a progressive sense of time, their magical thinking, while at the same time introducing them into the flow of history precisely through the act of representation.

Levi's problematization of time and history as progressive forces continues explicitly in the 1950 novel *L'Orologio*, which is the object of inquiry in Chapter 2. At the beginning of the novel, the watch of the title breaks, causing the category of linear time to collapse. In its stead, a circular temporality of memory and self-investigation imposes itself, calling into question the linearity of the plot by constantly interrupting it with digressive pauses, flashbacks and apocalyptic vaticinations. Levi's main instrument to achieve this powerful destabilization of narrative is, again, his ekphrastic writing. The dialogic tension between temporal and spatial dimensions that his pictorial style introduces repeatedly challenges and hinders the unfolding of consecutive temporality. In *L'Orologio*, as in *Cristo si è fermato a Eboli*, Levi's aesthetics are never severed from his political concerns. By questioning the very possibility of progress and change, he laments and denounces the failure of the Resistance movement to fulfill its revolutionary promises and radically transform Italian society after World War II.

If Levi's poetics of the visual constitutes a stylistic thread in his literary production, a thematic one is the image of the journey. All Levi's writings are, in some measure, travel literature. *Cristo si è fermato a Eboli* has been connected to the tradition of ethnographic journeys of discovery; *L'Orologio*'s main character takes a literal trip from Florence to (and through) Rome and later to Naples; *Quaderno a cancelli* is a more modernist journey into the self. Levi also wrote travel pieces for *La Stampa* and published travel books, which I examine in the third chapter, "Portraits of the South in *Le parole sono pietre* and *Tutto il miele è finito*." These texts embody the paradox of Levi's visual poetics. On the one hand, through a highly visual language Levi intensifies the descriptive nature of the travel genre, reproducing in words natural and urban landscapes, human faces, and animal forms. On the other, their narratives reproduce the traveler's movement in space, demonstrating a dynamicity that other books by Levi do not have. Levi's renewed attention to narrative movement reflects the changes that occurred in the South between his first contact with its culture, under fascist rule, and the 1950s, when he visited Sicily and Sardinia during the height of the agrarian reform. His writings witness the struggle of Sicilian and Sardinian mine workers and agricultural laborers, armed with a newly acquired class consciousness, to conquer for themselves a place in a history that for centuries had effectively excluded them, and his style reflects a more optimistic outlook toward historical progress.

This optimism translated, in the 1950s and 1960s, in Levi's political activism as a senator and the founder of the FILEF, the Italian federation of emigrants and their families. Levi believed that the South had suffered tremendously from the hemorrhage of workers that had left it for northern Europe and the Americas, and knew how these emigrants felt, alienated and abandoned by the state once they left the country. In 1973, Levi underwent surgery for a detached retina. During his hospitalization, Levi kept a private diary, which represents a *unicum* in his production, for he abandoned the realist mode in favor of quasi-surrealist self-analysis. Unable to observe the world outside, he turned his gaze inward to detect the landscape of his soul. Even the drawings from this period are completely new in terms of style and subject. Some of them are situated at the verge of abstraction, while others obsessively explore the symbolic dream-images of the owl, the lovers, Narcissus, or the Birmanian warrior. These images appear insistently in his writing as well and seem to spring from the innermost dimension of Levi's psyche. This is the originality of *Quaderno a cancelli*, where the imagistic and verbal dimensions are engaged in constant dialogue, aimed at exploring the author's own self. Yet as I argue in the final chapter, titled "*Quaderno a cancelli*: The Space of Memory," even this quasi-surrealist book, which explores the realm of dreams, memories, and visions, does not represent a retreat from extra-artistic reality. On the contrary, the book's last words, "I wake up again," signal Levi's return to an active engagement with the social, political, and cultural reality of his time, a form of *impegno* constantly nourished and sustained by his enduring faith in the possibility of creating "a new humanism."

to Natalino Sapegno and Carlo Levi. In turn, Benedetto Croce, Gaetano Salvemini, and Luigi Einaudi were fundamental to Gobetti's own formation. Gobetti admired Croce's resistance to the deterministic approaches of nineteenth-century positivism and his faith in the individual's potential for creativity (Ward, *Piero Gobetti* 19). From Croce he also learned the passion for a humanistic totality of vision that Levi considers the most attractive and singular feature of Gobetti's intellect (Levi, "Piero Gobetti" 86). Gobetti read avidly and absorbed anything of value that contemporary manifestations of Italian culture could offer. His desire for a unifying cultural perspective, as well as his energy and drive, were charismatic for many budding intellectuals, who surrounded him in a free school of self-education (94) characterized by a constant exchange of ideas and strong intellectual friendships. Politically, Gobetti embraced a liberalism that encouraged creative forms of political action, involving the popular masses in active and autonomous historical agency (98). Never a Communist, he nonetheless admired Antonio Gramsci and his work with the factory councils in Turin, which he saw as proof of the leading role that the industrial working class must take to effect political reform (Martin 49).[9] His liberalism implied a passion for freedom and autonomy in its broadest terms and was thus naturally opposed to fascism, which for Gobetti was "l'ultima e più totale espressione dell'incapacità alla libertà degli italiani" ["the ultimate and most complete expression of the Italian inability to be free"] (Levi, "Piero Gobetti" 102). In this respect, he departed from Croce's understanding of fascism as a temporary national illness and claimed instead that Mussolini's form of totalitarianism was nothing but the "autobiography of the Italian nation," the direct consequence of Italians' anxieties in the face of civic passion and responsibility (Levi, "Seconda lettera" 53). To the Italians' fear of freedom, Levi countered "[l]a libertà, l'aspro, consapevole sforzo di autonomia, [che] costituiscono l'unità della figura di Gobetti, sia nella sua vita morale, sia nel suo pensiero, sia nella sua azione politica" ["the freedom, the harsh, conscious effort to be independent (which) constitute the unity of Gobetti's figure, in his moral life, thought, and political action"] ("Piero Gobetti" 86).

Like Gobetti, Levi rejected determinism and embraced a view of man as the center and subject of history in his search for freedom (Marcovecchio 100). In this sense, Levi's outlook is close to the idea of humanism proposed by another influential figure of European thought, Jean-Paul Sartre. Levi and Sartre met in Paris and remained friends for their entire lives.[10] The French philosopher consistently recognized in Levi's work the same engagement with human existence that he proposed as the essence of existentialism as a form of humanism. According to Sartre, Levi's curiosity for human experience emerged from a passion for life that allowed him to recognize the value of every lived experience. His multifaceted activity as a doctor, writer, and artist was motivated by the same respect for life that gave unity to his work as an intellectual and as a politician (Sartre, "L'universale singolare" 259). Sartre's words about Levi parallel the French philosopher's argument in defense of existentialism in *The Humanism of Existentialism*. Despite existentialism's distrust of the positivistic optimism toward history and faith in progress, Sartre wrote, far from encouraging a withdrawal from social reality existentialist philosophy demanded of man a full engagement with the world, since "man is nothing else than what he makes of himself" (*Humanism* 18). Man bears full responsibility for his own destiny and for the destiny of all humanity. It is the burden of this responsibility that generates the angst that existentialism recognizes as profoundly human (21–22). Rather than freezing man into inaction, however, this existential anguish pushes him toward a full engagement with life (25).

Discussions about humanism were an essential part of postwar European philosophical debates. Particularly important was the *querelle* between Sartre and Martin Heidegger.[11] In reaction to Sartre's representation of existentialism as a form of humanism—and his enthusiastic appropriation of Heidegger's thought—Heidegger published his own *Letter on Humanism*, in which he condemned the humanistic man-centered position as the worst crime of Western philosophy since Plato. In the letter, the German philosopher claimed that all the evils of the modern world, from capitalism to communism, derived from the humanistic "anthropologization" of Being. Unlike Sartre, Heidegger stayed ostensibly clear of politics and political engagement. Indeed, "[t]he language of the Letter extricates thought from action" (Rabinbach 9)—a political statement in itself, as many readers have observed, which Heidegger conceived as a strategy to exonerate himself from his involvement with National Socialism since the early 1930s.[12] Although Levi remained suspicious of what he perceived as Heidegger's dangerously irresponsible antihumanist relativism, his critical and theoretical writings resonate deeply with the philosopher's reevaluation of poetic language and art. In this introductory chapter I propose that, through his multifarious and even paradoxical discussions of *umanesimo*, Levi in effect delineates a productive middle ground between Sartre's and Heidegger's contrasting views of humanism. Levi's philosophy, as it emerges in his more theoretical works, is based on a reinterpretation of Giambattista Vico's thought—which, as Ernesto Grassi writes, represents the height of Italian humanism[13]—and is rooted in a profoundly ethical concern for the Other that anticipates, in many ways, Emmanuel Levinas's "humanism of the Other."[14] I maintain that this concern for the Other lies at the core of Levi's intellectual project and that a careful examination of Levi's humanism opens new perspectives on his work as a painter and a writer.

Levi elaborated his philosophy of history for the first time in the essay *Paura della libertà*, which he wrote while in exile in France in 1939 and the intellectual roots of which he traced back to his experience of political confinement in Lucania a few years earlier (*Cristo* xix). In Lawrence Baldassaro's felicitous phrase, this essay constitutes the "unfinished preface" to the whole of Levi's work (143). In this *poema filosofico*,[15] written in a Biblical style and pervaded by echoes of Vichian thought, Levi formulates an analysis of the moral and intellectual crisis of interwar Europe, indirectly constructing a "theory of Nazism" without ever mentioning it.[16] Levi's perspective in *Paura della libertà* is not socioeconomic or specifically political. Rather, like Albert Camus, he is interested in tracing the roots of totalitarianism in the depths of the human psyche (Farrell 12). His point of departure is the distinction between *sacro* and *religioso*, the sacred and the religious. All human beings possess a metaphysical sense of the sacred, an awareness of the transcendent and of their connectedness with totality. The sacred is associated with the feminine as the source of all life. It is all-encompassing and thus paradoxical in nature, at once the "oscura continua negazione della libertà e dell'arte" and the "generatore continuo della libertà e dell'arte" ["continuous dark denial of freedom and art," and the "continuous creation of art and freedom"] (*Paura della libertà* 132, *Fear of Freedom* 1). The sacred is linked to original chaos, to undifferentiation, and to the ineffable, and as such it generates awe. Normative religion is born of the attempt to banish this awe. Religion belongs to the realm of rationalism insofar as it transforms the unknowable and the unspeakable into concrete facts and words. It turns myths into rites, institutionalizing human experience, from erotic desire to death, and assigning to each a precise function within its system. For Levi, religion is a "[r]elegazione del dio nel legame delle formule, delle evocazioni, delle preghiere, perché non sfugga, secondo la sua inafferrabile natura" ["(r)elegation of a god into a web of formulas, conjurations, invocations, prayers, so that he may not, as is his way, elude us"] (132, 1). Religion replaces transcendence with visible symbols, in contrast to the sacred, which is the trembling and reverent acceptance of the awesome mystery of existence (134–35).

If every religion is aimed at controlling and limiting the elusiveness of the sacred, the first strategy employed to achieve this aim is turning the sacred into the sacrificial. Through the institution of sacrifice, religion imposes a rule upon the sacred, thus exorcising the threat against the social order that its incommensurability represents.[17] Similarly, desire is regulated through the institution of marriage, whose purpose is the reinforcement of paternal law. Language, as well, is deprived of its creative purpose in order to assume an exclusively denotative value. Religion is, then, opposed to poetic language, where the sacred finds expression in a form that asserts human freedom and creativity. In sum, "[r]eligione è la sostituzione all'inesprimibile indifferenziato di simboli, di immagini reali e concrete, in modo da relegare il sacro fuori della coscienza" ["(t)he way of religion is to substitute that which is undifferentiated and inexpressible with concrete images and symbols—so that the sacred may be cast out of our consciousness"] (135, 4).

The paternalistic rule imposed by religion finds its secular form of expression in the worship of the state and the consequent transformation of the individual into an anonymous element of the masses. The state appropriates the institutions established by religion and utilizes them as equally effective instruments of power. The attraction that the masses feel for authoritarian regimes is nothing but the equivalent of their allegiance to organized religion as "a means of avoiding the fear of confrontation with the self, without which there can be no sense of identity or freedom" (Baldassaro 147). Levi's contempt toward the masses is tantamount to Gobetti's own feelings toward those that he considered "sheep, slaves, non-beings" (Ward, *Piero Gobetti* 33), which moved him to take as the motto for his press the Greek phrase "Ti moi syn doilisin?" ("What do I have in common with slaves?"). But it is precisely in this discussion that Levi's shift from the Kantian intellectual framework that defined Gobetti's thinking to a more organic, Vichian perspective emerges.[18] It is in *Paura della libertà* that Levi first explores the limits of rationalistic thought and manifests his interest in psychoanalysis. He returns to these themes in "Crisi di civiltà," an article published in 1944 in *La Nazione del popolo*, where he exposes the ultimate inability of rationality to conquer the unconscious drives of the human soul, which, when repressed, eventually explode into the monstrous and idolatrous ideals that Nazism and fascism incarnate:

> Il nazismo, e il fascismo ... furono una rivolta interna delle forze irrazionali compresse in questo mondo sclerosato ... Di fronte a un mondo inaridito di sola ragione essi suscitarono dal profondo dell'incosciente collettivo gli antichi mostri, gli spaventosi idoli del sangue e della razza. Era il rovescio della medaglia: il mondo sotterraneo degli istinti caotici e della disperazione senza forma che si agitava sotto quell'altro mondo tutto determinato, ottimista e progressivo. (62)

> *Nazism and fascism ... were the internal revolt of irrational powers trampled in this rigid world ... Facing an arid world, based on reason alone, they resuscitated the ancient monsters, the fearsome idols of blood and race from the depths of the collective unconscious. It was the other side of the coin: the subterranean world of chaotic instinct and shapeless desperation, which was simmering under the other, determined, optimist, and progressive world.*

The optimistic rationalism that characterized Western civilization at the beginning of the twentieth century failed to recognize the presence, in the human mind, of instinctive impulses and unconscious desires. It chose to ignore, in other words, the existence of irrationality, thus censoring an essential part of human experience.[19] The only remedy to the limitations of rationalism and the consequent enslavement to authoritarian states is art:

> L'arte è totalità, perché in lei nascono insieme il momento dell'indifferenziato e quello del particolare, l'abisso vi prende forma senza diminuirsi, la passione vi si esprime senza urlo, l'uomo vi è intero, senza legami, sufficiente a se stesso. Non esiste dunque, a rigore, un'arte religiosa: contraddizione in termini. L'arte risolve in sé senza residui tutto il mondo morale e religioso, e i territori vaghi del senso e del sentimento. E, in quanto la religione si racconti [sic] in miti poetici, essa è poesia, e non è più religione. (*Paura della libertà* 165)

> *Art is a totality, for both the element of indeterminateness and that of particularity originate there, and the abyss takes shape without losing depth, and passion expresses itself without howling, and man appears entire, unfettered, sufficient unto himself. Strictly speaking, there is no religious art: to say there is would be a contradiction in terms. Art resolves within itself, without residue, the entire moral and religious world, as well as the vague areas of sentiment and feeling. And, whenever religion is told in terms of poetical myth, it is mere poetry, and no longer religion. (43–44)*

Art is thus the only guarantee of freedom, as Levi further argues in "Paura della pittura," where he applies to painting the philosophical, political, and linguistic principles explored in *Paura della libertà*.

The origins of "Paura della pittura" can be traced to 1935, when Levi was arrested and briefly detained in the Roman prison of Regina Coeli. In a letter to his family, he outlined his plan to write a book on modern painting. He did not intend the book to be an exercise in erudition, a work of historiography, philosophy, or even criticism. Levi was interested in creating an "autobiografia pittorica, delle confessioni proiettate nel tempo, un racconto di viaggio attraverso un mondo tutto reale che è quello delle idee e dei sentimenti" ["a pictorial autobiography, a series of confessions, projected in time, the narrative of a journey through the completely real world of ideas and feelings"] (*È questo il carcer tetro?* 124). In writing, he would rely exclusively on his memory, which would lend unity and coherence to a "disordinatissimo" and chaotic text that would contain poems in addition to prose with many drawings to illustrate it (125). The book was partially realized in "Paura della pittura," in which Levi proposes an analysis of modern painting—from Cézanne to Picasso to the apocalypse of the fall of Paris into Nazi hands—as the mirror of the cultural and existential crisis of Western man in the first decades of the twentieth century.

For Levi, fear is the ultimate meaning of contemporary painting ("Paura della pittura" 25). While the individual is ontologically a work of art, infinite in his breadth as the site of all possible relationships (23), the experience of modernity has turned him into an isolated, fragmented being, estranged from the world. The defining factor of modernity is a dramatic loss of connection and meaning: "Il mondo, vuoto di noi, si riempie, per noi, di mostri: e l'uomo stesso diventa un mostro a se stesso, poiché egli è assente da sé" ["The world, emptied of us is refilled for us with monsters: man himself becomes a monster to himself, because he is absent from himself"] (24, *Fear of Freedom* 94–95). In the face of the monstrosity of a fundamentally alien reality, man experiences a solitude that generates only fear and causes him to withdraw into himself. Abstract art is the ultimate symptom of this loss, for it is the art of the abstract individual (24). Its objects are no longer people and things but empty idols endowed with illusory magic powers. Even when painting is meant as a protest against tyranny and alienation, as in Picasso, ultimately "[o]gni quadro è un grido, un urto contro invisibili mura fatate" ["(e)very painting is a cry, an onslaught against invisible enchanted walls"] (25, 97).

Levi acknowledges in Picasso the manifestation of a heroic attempt to escape from the abstraction of the modern human condition, albeit a tragic one because it lacks "il senso dell'esistenza come creazione, dell'identità dell'uomo col mondo, di ogni relazione come atto d'amore" ["the sense of existence as creation, of the identification of man with the world, of every relation as an act of love"] (23, 94). The only emotion left to the man whose amorous relationship with the world has been severed is, in fact, fear. In Picasso's paintings color no longer adheres to shapes; each element of pictorial composition exists in isolation, disconnected from all others. Every object becomes incomprehensible and frightening (24). Thus each of Picasso's paintings is a desperate cry in the face of the monstrous strangeness of a reality in which humanity can no longer find meaning (25). For Levi, Picasso's antirealist portrayal of a world of abstraction inevitably leads to an equally abstract form of art, in which the individual gets lost in the anonymous undifferentiation of the mass: "l'arte della massa" ["the art of the mass"] (24, 96). It is a form of rebellion that is inevitably destined to fail because its signs can no longer establish connections among the fragments of the world and are thus unable to create meaning. In his valiant battle against the horrors of history Picasso becomes, in Levi's eyes, an accomplice to the very forces that provoked them, for the consequence of his challenge to realism is ultimately the withdrawal from any serious engagement with historical reality and the reduction of the tragedy of modern man to a mere play of form (*Quaderno* 199–201).

As an antidote to the mystifications of modern art, Levi advocates a form of art that is utterly relational, generated within a positive relationship with reality. In direct opposition to abstractionism, authentic art derives from a sense of man's identity with the world, of man's existence as an amorous bond with nature ("Paura della pittura" 23). For Levi, authentic art has the power to attribute existence to the world by representing it: "[Q]uesta, di dare realtà, di aggiungere agli aspetti del mondo la categoria della realtà e dell'esistenza, il loro nome, la loro forma, è sempre stata la natura stessa dell'arte: la sua necessità; il suo valore esistenziale" ["This has always been the nature itself of art, its necessity, its existential value: giving reality, adding to the other aspects of the world the category of reality and existence, their names, their forms"] ("Riflessioni" 29). In an original reelaboration of Vico's category of *verum-factum*, Levi attributes to art—poetry, but also prose, painting, plastic arts, music, and architecture—the invention of truth ("L'invenzione" 51). Once again refusing to explain this statement in rigorous philosophical terms,[20] Levi draws on psychoanalytic theory to illustrate the concept in narrative terms: in the earliest stages of child development, no distinction is made between the child's subjectivity and the objects surrounding it; eventually, the child will recognize the existence of, say, the family's pet dog, but he will indicate it by imitating its voice—that is, by identifying with it. Only later, when the child is ready to differentiate himself from the dog, will he be able to designate it with the word *dog*. With this word the child will have placed the dog outside his consciousness, establishing himself as separate and at the same time laying the grounds for a relationship with the dog: "Così con la parola, con l'espressione il cane e il bambino, che prima non esistevano, diventano reali e diventa reale il rapporto fra di loro" ["Thus with the word, with the expression, the dog and the child, who did not exist before, become real and the relationship between them becomes real"] (52; emphasis mine).

The origin of the poetic event coincides, then, with the moment in which self-individuation occurs and object relations are established. As Levi puts it, the poetic word allows for "la conoscenza [in] un oggetto di un altro da sé, che acquista in quello stesso momento realtà" ["the knowledge of an Other that acquires reality in that same moment"] (53). By speaking of the power of art to create reality, whether in prose, poetry, or visual images, Levi exalts its capacity to make the observer aware of the existence of the world and of his own self. The object depicted or described comes into being, as it were, because its presence is recognized consciously for the first time. In this respect, Levi's argument parallels Heidegger's claim that poetry—as a metonymy for all art—permits "the naming and saying through which the Beyng [sic] of things first comes to be expressed, and through which the unspeakable enters the world with the speakable" ("On the Origin of the

Work of Art" 139). As for Heidegger, for Levi the work of art is no mere representation of something objectively existing outside of it. In *Cristo si è fermato a Eboli*, for example, Levi describes how, when looking at one of his canvasses at the end of a day's work, the peasants would be "meravigliati di vedere Grassano, nato così dal nulla" ["surprised to see Grassano where there had been nothing before"] (154, *175*).[21] In another of his favorite anecdotes, he remembers the amazement that the peasants would feel when they visited his house in the evenings and saw his paintings of people and landscapes. Although these pictures were neither naturalistic nor photographic in style, the peasants recognized the hills, the woods, and the animals they knew with the same wonder they would show if they were seeing or becoming aware of them for the first time ("Il contadino e l'orologio" 31).[22] In *Cristo si è fermato a Eboli*, then, art allows the "subaltern world" of the people of Lucania to become conscious of its own being in history. As Grassi writes of Dante, "the poetic word permits reality to appear in terms of historicity" (104).[23] For Levi, this recognition has political implications, as it founds the possibility of a productive relationship with society, one in which the peasants will no longer be mechanical instruments, fragmented bodies whose value is measured in terms of capitalist productivity, but rather agents in the construction of their own historical project ("L'invenzione" 54). As I argue in subsequent chapters about *Cristo si è fermato a Eboli* and Levi's travel writings, Levi's literary project consists precisely in shaping a poetic language that will give the people of southern Italy a sense of being in history on their own terms.

Levi's discussion of the relationship of southern peasantry with art is evocative of Vico's account of the birth of poetic language. Indeed, in his examination of Lucanian mythopoiesis in "Il contadino e l'orologio," Levi frames his discussion in neo-Vichian (and Jungian) terms.[24] For Levi, the peasants' forms of poetic narration correspond to the discovery of language itself:

> [L]a civiltà contadina è posta al limite dell'indistinzione, vive e perdura in quell'ambigua regione nella quale per la prima volta l'individuo si distacca, si forma e prende coscienza di sé, ed attorno a lui è sempre presente e incombente il senso del sacro, della originaria indistinzione, e ogni azione, ogni pensiero, ogni parola, ogni immagine hanno il carattere delle cose per la prima volta pensate, sono una affermazione di libertà nei riguardi della circostante, indeterminata, natura. ("Il contadino e l'orologio" 27)

> *Peasant civilization is located at the margins of indistinction. It lives and endures in the ambiguous region in which for the first time the individual detaches himself, acquires a form and consciousness of himself, and around him remains present and hovers the sense of the sacred, of the original indistinction,*

and every action, thought, word, image has the quality of things that are thought for the first time and is an affirmation of his freedom in relation to the indeterminate nature that surrounds him.

Peasant forms of narrative enable the process of individuation from undifferentiation, while extracting distinct objects from primordial chaos: words, writes Levi, "non sono altro che la memoria dei nomi che rappresentano l'atto della distinzione da un oggetto, la creazione, cioè, degli oggetti dalla indifferenziazione" ["are but the memory of the names that represent the distinction from an object, the creation, that is, of the objects from undifferentiation"] (27). Like Vico's *vera narratio*, Levi's notion of peasant poiesis consists in the act of creating things for the first time, in the perfect coincidence of signified and signifier: "[L]a parola è pienamente significante" ["The word signifies fully"] (28). In Grassi's words, "linguistic images—tropes, metaphors, and other figures of speech based on a discovery of similarities—are not witty inventions of writers . . . but the first forms of expression through which the human world came into being" (68).[25] According to Levi, the proper aesthetic mode for this kind of poetry is realism ("Il contadino e l'orologio" 31). In Levi's painting, the encounter with peasant poiesis during his exile in Lucania marks, indeed, a realist shift. His exilic painting makes evident his search for a more direct adherence to material reality, restoring to it substance and concreteness. Levi's painting in Lucania is linked to its natural and human environment. Portraying the passion, labor, grief, death, and life of the peasants, it shares the tragic dimension of their experience. At the same time, though, his *realismo contadino* "non ha nulla di veristico o di fotografico" ["is not at all naturalistic or photographic"] (31). In his landscape painting, the novel configuration of the terrain as well as its unusual chromatism assert themselves and impose new coloristic choices. However, the color is fragmented and uneven, contributing to the dynamism of the compositions. His broad brushstrokes allude to—more than represent—the physical concreteness of landscapes and faces, without enclosing them within clearly defined dimensional plans.[26] The presence of the Expressionist influence is clearly recognizable in the grotesque deformation of the human figure in some of his portraits and in the shocking repugnance of certain animal subjects.[27] Appropriating Vico's critique of art as mere imitation of reality,[28] Levi theorizes a form of realism that is unconcerned with mimetic fidelity, because "crea la realtà per la prima volta nell'atto dell'espressione" ["it creates reality for the first time in the act of expressing it"] (31).[29]

If Levi's understanding of realism does not coincide with mimesis, it remains rooted in a humanist philosophy of art. In "Sul nuovo umanesimo," Levi reelaborates some of the ideas he had expressed twenty years earlier in

"Paura della pittura." The abstractionism of those times no longer reflects a living artistic experience. The paths of art are now open to individuals who, like Levi's Lucanian friend, the political activist Rocco Scotellaro, for the first time have left the margins of history to become active participants in it. Their art bears witness to their new discovery of the world of history. It thus cannot but be realistic ("Sul nuovo umanesimo" 81).[30] As Levi further observes in a series of personal notes, in the aesthetics of realism the world is historical and dialectical. It is constituted as a relationship in which the I and the world objectively coincide. For Levi, in fact, the individual I does not exist in isolation or abstraction but is objectified in the encounter with the reality of the world, which in turn does not exist in and of itself but becomes real through an act of knowledge (Manuscript, April 6, 1955). From this perspective, artistic realism is the expression of a relational hermeneutics: Landscapes, objects, and faces "diventano pittura per opera dell'amore con cui sono guardati, dell'interesse, della energia vitale che fa di essi una scoperta . . . (La scoperta della verità, la poesia). Questo è il realismo" ["become painting thanks to the love with which we look at them, thanks to the interest, the vital energy that makes them into a discovery . . . (The discovery of truth, poetry). This is realism."] (Manuscript, April 28, 1957).

Levi understood his own artistic itinerary in relational terms, and created a taxonomy of his paintings based on the kind of rapport with the Other that they describe. In a 1955 manuscript he characterizes the series *Gli Amanti* as the symbolic epitome of his pictorial production, for in these works the subject of representation is the nature of the relationary process itself. The paintings of *contadini* have as their object, instead, the peasants' concrete experience of the world as a creative relationship, in which poetic expression acquires an existential value. Levi thus considers his depictions of peasant lives the dramatic apex of his painting. His portraits add another dimension to this artistic exploration of otherness, as here a complex reciprocal relationship is established with a full personality that consciously becomes a character in a painting. The last category Levi discusses includes still lives and landscape paintings, which express the artist's relationship with nature as a still and empty object to be shaped in the infinite forms of human thought. In these pictures, "libertà e amore sono conoscenza, distaccata invenzione della verità di quelle forme e di questi oggetti" ["freedom and love are knowledge, dispassionate invention of the truth or those forms and these objects"] (Manuscript, April 6, 1955).

The investigation of otherness that Levi proposes as the interpretive key of his work as a painter continues in his literary oeuvre. Beginning with *Cristo si è fermato a Eboli* (xviii, *x*), Levi's writings can be read as the chronicle of his delving into the relational essence of the self, culminating in the experience of perceiving his own self as Other in *Quaderno a cancelli*.

For Levi, art is generated in the awareness that the image reflected on the lake and recognized by Narcissus corresponds, in fact, to the self as Other (Vivarelli, *Lo specchio* xiv). All poiesis thus entails this discovery of the existence of the Other: "[S]oltanto il rapporto con l'altro, soltanto l'amore, crea l'esistenza, e la poesia" ["Only the relationship with the other, only love, generates existence and poetry"] (Levi, Manuscript, April 28, 1957). Here, I would like to propose that Levi's emphasis on love as the condition for the self's existence strongly resonates with the ethical writings of Levinas, for whom, too, the self is realized only in loving the Other (Cohen xxvii).

The main notion of Levinas's thought is that ethics is first philosophy, a concept developed in *Totality and Infinity* and further refined in *Otherwise than Being*. Situating himself within a broadly phenomenological framework, Levinas argues that ethics does not consist in the practice of a set of preordained universal moral rules, but is a primal experience. As such, it precedes all moral and philosophical formulations of prescriptive norms of behavior and "is lived in the sensibility of an embodied exposure to the other" (Critchley 21). According to Levinas ethics coincides with the self's infinite responsibility to the Other, with saying "here I am" (*Otherwise* 114). This responsibility does not allow totalization, for the Other remains ultimately enigmatic, an excess with regard to the categories of the self (Nealon 135). In *Totality and Infinity*, Levinas discusses this absolute otherness in terms of a challenge to the self:

> A calling into question of the same . . . is brought about by the other. We name this calling into question of my spontaneity by the presence of the Other, ethics. The strangeness of the Other, his irreducibility to the I, to my thoughts and my possessions, is precisely accomplished as a calling into question of my spontaneity, as ethics. Metaphysics, transcendence, the welcoming of the other by the same, of the Other by me, is concretely produced as the calling into question of the same by the other.[31] (43)

The locus of this challenge, in Levinas, is the face of the Other, which is "precisely the unique opening where the significance of the trans-cendent does not cancel out transcendence to make it enter into an immanent order; on the contrary it is where trans-cendence refuses immanence" (*Humanism* 40). Although the otherness of the Other remains ultimately irreducible, for Levinas "the Ego is through and through, in its very position, responsibility or diacony, as in chapter 53 of Isaiah" (33). This responsibility exists before and beyond freedom (54). Without becoming servitude, subjectivity is responsibility to the point of being *hostage* for the Other (*Otherwise* 59), of substituting oneself for the Other (114). Appropriating Arthur Rimbaud's famous phrase, Levinas concludes, "I am an other" (118).

Levi uses almost exactly the same language in an essay on portraiture written over the course of more than thirty years, between 1935 and 1968. For Levi, the portrait is the image of the self as Other ("I ritratti" 9). It is the product of adulthood, when the self is free and no longer needs to define itself "con cose di fuori, da cui essere posseduti (pesi) o da possedere (potere)" ["through outside things, by which to be possessed (weights) or to possess (power)"] (19). For Levi, as for Martin Buber, the adult I is fundamentally relational: the person comes really into being only through the encounter with another, who becomes an equal partner in a relationship and can be addressed as "thou" (Buber 80). Such a relationship is defined by reciprocity. There is no room for possession in it (62–63). A relationship lies at the origin of artistic expression as well: The artist "confronts a form that wants to become a work through him ... Not as a thing among the 'internal' things, not as a figment of the 'imagination,' but as what is present" (60–61). In Levi's view, too, art is born from the loving recognition of the Other's presence, and as such, all art is fundamentally a form of portraiture ("I ritratti" 21). This recognition, he explains, is not based on authority and power: "Il potere non comporta il Ritratto. Il Ritratto è l'opposto del potere" ["Power does not comprise the Portrait. The Portrait is the opposite of power"] (19). The portrait requires, in fact, the establishment of a real collaboration, a mutual relationship with the object of representation (20). Analogously to Levinas's responsibility, the result of this generative relationship precedes consciousness: "[N]on può neppure essere un atto di consapevolezza, essendo una condizione precedente alla coscienza" ["It cannot be a conscious act, for it is a condition that precedes consciousness"] (11). When the artist attempts to define his relationship with the subject of the portrait in terms of pure, rational form, it dissolves into abstraction (11).[32]

Despite Levi's theorizing in these texts of the portrait as a genre that is excluded from a hierarchical structure, elsewhere he does not hide his anxiety in regard to the question of power relations as they play out in the process of representation. His concerns emerge explicitly in an episode of *Cristo si è fermato a Eboli*, in which Levi vividly describes his difficulty in persuading the local peasants, and his housekeeper in particular, to pose for a picture. Levi explains that, according to the *contadini*, a portrait gives its painter absolute power over his subject, whose image he fixes in time and space. Thus Levi's housekeeper, Giulia, refuses to be portrayed precisely because she is afraid of "l'influsso e la potenza che io avrei esercitato cavando da lei un'immagine, come lo esercitavo certamente su persone e cose e alberi e paesi, con le pitture che andavo facendo ogni giorno" ["the tangible sway I could exercise over her just as, to her mind, I undoubtedly exercised it over the people and things and trees and villages that were the subjects of my paintings"] (*Cristo* 136, *154*). Levi suggests that only through violence—that is, by asserting his authority over her—can he convince her to pose for him. I shall return to this episode in more detail in Chapter 1, where I also examine the question of gender that underlies Levi's description of this scene. Here, I believe it is important to consider how Levi foregrounds, in this passage, the problem of the ethics of representation in a more nuanced manner than he does in his essays on portraiture and more closely in line with his reflections about the sacred and the religious in *Paura della libertà*.

For Levi, the rural civilization of southern Italy is immersed in the indistinctness of the sacred, and given this it lacks the consciousness of its own being that it needs to become a free historical agent. In representing the southern experience in *Cristo si è fermato a Eboli* and in his paintings from the exile, Levi has a double purpose: He aims, first of all, to facilitate the process of differentiation, making the peasants aware of their own existence as separate from the original chaos of nature. Second, he wants the Italian public to acknowledge the reality of this "other Italy" and to consider it on its own terms ("Il contadino e l'orologio" 18). Levi's intent is, thus, political, as he believes—in accordance to the principles of autonomy theorized by Gobetti—that the peasant classes should become independent actors on the stage of Italian politics, rather than puppets in the hands of an alien political leadership. Yet as the episode of Giulia's portrait shows, Levi is both sensitive to the dangers of representation and aware of his own unavoidable complicity with the power dynamics at work within its process. He realizes that his desire to project the peasant civilization out of its ahistorical existence through artistic representation subjects it to his power, as an artist, a member of the cultural and political élite, and, in the case of Giulia, as a man.[33] Representation constitutes an attempt to give form to what is formless, to define the contours of its shapeless fluidity, and thus inevitably involves a reduction of its object's depth and scope. In this respect, it is analogous to religion, as Levi understands it in *Paura della libertà*. As we have seen, in *Paura della libertà* Levi describes religion as the formalization of the sacred: religion forces the sacred into fixed formulas and boundaries, in order to control its vertiginous chaos. Religion is, then, an authoritarian system, which finds its political equivalent in totalitarianism (135). By admitting to his despotic treatment of Giulia, sacrificed to the needs of his painting, Levi more generally acknowledges the violence implicit in every act of representation of the Other. This reduction of the Other's experience to an image is the inevitable price of both knowledge and art—and, throughout his writings, Levi wrestles with the inconsistency between the imbalance of power implicit in representation and his vision of artistic creation as infinite openness to the freedom of the Other (*Paura della libertà* 154).

This humanistic respect for the Other's difference, and the consequent apprehension about the limits of the representation of otherness, also defines the work of Pier Paolo Pasolini, Levi's contemporary and friend. Passionate about giving voice to the experience of those who live at the margins of society, Pasolini theorizes free indirect discourse as a strategy that can open up the language of literature to welcome difference. Pasolini's reflections on free indirect discourse thus shed light on Levi's own attempts in *Cristo si è fermato a Eboli* to shape a literary language that would be hospitable to otherness. In "Intervento sul discorso libero indiretto," one of the essays collected in *Empirismo eretico*, Pasolini reprimands the bourgeoisie for its inability to acknowledge other life experiences, a trait that he sees reflected in the national literature: "La cosa più odiosa e intollerabile, anche nel più innocente dei borghesi, è quella di non saper riconoscere altre esperienze vitali che la propria: e di ricondurre tutte le altre esperienze vitali a una sostanziale analogia con la propria" ["The most odious and intolerable thing, even in the most innocent of bourgeois, is that of not knowing how to recognize life experiences other than his own: and of bringing all other life experiences back to a substantial analogy with his own"] (89–90, *Heretical Empiricism* 87). In contrast, Pasolini proposes free indirect discourse as a profoundly dialogic strategy, one where the author's language, insofar as it is the expression of a conception of the world, must confront the different idiom and experience of his character.[34] "Il discorso libero indiretto," Pasolini writes, "non può che essere scritto in una lingua sostanzialmente diversa da quella dello scrittore . . . e la poesia, in quanto lirismo o espressività, nasce dalla contaminazione, nell'urto tra due anime, tavolta profondamente diverse" ["'free indirect discourse' can only be written in a language substantially different from that of the writer . . . and poetry, as lyricism or expressiveness, is born of the blending in the collision of two, sometimes profoundly different, spirits"] (91–92, 89). In this sense, for Pasolini the notion of free indirect discourse must be broadened from that of a structure, clearly defined in syntactic and grammatical terms, to encompass the total style of a literary text (86).

In this essay Pasolini advocates the use of free indirect discourse as a form of openness to the Other, a recognition and acceptance of the Other's voice that goes beyond a merely sentimental position of sympathy (Ricciardi 148). For Pasolini, free indirect discourse is an instrument of political revolution as well as a literary practice in his Roman novels. In his fictions of the 1950s, in fact, he employs this technique in order to give the *borgatari* that populate his stories an autonomous voice. Through free indirect discourse he asserts the literary dignity of the Roman dialect they speak. Moreover, he calls into question the notion of standard Italian, which he denounces as a bourgeois construct that promotes through its very existence a class agenda (6). In his representation of the experience of Lucania's peasants in *Cristo si è fermato a Eboli*, Levi pursues the same openness and welcoming of the otherness of southern civilization. In keeping with the visual nature of his painterly calling, he does so in a way that moves beyond the Friulan writer's literary theories and anticipates their development into cinematic semiotics with "Il cinema di poesia," adopting what I have called a "visual poetics."

To classic narrative cinema, Pasolini opposes a "cinema of poetry," based on the semiotic unit of the *im-segno*, or image-sign (*Empirismo Eretico* 170). In the cinema of poetry, the camera's dominant stance is the free indirect point-of-view shot, which represents the equivalent of free indirect discourse (177).[35] Through its obtrusive presence, the camera disrupts the illusory naturalness of narrative development and reveals it as an artificial construct.[36] Pasolini emphasizes the subversive power of the language of images as opposed to the language of words, too compromised with established power structures and bourgeois ideology. In a later essay, "Osservazioni sul piano-sequenza," Pasolini continues to expand his theory of cinema, explaining how "il cinema ... è sostanzialmente un infinito piano-sequenza, come è appunto la realtà ai nostri occhi e alle nostre orecchie ... : in altre parole è la riproduzione del presente" ["cinema ... is in essence an infinite sequence shot, precisely as reality is to our eyes and ears ... : in other words, it is the reproduction of the present"] (*Empirismo Eretico* 240, *235–36*). For Pasolini, cinema records the unfolding of life as it happens, in its chaotic formlessness and meaninglessness. In order to "ricondurre allo studio della realtà ... come se la realtà fosse stata scoperta attraverso la sua riproduzione" ["(bring) us back to the study of reality ... as if reality had been discovered through its reproduction"] (232, *228*), cinema must become "film"—that is, must be given a narrative order and meaning (241).

Pasolini's theories of cinema illuminate Levi's own understanding of art as the discovery of reality. As we have seen, for Levi the act of representation brings the represented onto the level of consciousness both for the audience and, if it is human, for the object, too. In doing so, however, representation imposes a form over the fluidity of the unconscious and thus foreshortens its infinite potentiality. Levi speaks of the moment of self-individuation and differentiation, which art makes possible, as an experience akin to death (*Paura della libertà* 134)—precisely as Pasolini writes of film: "Il montaggio opera dunque sul materiale del film (che è costituito da frammenti, lunghissimi o infinitesimali, di tanti piani-sequenza come possibili soggettive infinite) quello che la morte opera sulla vita" ["Editing therefore performs on the material of the film (which is composed of fragments that can be extremely long or infinitesimal, of many sequence shots understood as possible infinite subjective shots) the operations that death performs on life"] (*Empirismo Eretico* 241, *237*). In other words, by imposing narrative closure, editing and montage allow for the retrospective gaze that gives meaning to a life when it ends. Similarly, Levi defines death both as the inability to separate oneself from the raw material of life and as the individual's complete detachment from it. On the contrary, a human being should long for "il prodotto dell'attività umana in quanto creatrice, ricca cioè nello stesso momento di differenziazione e di indifferenziazione, di individualità e di universalità" ["achievement, which results from creative human activity, and blends at the very same moment individual riches and the treasures of universality"] (*Paura della libertà* 134, 3). The only authentic human position, then, is the precarious balance between the connection with original chaos of nature and the consciousness of one's own distinct being in the world.

In his essays on film theory, Pasolini manifests the precariousness of this position by seemingly embracing, at times, the meaning-making power of narrative film, while, on other occasions, privileging the possibilities offered by poetic cinema (Ward, *A Poetics of Resistance* 139). In Levi's literary works, this same instability plays out as a productive tension between the visual and the verbal, which defines his visual poetics. As I argue in the following chapters, Levi's writing is based on an original narrative code, in which word and image participate equally in the creative process. Beginning with *Cristo si è fermato a Eboli*, Levi adopts his own painting as the original semiotic unit of narration, whose principal rhetorical strategy is ekphrasis—that is, the verbal representation of visual experience. By choosing to construct his text on the fundamentally antirationalistic cornerstone of art, Levi creates a novel literary language that foregrounds the dialogue between the original chaos of indistinctiveness and the rational order of individualization, between the magic mentality of the southern Italian peasants and the post-Enlightenment culture of which he is a representative. In *Cristo si è fermato a Eboli*, he associates visual experience with the indistinctiveness of peasant civilization and introduces it as a dialogic element in the narration, as a way to give voice to this marginal experience, in a manner that, as we have seen, is analogous to Pasolini's "cinema of poetry."

Like Pasolini, though, Levi does not reject tout court the power of the word to define and convey meaning. The pages of *L'Orologio*, in which he offers a reflection on language and creativity, clarify that the issue for him is not whether verbal or visual representation is more powerful but rather the need to shape a new expressive code that gives space to difference. In speaking of the *contadini*—the peasants, who include, for Levi, all those who lovingly exercise their creativity in every field of human activity—he deplores their lack of a language to express themselves: "Il problema è tutto qui. La lingua degli altri, il loro Stato, bandiere, partiti, non conviene a loro: non ha senso sulle loro bocche. Devono parlare, ma a modo loro" ["The language of the others, their state, flags, parties, do not suit the Contadini and have no meaning in their mouths. They too must speak, but in their own way"] (167, *The Watch* 186). Levi's visual poetics is, thus, an attempt to open up literary language to the voice of otherness. The cost of this radical openness is a certain theoretical instability about the exact terms of the relationship between word and image. In "L'invenzione della verità," Levi speaks of both painting and literature as "poetry," as both contributing, that is, to the process of poiesis that takes place in the creative act. This harmonious dialogue between the visual and the verbal is, however, ostensibly contradicted in the crucial episode of Giulia's portrait in *Cristo si è fermato a Eboli*. There, Levi seems to embrace the long-established hierarchical view of language as being associated with rationality—and masculinity—versus the feminine irrationality of the image and reveals the contradictions implicit in all forms of representation. In the chapters that follow, I propose a reading of Levi's literary work that attempts to respect its dialogic inclusiveness, which I see as the manifestation of his humanistic comprehensiveness. Indeed, all Levi's philosophy can be understood as an ongoing dialogue with the contrasting and apparently irreconcilable philosophical positions of his times, an exchange in which no theoretical system is allowed to have the last word. The openness and inclusiveness that characterize Levi's intellectual conversation with the most influential voices of twentieth-century philosophy are made possible by his constant preoccupation with and welcoming of otherness. Levi's discovery of concrete alterity during his exile in Lucania, chronicled in *Cristo si è fermato a Eboli*, has an enduring aesthetic and existential impact on him. His arrival in Lucania coincides with his encounter with the peasants' experience, their land, their world, which impose themselves on his imagination and compel him to break the endless circle of self-representation in his art and lovingly to recognize and embrace the presence of the Other. Since this "traumatic" moment of recognition, Levi's philosophy of art, like Levinas's "humanism of the Other," asserts the unreserved affirmation of the Other's being as the condition for the existence and realization of the self. It is this ethical commitment to the Other that Levi recognizes as the root of his painting and literary work, ultimately as the origin of his project of "una nuova cultura che è un fatto poetico nel senso etimologico greco del *poiein*, del fare, dal fare, dall'azione creatrice" ["a new culture that is a poetic event in the etymological sense of the Greek *poiein*, of making through creative activity"] ("L'invenzione" 54).

1

The Magic of Painting in *Cristo si è fermato a Eboli*

When, in 1935, Carlo Levi was confined to Lucania by the fascist government, he had prepared himself for a sojourn in a "terra antica, abituata alla solitudine" [an "ancient land, used to its own loneliness"] (*È questo il carcer tetro?* 141)[1] where he could pursue his philosophical and intellectual meditations in peaceful retreat from the world.[2] His romantic musings clashed, though, with the harsh reality he faced upon his arrival in the South. The exile in Lucania coincided for the Turinese intellectual with the discovery of another Italy, completely foreign to the industrialized and progressive North with which he was familiar.[3] Gagliano and Grassano, the locations of Levi's political exile, belong to another world, "serrato nel dolore e negli usi, negato alla Storia e allo Stato, eternamente paziente" ["hedged in by custom and sorrow, cut off from History and the State, eternally patient"] as he writes in the prologue to *Cristo si è fermato a Eboli* (3, *Christ Stopped at Eboli* 3).[4] The villagers and peasants of Lucania appear to him locked within the circular repetition of a seasonal temporality, ceaselessly performing the gestures their ancestors carried out for centuries. They are fundamentally alien to the values of modernity: the progress of time, the worth of individual endeavor, the idea of the State remain abstract notions, with no actual meaning for their daily existence. Thus the proverbial expression "Christ stopped at Eboli," used by the *contadini* to describe their own condition, acquires a quite literal meaning:

> Cristo si è davvero fermato a Eboli, dove la strada e il treno abbandonano la costa di Salerno e il mare, e si addentrano nelle desolate terre di Lucania. Cristo non è mai arrivato qui, né vi è arrivato il tempo, né l'anima individuale, né la speranza, né il legame tra le cause e gli effetti, la ragione e la Storia ... Le stagioni scorrono sulla fatica contadina, oggi come tremila anni prima di Cristo: nessun messaggio umano o divino si è rivolto a questa povertà refrattaria. Parliamo un diverso linguaggio: la nostra lingua è qui incomprensibile. (3–4)

> *Christ did not stop at Eboli, where the road and the railway leave the coast of Salerno and turn into the desolate reaches of Lucania. Christ never came this*

far, nor did time, nor the individual soul, nor hope, nor the relation of cause to effect, nor reason nor history . . . The seasons pass today over the toil of the peasants, just as they did three thousand years before Christ; no message, humane or divine, has reached this stubborn poverty. We speak a different language, and here our tongue is incomprehensible. (4)

The peasants' incomprehension is not simply metaphorical, as for the *contadini* Italian is not the "mother tongue." Rather, they associate the use of the national language with the impositions of a government they perceive as a distant entity, a mysterious mechanism whose workings are fundamentally irrelevant to their own lives.[5] Italian is the language of political speeches and fascist rhetoric. It is the idiom of the intellectual and economic élites of the country. Finally, it is the adopted language of the local *galantuomini*, the petit bourgeois who oppress the peasants and despise them as well-meaning but primitive people (13). Thus Levi reveals language to be the site of a dramatic conflict taking place between the industrial, progressive, post-Christian Italy he belongs to and the agrarian, immobile, pre-Christian Italy of the South. As Antonio Gramsci explains, language is indissolubly connected with culture and philosophy (*Gramsci Reader* 347). The question of language cannot be reduced to a theoretical issue but must be recognized as the privileged locus of the intersection of culture and politics, always socially and historically determined (354–55).

By making explicit reference to the linguistic problem in the prologue, Levi foregrounds it as a central concern of *Cristo si è fermato a Eboli*. The question of language emerges as fundamental in the book in both theme and form. The encounter with the absolute otherness of Lucania's rural civilization forces Levi to transform radically his writing and define a new narrative language. He shuns the betrayal that inevitably seems to occur in the Italian literary representations of the peasant world, in which their existence is drained of meaning and value. Even "uno dei loro" like Gabriele D'Annunzio, born in rural Abruzzo, Levi writes, "era un letterato italiano, e non poteva non tradirli" ["when he became a literary figure he was bound to betray them"] (*Cristo* 162, 184).[6]

> Egli era partito di qui, da un mondo senza espressione, e aveva voluto sovrapporgli la veste brillante della poesia contemporanea, che è tutta espressività, sensualità, senso del tempo. Aveva perciò degradato quel mondo a puro strumento retorico, quella poesia a vuoto formalismo linguistico. Il suo tentativo non poteva essere che un tradimento e un fallimento. Da quel connubio ibrido non poteva che nascere un mostro. (162)

> *His beginnings were in a mute world like this one, among the Abruzzi Mountains, but he sought to superimpose on it the many-colored coat of contemporary*

verse, which is primarily wordy, sensual, and haunted with a sense of time. In so doing he degraded this world to a mere instrument of rhetoric and its poetry to futile verbal acrostics. His efforts could only result in betrayal and failure; from such a hybrid combination only a monstrosity could be born. (184)

In contrast, in giving artistic form to his memories of exile, Levi creates an original expressive code through which to overcome the artificiality and inadequacy of conventional literary forms and give a voice to the marginalized experience of the peasants, excluded from the *logos*, strangers to Christ, the word made flesh. Faithful to his painterly vocation, he chooses a technique that places the visual image at the core of the narrative structure—a strategy that, in classical rhetorical terms, is called *ekphrasis*.

Now understood as the verbal representation of a work of visual or plastic arts within a literary text, *ekphrasis* originally indicated simply a verbal description of an object. Its main qualities were required to be "extravagance in detail and vividness in representation" (Krieger 7), according to its etymological origins, from the verb *phrazein*, "to show," "to make known," and its derivate *ekphrazein*, "to show very clearly." Writing in the first century AD, the master of oratory Quintilian treats ekphrasis as an established figure of discourse but does not yet provide precise criteria to identify it, except that the audience must have the distinct feeling of being turned from readers into spectators (8.3). Ekphrasis must, in other words, exhibit *enargeia*, defined in classical manuals of rhetoric as the capacity of words "to yield so vivid a description that they . . . place the represented object before the reader's (hearer's) inner eye" (Krieger 14). The Hellenistic era witnessed the beginning of the practice of focusing such exercises in description on works of art, which rapidly flourished and developed into a separate poetic genre called *ekphrasis*. Later on, the term also came to designate the description of a work of art incorporated in another text (Clüver 35). Due to its visual nature, the use of ekphrasis in a narrative text introduces a suspension in the development of the plot, an interruption in the temporality of discourse that generates a productive tension between the narrative thrust and the exploration of spatiality associated with a work of art, implying a self-conscious reflection on the specificity of the literary medium (Krieger 7).[7]

In this sense, ekphrasis appears to be a singularly suitable technique to represent the timelessness and the exclusion from history as progress of Lucania's "immobile civiltà" ["motionless civilization"] (*Cristo* 3, 3). By calling into question the linear development of the narrative plot, constantly disrupted by descriptive and ekphrastic digressions, Levi gives literary form to the peasants' alienation from Western thought, with its faith in humanity's capacity to shape the future. The dialogue between the verbal and visual semiotic systems introduced by ekphrasis in the text acquires, then, a dual significance. On one level, it reflects formally the dialogue taking place throughout the book between Levi's received rationalistic attitude and peasant folklore, intended in Gramscian terms as the multifarious and often contradictory worldviews typical of subaltern classes and fundamentally (if only implicitly) opposed to dominant ideological positions (Gramsci, *Selections* 189). While Levi's Enlightenment intellectual stance is associated with the dominance of the word, the peasants' folkloric thinking, in its extraneity to the hegemonic social order, is akin to the realm of the image. The antagonism between word and image is, in fact, perceived to be equivalent to the opposition of culture and nature, of signs and things (Mitchell, *Iconology* 43). The word is traditionally associated with history, consciousness, and symbolic mediation, in opposition to the immediacy and naturalness of the image (43). On another level, then, the ongoing dialogue between word and image constitutes by extension an act of defiance against the modern idolatry of rationality, giving equal weight to the mythical imagination of Lucania's *contadini*. It becomes an expression of political resistance, as the Russian thinker Mikhail Bakhtin reminds us when he suggests that challenging established linguistic codes is equivalent to challenging official law and that the subversion of conventional narrative discourse is a form of social and political protest.[8]

Grounded in the dialogic relationship between word and image, Levi's visual poetics is thus revealed to be an instrument of political subversion. The political aspect of Levi's aesthetic choices is further illuminated by the critical writings of another "resistant"—to echo David Ward's phrase—Pier Paolo Pasolini.[9] Pasolini and Levi indeed share many of the same preoccupations as engaged intellectuals and artists, both passionate about giving voice to marginal experiences within Italian society. As Alessia Ricciardi has argued, Pasolini's intellectual project coincides with a veritable poetics of hospitality, which implies "an incorporation of the Other's speech and thoughts that greets the unfamiliar with hospitality, while acknowledging its alterity and hence its unknowability" (148).[10] In "Intervento sul discorso libero indiretto," Pasolini theorizes free indirect discourse as the literary strategy that, by introducing the voice of the Other into an author's writing, subverts from within the bourgeois structures of literature and opens them up to otherness. In representing the experience of Lucania's peasants in *Cristo si è fermato a Eboli*, Levi pursues the same "poetics of hospitality" that Ricciardi attributes to Pasolini, recognizing and embracing the difference that he has encountered in southern civilization. As a painter, he does so by adopting a visual poetics that opens up verbal expression to its Other, the pictorial sign, at the same time that it introduces the speech and mentality of the Lucanian peasants into the bourgeois space of literature. With its emphasis on the visual, Levi's poetics also anticipates the development of Pasolini's cinematic theories, in particular his concept of the "cinema of poetry." Pasolini defines the cinema of poetry as a specifically visual form of filmmaking that is based on the *im-segno*, or image-sign, and that constitutes an alternative to classic narrative cinema (*Empirismo Eretico* 170). Whereas the cinema of prose aims to achieve a naturalistic form of narration that moves seamlessly from sequence to sequence and thus privileges the impersonality of objective shots, in the cinema of poetry the camera tends to take the semisubjective stance, which is tantamount to the cinematic equivalent of free indirect discourse (177). Beginning with *Cristo si è fermato a Eboli*, Levi constructs a literary equivalent of Pasolini's "cinema of poetry" and adopts his own painting as an original im-sign, the semiotic unit of a novel narrative code born from the ekphrastic transposition of the visual into the verbal.[11] By constructing his text on a foundation that stems in the art of painting, as the im-sign that reveals the "the world's poetic substratum" (Ward, *A Poetics of Resistance* 117), Levi creates a profoundly dialogic literary language that welcomes and gives voice to the subaltern civilization of rural Lucania, with its antirationalist, poetic mentality.

In the prefatory letter to Giulio Einaudi that opens the 1963 edition of the book, Levi explicitly places painting at the origins of his narration: "Il *Cristo si è fermato a Eboli* fu dapprima esperienza, e pittura e poesia, e poi teoria e gioia di verità (con *Paura della libertà*), per diventare infine e apertamente racconto" ["Thus *Christ Stopped at Eboli* was, first, experience and painting and poetry; secondly, together with *Fear and Freedom* (sic), theory and joy in truth; becoming finally and openly a story"] (xix, *xi*). Painting's fundamental function is confirmed in a private note to a friend, where he remarks that his pictures "furono in verità i soli appunti sui quali anni dopo il libro fu elaborato e costruito. Essi sono non solo illustrazioni, ma la sua interpretazione autentica" ["were, indeed, the only notes upon which, years later I elaborated and constructed the book. They are not simple illustrations, but its authentic interpretation"] (qtd. in Wells, "Carlo Levi e la Lucania" 167).[12] Indeed, painting informs every aspect of Levi's prose, as Natalia Ginzburg observes in lyrical terms: "Avevo avuto la sensazione, leggendo [*Cristo si è fermato a Eboli*] la prima volta, che lui scrivendo non raccontasse, ma dipingesse e cantasse" ["When I read (*Christ Stopped at Eboli*) for the first time, I had the feeling that, while writing, he was not recounting a story, but painting and singing"] (13). The identity of painting and writing implied in Ginzburg's words is confirmed in Manlio Cancogni's testimony of his almost daily visits to Levi while the artist was hiding in Nazi-occupied Florence between 1943 and 1944, at the same time that he was writing *Cristo si è fermato a Eboli*.[13] During these visits, Cancogni heard from Levi endless stories of his confinement in Lucania, filled with vivid images, "sorelle di quelle che realizzava sulla tela con i colori e i pennelli" ["sisters to those that he created on canvas with colors and brushes"] (10). Verbal and visual images are noticeably seen as peers and not competitors in Cancogni's account, contributing equally to the concreteness and vibrancy of Levi's narration. Levi painted and wrote at the same time: "Cominciò a scrivere 'Cristo s'è fermato a Eboli' [sic] a matita come se disegnasse, con un tratto ampio e agile, arrestandosi di tanto in tanto per porre mano ai pennelli, e riprendendo più avanti la matita come se lo scrivere e il dipingere fossero parti dello stesso discorso ininterrotto" ["He began writing *Christ Stopped at Eboli* with a pencil, as though he were drawing, with broad and light gestures, and he stopped once in a while to pick the paint brush, later taking the pencil again, as though writing and painting were part of the same uninterrupted discourse"] (Cancogni 10). Furthermore, the emergence of the visual in the text authorizes a reading of the entire narration as a textual object, in the tradition of visual or spatial poetry (Arouimi 51). Indeed, thanks to Levi's use of ekphrasis, in *Cristo si è fermato a Eboli* painting and writing literally belong to the same discursive practice.

In the book, ekphrasis functions both in its narrow sense of verbal representation of a work of visual art—when, for example, Levi directly reproduces one of his paintings in a passage—and in its broader definition as a literary principle, whose aim is to transform the reading experience into a visual one, turning readers into spectators (Krieger 14). This pictorial drive affects language as well, concretizing the visual metaphors that the discourse of literary criticism has appropriated for centuries, when treating the writer as though he were a painter. Critics constantly collapse the distance between writing and painting in describing how an author "paints" vibrant "portraits" of her characters or by saying that she "depicts" scenes and settings in a few touches or that she "paints frescoes" of a certain society. In *Cristo si è fermato a Eboli* these metaphors acquire a more literal meaning; the generic categories of painting, from the portrait to the landscape, apply equally well to Levi's artistic work and his writing.

The beginning of *Cristo si è fermato a Eboli* constitutes a masterly example of what I will call Levi's "landscape writing:"

> Grassano, come tutti i paesi di qui, è bianco in cima ad un alto colle desolato, come una piccola Gerusalemme immaginaria nella solitudine di un deserto. Amavo salire in cima al paese, alla chiesa battuta dal vento, donde l'occhio spazia in ogni direzione su un orizzonte sterminato, identico in tutto il suo cerchio. Si è come in mezzo a un mare di terra biancastra, monotona e senz'alberi: bianchi e lontani i paesi, ciascuno in vetta al suo colle, Irsina, Craco, Montalbano, Salandra, Pisticci, Grottole, Ferrandina, le terre e le grotte dei briganti, fin laggiù dove c'è forse il mare, e Metaponto e Taranto. (5)

> Grassano, like all the villages hereabouts, is a streak of white at the summit of a bare hill, a sort of miniature imaginary Jerusalem in the solitude of the desert. I liked to climb to the highest point of the village, to the wind-beaten church, where the eye can sweep over an endless expanse in every direction, identical in character all the way around the circle. It is like being on a sea of chalk, monotonous and without trees. There are other villages, white and far away on the tops of their hills, Irsina, Craco, Montalbano, Salandra, Pisticci, Grottole, Ferrandina, the haunts and caves of the brigands; and beyond the reach of the vision lies the sea, and Metaponto, and Taranto. (5)

In his description of Grassano and its countryside, Levi privileges spatiality and chromatism. White is the predominant color: the small town, the land, and the other villages that dot the surrounding territory are all characterized as white, giving verbal dimension to the monotonic, chromatic quality of the landscape through the repetition of the adjectives "bianco," "biancastra," and "bianchi." In this passage, the reader is called to assume the position of the viewer in the text, as Levi marks linguistically the shift from his own memory of Grassano ("amavo salire in cima al paese") in the past tense to the present tense and inclusiveness of the third person singular: "l'occhio spazia," "si è come in mezzo a un mare" (5). By adopting the impersonal form of the verb, Levi effectively universalizes his personal experience, involving the reader in the process of making present, through *enargeia*, the visual basis of his narration. In this sense, this verbal depiction of the landscape conforms to Quintilian's specifications of the requirements of ekphrasis: it self-consciously places at its center the act of seeing itself and urges its readers to metamorphose into viewers (Krieger 14).

But this descriptive passage is ekphrastic in the stricter sense as well, since it possesses a direct pictorial referent in a 1935 painting, titled *Grassano come Gerusalemme* (Figure 1).[14] In this picture, Grassano is represented from a low angle, which emphasizes its dominating position over the clayey valleys below. The wide and vigorous brushstrokes confer dynamic tension to the monotony of the landscape, in which, as Levi writes in a letter to his mother, "nessun contrasto interrompe l'orizzonte sempre uguale, e il seguirsi dei campi e delle valli, a perdita d'occhio" ["there is no contrast to interrupt the always identical landscape, and the fields and valleys that follow each other as far as one can see"] (*Carlo Levi e la Lucania* 101). Indeed, Grassano's whiteness produces a stark chromatic contrast within the countryside, painted in earth tones: "Ho dipinto ieri il primo paesaggio grassanese, una distesa di colline e di campi bianco-giallastri, con radi alberi grigi, e le prime case bianche e grigie del paese. Mi pare di averne reso abbastanza bene il carattere, e mi sono servito di una gamma di colori per me inusitata e che vi stupirebbe, che va dal giallo al violetto, senza conoscere né l'azzurro né il rosa" ["Yesterday I painted my first landscape of Grassano, an expanse of yellowish-white fields and hills, with scarce gray trees and the first grey and white houses of the village. I think I rendered its character quite well, and I used quite an unusual scale of colors, which would surprise you, going from yellow to violet, without touching either blue or pink"] (101). In the painting, a few trees dot the landscape, broken by ravines and gorges, apparently untouched by human hands except for a white road that winds up the hill from the lower left side. The road counterbalances the brightness of Grassano's buildings, at the opposite end of the painted surface, with its own whiteness, before disappearing into the space outside the picture, ending nowhere and emphasizing in this way the isolation and remoteness of the land. The scene thus acquires the additional quality of a visual equivalent for Levi's own feelings of exclusion and solitude as an exile, exacerbated by the utter unfamiliarity of the places of his confinement.[15] In its psychological aspect, the painting recalls another spiritual landscape, the dark wood of Dante's *Commedia*, whose presence in Levi's thoughts at the time is confirmed in the same letter to his mother.[16] The road, with its twisting appearance, evokes through absence the lost *diritta via*, and the intimation of a Dantean model for the representation of Grassano is further strengthened by the title of the painting, *Grassano come Gerusalemme*, which conjures up precise images of the celestial Jerusalem as interpreted visually by numerous illustrators of the *Commedia*, from Botticelli to Baldassare Lombardi in his work for the Paduan edition of 1822.[17]

Levi explicitly reformulates the comparison between Grassano and Jerusalem in the description that opens *Cristo si è fermato a Eboli*, highlighting in this way the visual nature of his narrative inspiration, which finds its referent not directly in Dante's poem but in its iconography. By means of this analogy, Levi implicitly establishes a parallel between his own journey in Lucania and Dante's infernal itinerary, drawing literary authority for his own book from the pictorial interpretations of Dante's *poema*.[18] Moreover, by collapsing the distance between Dante's text and its visualizations, Levi confirms the absolute correspondence of word and image in his own poetics. As he observes in a private note, his thoughts "nascevano insieme ai quadri, venivano dalla stessa radice, dicevano, col diverso linguaggio delle parole, in ragionamenti o racconti, in teorie o fantasie, le stesse cose che nella pittura erano pittura" ["were born at the same time as the paintings; they came from the same root. They said with the different language of words, through reasonings or stories, through theories or imaginations, the same things that, in painting, were painting"] ("I ritratti" 15).

In Lucania, painting represents for Levi the "magic key" that grants him access to the closed world of the peasants and prevents him from becoming

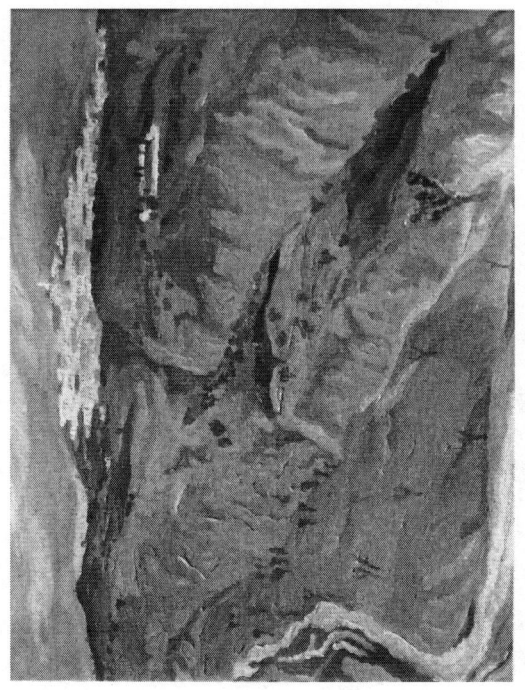

Figure 1. Carlo Levi, *Grassano come Gerusalemme* (1935)
© 2012 Artists Rights Society (ARS), New York / SIAE, Rome.

yet another foreign conqueror in this southern land.[19] As he explains in the preface, painting, together with poetry, constituted the primary mediating force between his consciousness and the world of lived experience. Thanks to painting, he discovered the existence of the Other and abandoned the solipsism of his earlier art. Indeed, Levi's exilic painting signals a shift in Levi's style, which acquires a more mature and distinct quality, compared to the still tentative and somewhat derivative experiments of his previous production (Vivarelli, "Diaro pittorico" 24). The painter's Lucanian works manifest the abandonment of the stylization of the 1920s (Figure 2) toward a more direct adherence to material reality, enriched by a reelaboration of expressionistic elements from the early 1930s (Figure 3).

This new painting is linked "all'ambiente, alle passioni, alla vita, al lavoro, alla fatica, al dolore, alla morte" ["to the environment, human passions, life, work, toil, grief, death"], as he writes in another essay, "Il contadino e l'orologio" (31); it is not separate from peasant life but rather participates in its tragic quality. His *realismo contadino*—as he defines his new style—also signals the detachment from the image of his own self, which frequently appeared in his prior work, and a new openness to the experience of otherness. In a 1954 conversation with the art critic Aldo Garosci, he confirms the aesthetic revolution that marked his production during the exile: "Nei quadri di prima, il soggetto ero io, un io nel suo farsi e specchiarsi nelle cose . . . e nel suo concludersi di ogni cosa su sé stessa, rispecchiata in ogni altra . . . La Lucania è stata la rottura di questo cerchio magico . . . Quelle terre, quelle persone . . . avevano una esistenza che rifiutava ogni specchio, ogni magica metamorfosi. Così cominciò il distacco, che è la libertà, la comprensione e l'amore" ["In my previous paintings, I was the subject, an I that was making itself and mirrored itself in objects . . . and every object completed itself, mirrored in all others . . . Lucania broke this magical circle . . . That land, those people . . . had an existence that rejected all mirrors, all magical metamorphoses. This was the beginning of the detachment that coincides with freedom, understanding, and love"] (qtd. in Vivarelli, "Diario pittorico" 27).[20] The arrival in Lucania, thus, had a philosophical and existential impact on Levi. The concrete experience of the peasants, their land, and their world imposed itself upon his imagination, compelling him to break the circle of self-representation and to recognize the presence of alterity.

In *Cristo si è fermato a Eboli*, the Other is epitomized by Giulia Venere, Levi's housekeeper. Her figure dominates the book, acquiring a symbolic valence as an emblem of Lucania's agrarian civilization. Her relationship with Levi, too, is fundamental in the book, as it carries important implications for the rapport he establishes with the *contadini*, making explicit the contradictions and ambiguities implicated in his attempt to comprehend

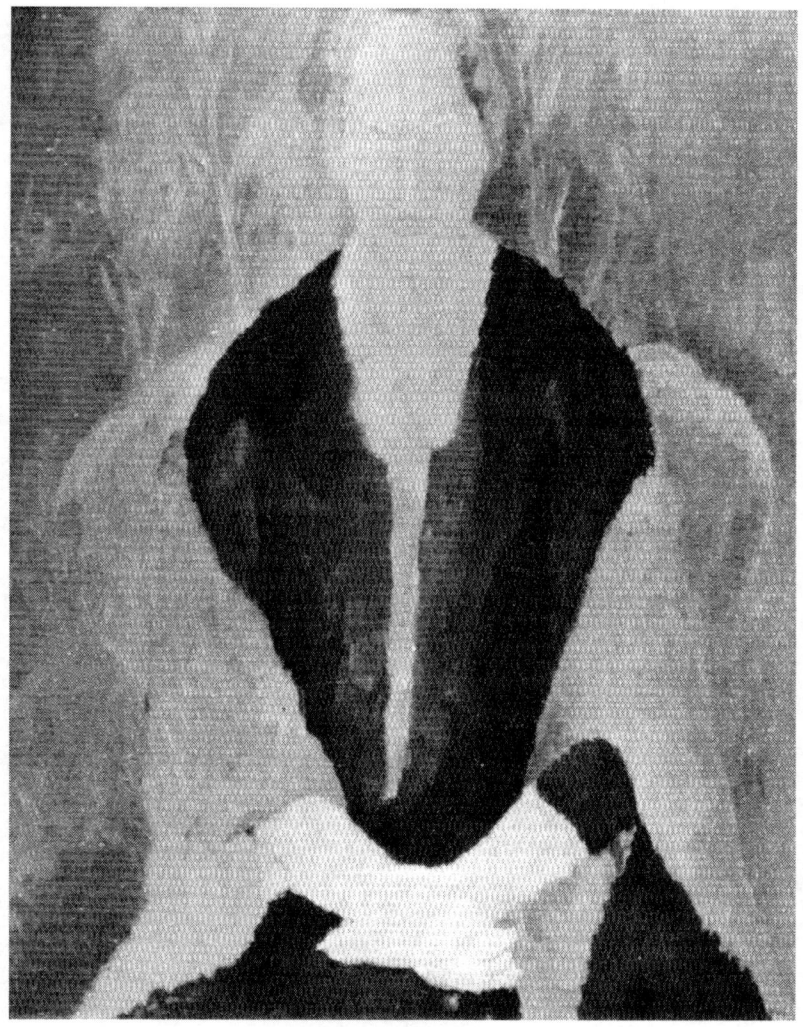

Figure 2. Carlo Levi, *Il ritratto della madre* (1930)
© 2012 Artists Rights Society (ARS), New York / SIAE, Rome

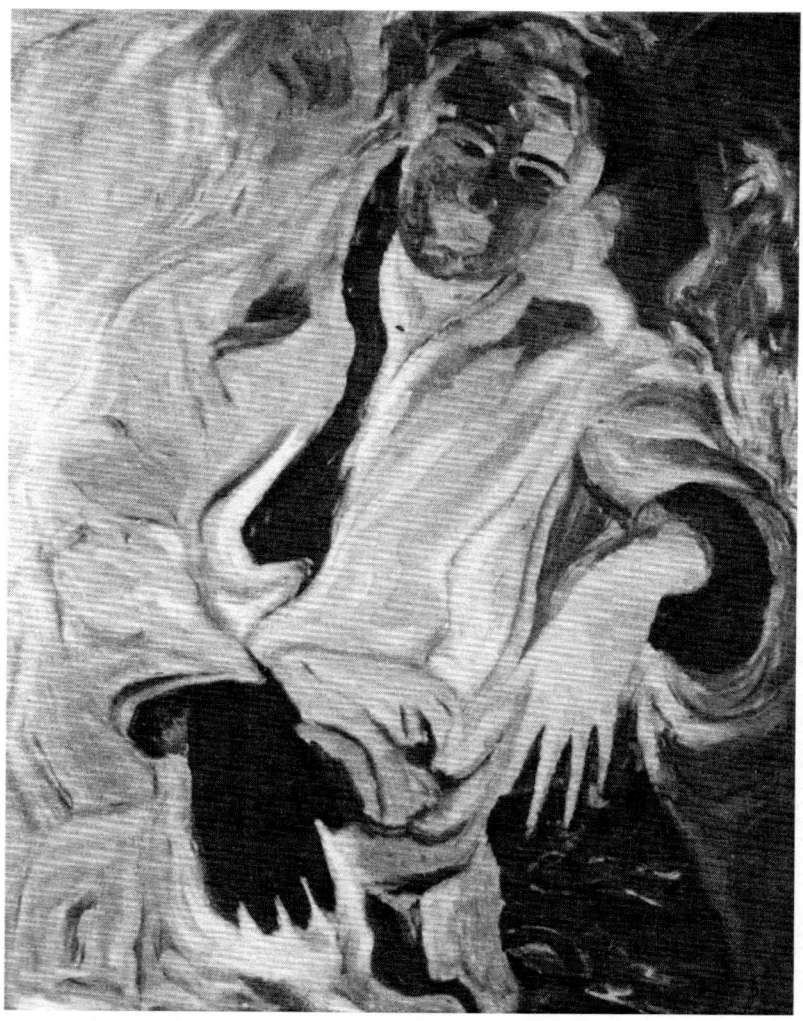

Figure 3. Carlo Levi, *L'eroe cinese* (1932)
© 2012 Artists Rights Society (ARS), New York / SIAE, Rome

their culture.[21] Giulia is the only woman in the village who can work in the house of a single man like Levi, since she has already lost her honor after having multiple pregnancies outside her marriage. Also called "La Santarcangelese," from the village beyond the hills where she was born, through her nickname she is openly labeled as an outsider in Gagliano's society. Her marginality is further confirmed by her widespread reputation as a witch. She is familiar with the secrets of all plants and herbs, the powers of magical objects, and the charms that can cure illnesses as well as provoke death. The young women of the village secretly approach her to learn how to make powerful love potions or remedial concoctions. Her life is completely governed by magical thinking, and in magic is rooted her stubborn refusal to be portrayed by Levi, who describes her reasoning thus:

> Un ritratto sottrae qualcosa alla persona ritrattata, un'immagine: e, per questa sottrazione, il pittore acquista un potere assoluto su chi ha posato per lui . . . La Santarcangelese, che viveva addirittura nel mondo della magía, aveva paura della mia pittura: e non tanto perché io potessi adoperare la sua figura dipinta, come una statua di cera, per qualche malvagia stregoneria ai suoi danni, quanto proprio per l'influsso e la potenza che io avrei esercitato cavando da lei un'immagine, come lo esercitavo certamente su persone e cose e alberi e paesi, con le pitture che andavo facendo ogni giorno. (136)

> *A portrait takes something away from the sitter—to be exact, an image of herself. By this means the painter acquires complete power over anyone who poses for him. . . . Giulia, who lived in a world ruled by magic, was afraid of my painting her, not so much because I might use the portrait as a waxen image and cast an evil spell upon her, but rather on account of the tangible say I should exercise over her just as, to her mind, I undoubtedly exercised it over the people and things and trees and villages that were the subjects of my painting. (154)*

For Giulia, there is no difference between the image that the painter projects onto the canvas and the object of representation. Indeed, as Levi writes in another essay, within the magical dimension of the peasant experience words and images are identical to their objects; signifier and signified fully coincide ("Il contadino e l'orologio" 31). On the basis of this identity, painting is a powerful instrument of magic, one that grants the artist possession of reality, by allowing him to capture its likeness and imprison it within the limits of the picture. Giulia's reticence is, thus, an act of resistance to being possessed and an assertion of her unmitigated difference in the face of Levi's attempts to conquer the distance between them. Her denial is perceived by Levi as a threat both to his masculine authority and to the system of rational philosophy to which he subscribes. Moreover, if the textualization of a work of art always introduces a self-reflective element in the text (Meltzer 11), then Giulia's refusal to be portrayed acquires a meta-artistic valence. Her struggle against Levi's wish to paint her image can be seen as symbolic of the difficulty, for the artist, of depicting otherness through modes of representation—be they verbal or visual—that are fundamentally alien to it.

Faced with Giulia's defiance, the writer makes a decision that poignantly illustrates the inescapable contradictions inherent in his position of sympathetic outsider. In order to overcome her fears, Levi decides to rely on "una magía più forte della paura; e questa non poteva essere che una potenza diretta e superiore, la violenza" ["a magic even stronger than fear, an irresistible power, namely violence"] (*Cristo* 137, 155). He admits reluctantly how he threatened to beat her and made the gesture: "[E] forse anche qualcosa di più dell'atto" ["(I)n fact I actually started"] (137, 155). Despite the thin veil of ambiguity in which Levi drapes this account, his description of the incident fully discloses the problematic side of his attitude toward Giulia and her culture:

> Appena vide e sentì le mie mani alzate, il viso della Giulia si coprì di uno sfavillío di beatitudine e si aperse ad un sorriso felice a mostrare i suoi denti di lupo. Come prevedevo, nulla era più desiderabile per lei che di essere dominata da una forza assoluta. Divenuta a un tratto docile come un agnello, la Giulia posò con pazienza, e di fronte agli argomenti indiscutibili della potenza, dimenticò i ben giustificati e naturali timori. (137)

> *As soon as she saw my raised hand and felt the first blow, Giulia's face filled with joy and she smiled beatifically, showing the full array of her wolf-like teeth. Just as I had imagined, she knew no greater happiness than that of being dominated by an absolute power. All of a sudden she became as gentle as a lamb and sat willingly for her portrait. Face to face with the unanswerable argument of brute force, she forgot all her natural and justifiable fears.* (155)

Levi's use of animal imagery in describing Giulia dehumanizes her and places her in a position of inferiority. Through an act of violence, asserting his power over her, he is able to transform her from a threatening wolf into a tame lamb, eager to be sacrificed on the altar of the painter's art.

In the context of Giulia's portrait, too, painting is evidently revealed to be the metaphoric site of complex power relations, inextricably linked with issues of gender and sexuality. The question of the "perennial gendering of the model as female" has "implications for priority, power, and value" (Steiner 15). Furthermore, the feminization of the model perpetuates and derives from "the analogy between creation and procreation and the age-old association of woman with matter (and man with spirit)" (15).

Levi explicitly deals with the question of sexuality in relation to Giulia. He writes that Giulia "si stupiva anche che io non le chiedessi di fare all'amore" ["was surprised that I showed no desire to make love to her"] (136, *154*). Within the peasants' Weltanschauung, erotic desire is perceived as an irresistible natural drive, which nobody can oppose: "Se un uomo e una donna si trovano insieme al riparo e senza testimoni, nulla può impedire che essi si abbraccino, né propositi contrari, né castità, né alcun'altra difficoltà può vietarlo" ["If a man and a woman are alone in sheltered spot, no power on earth can prevent their embrace"] (87, *99*). Levi and Giulia, sharing the same space with daily frequency, are expected to fall inevitably prey to the laws of attraction. Sexuality belongs exclusively to the instinctual sphere, and in their resignation to its fatal power, the women of Gagliano are "come animali selvatici," untamed animals (89). Yet the women's acceptance of sexual desire as natural and unavoidable situates them outside the codes of bourgeois morality and grants them a position of supremacy they would not enjoy in "civilized" society: "[L]'autorità delle madri è sovrana," writes Levi, and "il regime è matriarcale" ["(T)he mother holds absolute sway," and "a matriarchal regime prevails"] (89, *102*). Giulia's sexual bluntness is an expression of this alternative matriarchal order, which threatens Levi's masculinity by refusing to submit to his authority. In fact, the writer continues, although she was "disposta per me a qualunque servigio, . . . tuttavia, quando le chiedevo di posare, che le avrei fatto il ritratto, si rifiutava come di cosa impossibile" ["ready to render me any service, (she) absolutely refused to pose for her portrait"] (136, *154*). Within this perspective the portrait acquires the quality of a displaced sexual act, one where the male painter exercises his absolute rule over the female sitter, thus restoring the normality of gender relationships in the social order. Giulia's refusal to be depicted represents an attempt to assert her agency, a tentative form of resistance—albeit destined to fail—to Levi's efforts to impose his male dominance on her. Moreover, the motivation she gives for her denial is perceived as equally threatening by Levi, who sees the categories of Western rationalistic thought constantly called into question by her belief in the mysteries of magic. By obliging Giulia to pose for him, Levi asserts the hegemony of his own worldview, seemingly dismissing her fears as meaningless superstitions. In describing this episode, then, Levi effectively foregrounds the unavoidable objectification of Gagliano's peasants, implicit in any attempt to represent their existence, no matter how compassionate its intent.

Paradoxically, though, Giulia's portrait marks a positive turning point in Levi's narration. His skepticism toward the peasants' folklore begins to give way to acceptance and respect, even when their beliefs are radically at odds with the scientific basis of his medical training: "[I]o rispettavo gli abracadabra, ne onoravo l'antichità e l'oscura, misteriosa semplicità, preferivo essere loro alleato che loro nemico" ["I respected the amulets, paying tribute to their ancient origin and mysterious simplicity, and preferring to be their ally rather than their enemy"] (210, *238*). It is Giulia's portrait that allows Levi to initiate a dialogue with her and her world, eventually leading him to suspend his disbelief in magic and myth, and to enter her cultural realm. The portrait, in fact, gives substance and reality to the Other, as Levi argues in his essay on portraiture. The portrait is "il frutto di un rapporto e di una presenza: della collaborazione necessaria e preziosa della persona ritratta, che, momento di una relazione creatrice, dà quello che è anche senza saperlo" ["the result of a relationship and a presence; of the precious and necessary collaboration of the portrayed person, who, as a member of a creative relationship, gives all that he is, even if unconsciously"] ("I ritratti" 14). For Levi the source of all art is the creative relationship that the artist establishes with his subject, a relationship that is defined by mutuality and that excludes the dynamics of authority and power. In this respect, the portrait also represents a heuristic tool, a way of thinking of the world as fundamentally relationary (Vivarelli, "Carlo Levi tra impegno" n. pag.). By painting Giulia's portrait, then, Levi engages in cultural and epistemological dialogue with her. Although nothing can erase the fact that Giulia's portrait is only made possible through an action of forceful domination, at the same time it is painting that teaches Levi how to speak and understand the language of Gagliano's peasants. By posing for Levi, Giulia becomes his guide in his journey of discovery of her world, handing him the key that unlocks the gates to the magic imagination of peasant life.

Thus the connotation of art as a vehicle of power is entertained together with its opposite value as privileged entryway into Lucania's agrarian civilization, offering just one example of the many ambiguities of Levi's text. Indeed, *Cristo si è fermato a Eboli* resists all univocal interpretations, reflecting the complexity of the dialogue taking place between its author and the reality he faces. The reader must abandon binary thinking, which breaks down in the text as the categories of rational discourse are called into question. The folkloric dimension in which Giulia and her people live is ruled by another logic, based on analogy and relationality, in which opposites are never mutually exclusive but coexist without contradiction (Bakhtin, *Problems* 107). Levi describes vividly this multivalence of all things as seen from the peasants' perspective:

> Tutto, per i contadini, ha un doppio senso. La donna-vacca, l'uomo-lupo, il Barone-leone, la capra-diavolo non sono che immagini particolarmente fissate e rilevanti: ma ogni persona, ogni albero, ogni animale, ogni oggetto, ogni parola partecipa di questa ambiguità. La ragione soltanto ha un senso

univoco, e, come lei, la religione e la storia. Ma il senso dell'esistenza, come quello dell'arte e del linguaggio e dell'amore, è molteplice, all'infinito. Nel mondo dei contadini non c'è posto per la ragione, per la religione e per la storia. (102)

> To the peasants everything has a double meaning. The cow-woman, the werewolf, the lion-baron, and the goat-devil are only notorious and striking examples. People, trees, animals, even objects and words have a double life. Only reason, religion, and history have clear-cut meanings. But our feeling for life itself, for art, language, and love is complex, infinitely so. And in the peasants' world there is no room for reason, religion, and history. (116–17)

As Levi writes in *Paura della libertà*, religion and reason are connected insofar as they attempt to restrain and control the mystery of existence by institutionalizing it—whether through rituals or the laws and order of the state. The agrarian culture of the South resists the domestication of the sacred offered by organized religion, instead appropriating its ceremonies and transforming them into "riti pagani, celebratori della indifferenziata esistenza delle cose, degli infiniti terrestri dèi del villaggio" ["pagan rites, celebrating the existence of inanimate things, which the peasants endow with a soul, and the innumerable earthly divinities of the village"] (*Cristo* 102, *117*). The local Madonna, whose blessing is invoked every year to ensure a good harvest, is not the "pietosa Madre di Dio, ma una divinità sotterranea, nera delle ombre del grembo della terra, una Persefone contadina, una dea infernale delle messi" ["sorrowful Mother of God, but rather a subterranean deity, black with the shadows of the bowels of the earth, a peasant Persephone or lower-world goddess of the harvest"] (104, *118– 19*). Popular participation in the procession in her honor seems to lack an authentically religious sense, representing rather an example of carnivalistic suspension of the normal social order in favor of a Dionysiac abandonment to irrationality and sensuality: "[N]on si vedeva, negli occhi delle persone, felicità o estasi religiosa, ma una specie di follia, una pagana smoderatezza, e come uno stordimento a cui si lasciavano andare" ["(T)here was no happiness or religious ecstasy in the people's eyes; instead they seemed prey to a sort of madness, a pagan throwing off of restraint, and a stunned or hypnotized condition"] (103, *118*).

In *Cristo si è fermato a Eboli*, Levi renders this subversion of rational order in formal terms through ekphrasis, which challenges from within the verbal semiotic system by launching a dialogue with the immediacy of the visual image. Again, it is Giulia's painted image that helps illuminate the implications of Levi's poetics on the ethical and political level. Indeed, by giving her portrait such an important role in the narration and by repeatedly representing her in ekphrastic terms, Levi returns to her figure the revolutionary power that his violent imposition had previously annihilated. Through ekphrasis, in fact, the painted image rejects its role as an ornamental object and reclaims for itself a position within the order of verbal discourse (Mitchell, *Iconology* 110). Historically, the dialectic between word and image can be related to the opposition between culture and nature, mind and body, and ultimately, to the antagonism between genders: "Paintings, like women, are ideally silent, beautiful creatures designed for the gratification of the eye, in contrast to the sublime eloquence proper to the manly art of poetry. Paintings are confined to the narrow sphere of external display of their bodies and of the space which they ornament, while poems are free to range over an infinite realm of potential action and expression, the domain of time, discourse, and history" (Mitchell, *Iconology* 110). By integrating paintings into texts, ekphrasis grants them access to the "realm of potential action and expression," to "the domain of time, discourse, and history," thus questioning their roles as objects of pleasurable vision. Pictures are no longer silent but acquire voice and agency. The presence of imagistic and pictorial elements in a text can thus be read as a "transgression, an act of . . . violence involving an incorporation of the symbolic Other into the generic Self" (Mitchell, *Iconology* 157). The portraits of Giulia that Levi inserts in his narration, then, can be legitimately read also as manifestations of the painter's sincere attempt to recognize, accept, and give her otherness the power to speak.

Levi's ekphrastic portraits of Giulia in *Cristo si è fermato a Eboli*, which reproduce the numerous paintings of her, reflect the complexities and ambiguities of his attitude toward the South. In the first description of her, Levi transfigures her clearly into a symbol of Lucania as a land excluded from history, participating in the eternal dimension of myth:

> Giulia era una donna alta e formosa, con un vitino sottile come quello di un'anfora, tra il petto e i fianchi robusti. Doveva aver avuto, nella sua gioventù, una specie di barbara e solenne bellezza. Il viso era ormai rugoso per gli anni e giallo per la malaria, ma restavano i segni dell'antica venustà nella sua struttura severa, come nei muri di un tempio classico, che ha perso i marmi che l'adornavano, ma conserva intatta la forma e le proporzioni. Sul grande corpo imponente, diritto, spirante una forza animalesca, si ergeva, coperta dal velo, una testa piccola, dall'ovale allungato. La fronte era alta e diritta, mezza coperta da una ciocca di capelli nerissimi lisci e unti; gli occhi a mandorla, neri e opachi, avevano il bianco venato di azzurro e di bruno, come quello dei cani. Il naso era lungo e sottile, un po' arcuato; la bocca larga, dalle labbra sottili e pallide, con una piega amara, si apriva per un riso cattivo a mostrare due file di denti bianchissimi, potenti come quelli di un lupo. Questo viso aveva un fortissimo carattere arcaico . . . Nell'ondeggiare

dei veli e della larga gonnella corta, nelle lunghe gambe robuste come tronchi d'albero, quel grande corpo si muoveva con gesti lenti, equilibrati, pieni di una forza armonica, e portava, erta e fiera, su quella base monumentale e materna, la piccola, nera testa di serpente. (91–92)

> Giulia was a tall and shapely woman with a waist as slender as that of an amphora between her well-developed chest and hips. In her youth she must have had a solemn and barbaric beauty. Her face was wrinkled with age and yellowed by malaria, but there were traces of former charm in its sharp, straight lines, like those of a classical temple which has lost the marbles that adorned it but kept its shape and proportions. A small head, in the shape of a lengthened oval, covered with a veil, rose above her impressively large and erect body. Her forehead was straight and high, half hidden by a lock of smooth black hair; her almond-shaped, opaque, black eyes had whites with blue and brown veins in them like those of dogs. Her nose was thin and long, slightly hooked; her wide mouth with thin, pale lips, somewhat turned down at the corners in bitterness, opened when she laughed, over powerful, sparkling, wolflike teeth. Her face as a whole had a strongly archaic character . . . In billowing veils and a wide, short skirt, firmly planted on legs as long and sturdy as the trunks of trees, her large body moved slowly and with harmony and balance, bearing proudly and erectly on it monumental and maternal base the small, black head of a serpent. (105–6)

Giulia's body is maternal, strong, and monumental; she symbolizes the possibility of a total assimilation between humanity and nature, suggested by the comparison with a tree. Moreover, although the multiple animal similes that Levi adopts in this passage—where Giulia is compared to a dog, a wolf, and a snake, and the strength of her body is also given an animal quality—seem to reinforce the notion of her dehumanization as object of representation, they also powerfully communicate the peasant belief in the dual nature of all things. By underlining the animal aspect of Giulia's appearance, then, Levi offers her as a visual *trait d'union* between the reader's world and the different cultural dimension in which she lives, a dimension in which contradictions are not resolved but accepted as part of everyday existence.

This detailed description of Giulia's features constitutes the ekphrastic representation of one of her portraits, dated December 1935 (Figure 4). In this painting, Giulia looks frontally at the viewer. The perfect oval of her face is surrounded by the deep black crown of her hair and by the white kerchief that covers her head according to tradition. Her black, almond-shaped eyes contrast with the yellowish color of her skin, a sign of her age as well as of the malaria that affects the area. Her gaze is downcast, as though to resist being completely taken into the painter's representation,

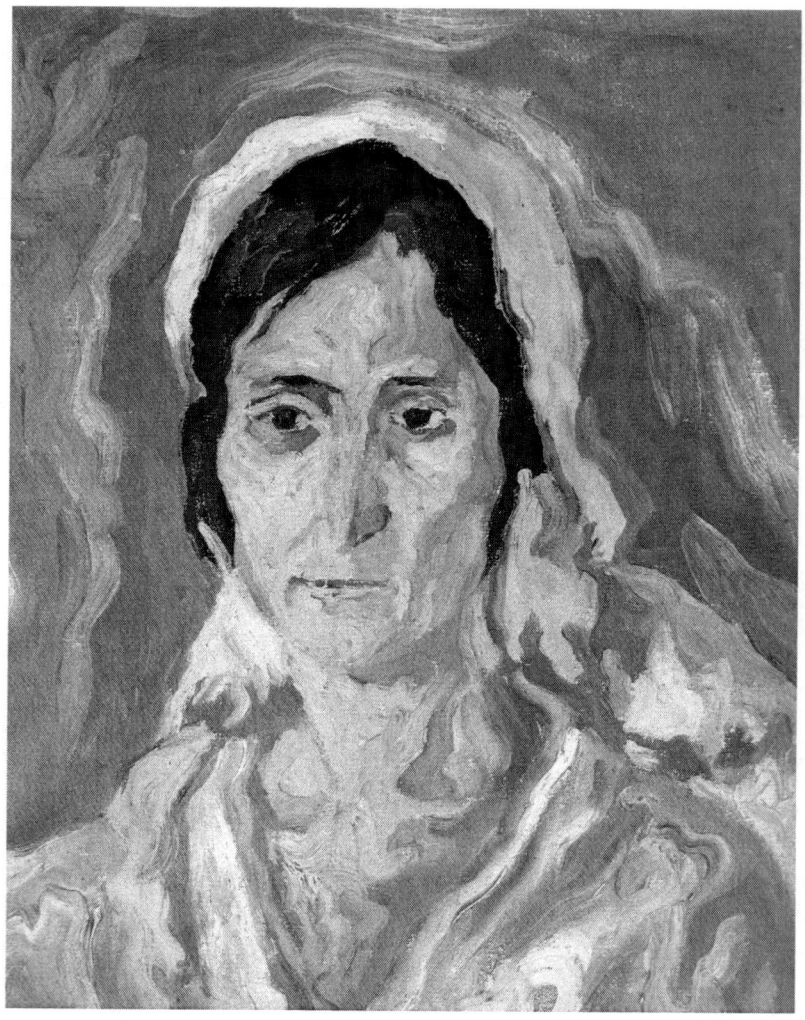

Figure 4. Carlo Levi, *Giulia la Santarcangelese (Ritratto di Giulia Venere)* (1935)
© 2012 Artists Rights Society (ARS), New York / SIAE, Rome

and reinforces the impression of sadness that her tightly closed mouth expresses. Immobile in her statuesque pose, against a neutral background, she forcefully asserts her existence in the world, as well as the existence of the civilization she incarnates. The dynamism of the brushstrokes creates an effect of depth that makes her emerge from the painting, imposing her presence outside the bidimensional space marked by the frame. Thus she seems to reclaim for herself a role that cannot be confined to her objectified image in the picture but that engages the viewer in an active cultural dialogue. The subversive potential of the representation of Giulia as a monument to peasant civilization is fully exploited in another picture, *La Santarcangelese*, dated at the beginning of 1936 (Figure 5). In this painting, Giulia is depicted according to the pictorial model of a Madonna with child, holding her youngest son on her lap. One arm around him, the other resting on her long and ample green skirt, Giulia is completely absorbed in the contemplation of her child, her gaze lowered as though to exclude the rest of the world. By replacing Christ's mother with Giulia, Levi both subverts the religious tradition, which wants her to be a virgin when Giulia is evidently not, and elevates the lives of the peasants to an object of sacred representation, inserting their images in the highly codified canon of Western painting. In this way, his painting parallels the same revolutionary challenge to established semiotic systems launched through his ekphrastic writing in *Cristo si è fermato a Eboli*.

The numerous ekphrases of Giulia's portraits are paralleled by the "ritratti di paesaggi e di persone," which functioned as painterly mediations between Levi's memory and its literary recreation of the past. They comprise different genres, from the epic portrayals of the peasants—the men compared to "figure italiche antichissime" ["most ancient Italic types"] (*Cristo* 123, *140*), the women in costume likened to "una flottiglia di barche tondeggianti e oscure, pronte a prendere tutte insieme il vento nelle piccole vele bianche" ["a fleet of dark round boats waiting all together for the wind to inflate their white sails"] (28, *31*)—to the caricatures of the *galantuomini*. As in *Ritratto del dottore* (Figure 6), Doctor Milillo, for instance, is "un buon uomo, completamente rimbecillito" ["a good man, gone completely to seed"], with "guance cascanti e gli occhi lagrimosi e bonari di un vecchio cane da caccia" ["flabby cheeks and kind watery eyes of an old hunting dog"] and grotesquely ugly with his "labbro superiore enormemente lungo, e uno inferiore cadente" ["upper lip, which was exaggeratedly long, and the hanging lower one"] (12–13, *13*). His daughters are "tarchiate, grassotte, esuberanti, nere come sacchi di carbone, con neri capelli corti arricciolati e svolazzanti, neri occhi che lancia[no] fiamme, neri baffi sulle grandi bocche carnose e neri peli sulle braccia e sulle gambe in perpetuo movimento" ["stocky and plump, as dark-skinned as coal

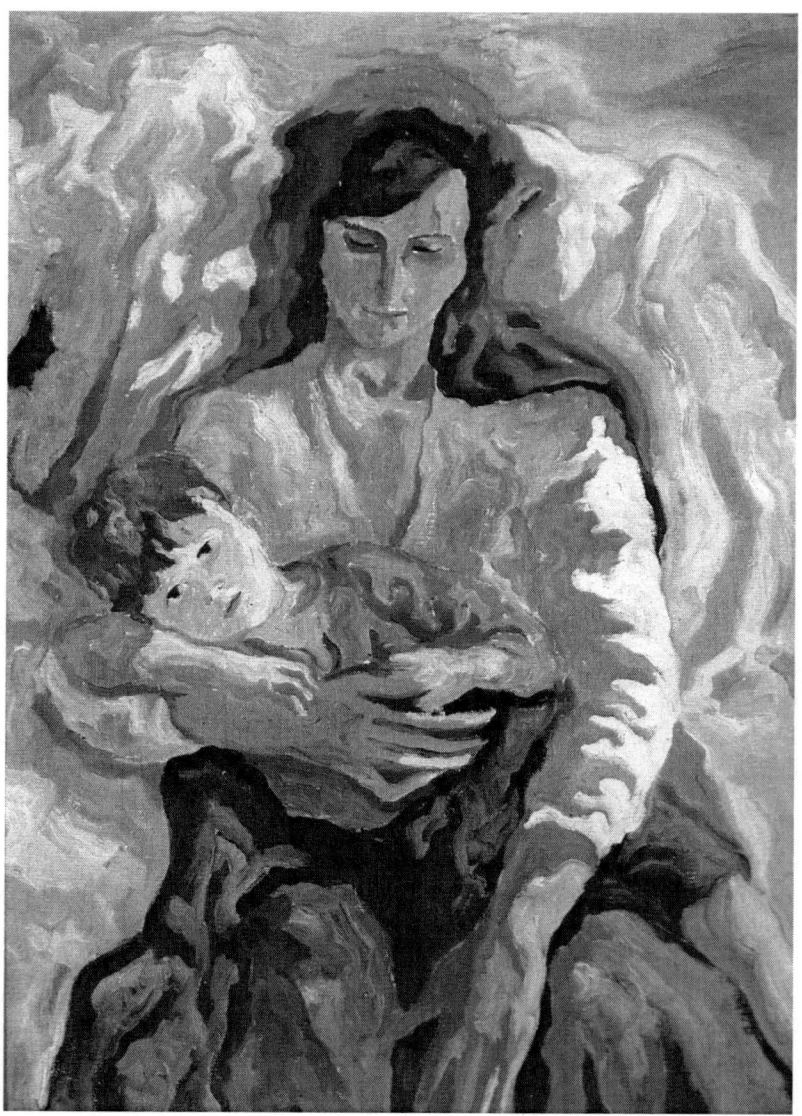

Figure 5. Carlo Levi, *La Santarcangelese* (1936)
© 2012 Artists Rights Society (ARS), New York / SIAE, Rome

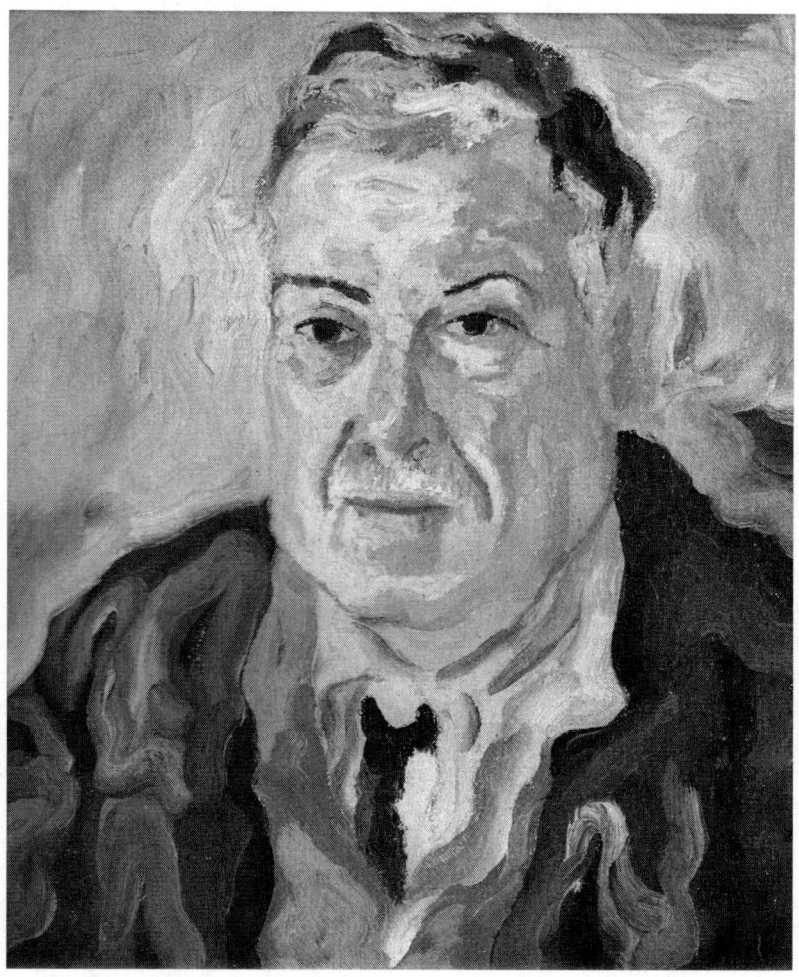

Figure 6. Carlo Levi, *Ritratto del dottore* (1936)
© 2012 Artists Rights Society (ARS), New York / SIAE, Rome

sacks, with short, curly, flying black hair, fiery black eyes, and black hairs above their full lips and on their continually moving arms and legs"] (52, 60). In these satirical portraits the members of the local *piccola borghesia* are clearly treated as Levi's ideological Other for their allegiance—or compromises—with the fascist regime. Their physical appearance carries a symbolic dimension, becoming a visible sign of the ethical and political flaws of their class.

Indeed, for Levi the portrait requires a search for both somatic and introspective likeness, implying moral indications (Trombadori 77). His depiction of the fascist mayor clearly exemplifies how his use of portraiture in the narration not only performs an aesthetic function but also plays an important role in the ideological world of the text. "Magalone Luigi," writes Levi, "è un giovanotto alto, grosso e grasso, con un ciuffo di capelli neri e unti che gli piovono in disordine sulla fronte, un viso giallo e imberbe da luna piena, e degli occhietti neri e maligni, pieni di falsità e di soddisfazione. Porta gli stivaloni, un paio di brache a quadretti da cavallerizzo, una giacchetta corta, e giocherella con un frustino" ["was an overgrown, corpulent young man with a lock of oily black hair tumbling over his forehead, a yellowish, beardless face and darting black eyes both insincere and self-satisfied in expression. He wore high boots, checked riding breeches, and a short jacket, and his hands were toying with a small whip"] (11, *12*). The discrepancy between the attention the *podestà* pays to his clothes—evidently intended as a sign of gentility—as opposed to the care of his person—which looks unhealthy and unkempt—reinforces the impression of falsity that his eyes immediately communicate. The duplicity that Levi exposes in Magalone is a direct reflection of the deceitfulness of Fascism, with its empty rhetoric, hardly able to mask its basic political flimsiness.

The theme of fascism's insubstantiality is further explored in the passage that follows, which expands verbally the condemnation visually present in Magalone's portrait. By skillfully alternating free indirect discourse and the first-person narrator's ironic perspective, Levi fully discloses the *podestà*'s narrow mentality and reveals how his allegiance to the Fascist Party is more a function of his social anxieties than a product of a political set of beliefs. Meeting Levi for the first time upon his arrival in Gagliano, in fact, Magalone gives him a basic picture of the social functioning of village life:

> Ci sono qui alcuni confinati, una diecina in tutto. Non devo vederli, perché è proibito. Del resto sono gentaglia, operai, robetta. Io invece sono un signore, si vede subito. Mi accorgo che il professore è orgoglioso di potere, per la prima volta, esercitare la sua autorità su un signore, un pittore, un dottore,

un uomo di cultura. Anch'egli è un uomo colto, ci tiene a farmelo sapere. Con me egli vuol essere gentile, siamo dello stesso rango. Ma come mai mi sono fatto mandare al confino? E proprio in quest'anno, che la Patria diventa così grande.... Ad ogni modo, qui mi troverò bene. Il paese è salubre e ricco. Un po' di malaria, cosa da nulla. I contadini sono quasi tutti piccoli proprietari, nell'elenco dei poveri non c'è quasi nessuno. (12)

> *There were quite a few political prisoners here, a dozen in all. I was not allowed to see them; this was forbidden. Anyhow they were of no account, workers and such, whereas it was plain to see that I was a gentleman.*
>
> *I realized that the professor was proud to exercise his authority for the first time over a gentleman, a painter, a doctor, a man of some culture. He too was cultivated, he hastened to assure me; he wanted to treat me well because we were of the same class. But how in the world had I got myself arrested? And this year, of all years, when our country was on the road to greatness? ... But I should be comfortable here; the village was healthful and prosperous. There was only a bit of malaria, nothing to speak of. Most of the peasants owned their own land and very few of them were listed as indigent. (12–13)*

"Professor" Magalone—in reality an elementary school teacher—cannot understand why Levi, who belongs to the same bourgeoisie he is proud to be a part of, opposes fascism, especially at a moment in which the regime promises to become stronger thanks to its imperial enterprise in Africa. Magalone is, thus, representative of a southern agrarian bourgeoisie of historically liberal leanings, who had simply followed the new political leadership without questioning its positions. In Levi's view, it was precisely the reliance of the post-Risorgimento Liberal Party on "questa base sociale essenzialmente reazionaria, illiberale" ["a social basis that is essentially reactionary and anti-liberal"] ("Antonio Salandra" 11) that opened the way to Mussolini's ascent to power. In a 1926 article on the former prime minister, Antonio Salandra, Levi criticized the liberal doctrine as a form of idolatry of the state: "Come il risorgimento fu opera di Stato, opera di Stato sarà la nostra politica nuova. Allo Stato tutti i compiti, dallo Stato tutte le soluzioni. Quindi problema sostanziale è quello dell'autorità" ["Just as the Risorgimento was the work of the State, so our new politics will be a work of the State. To the State all tasks, from the State all solutions. The fundamental problem is, thus, that of authority"] (4). This emphasis on authority, rather than on the people, created a fundamental incongruity within the texture of the nation, as Magalone's words illustrate. His loyalty to fascism is directly proportional to its perceived authority and has nothing to do with the validity of its message. The disjunction between words and their contents that characterizes the mayor's political discourse is further made evident by the contrast between his description of the village as salubrious and his own yellow complexion, a visible signal of the endemic malaria that afflicts the area. Although Magalone believes he can erase the reality of the disease by negating it verbally, the visible marks of the illness unequivocally disclose its presence to Levi's medical eye. Visual language, then, is proposed here as a more truthful mode of representation of the world, more faithful than words to its concreteness, less prone to be corrupted and manipulated.

To Magalone's distorted use of language, Levi opposes his own, where "le parole e le immagini non possono non essere identiche col loro oggetto, pienamente significative" ["words and images cannot but be identical to their objects, fully signifying"] ("Il contadino e l'orologio" 31) as he puts it in a later essay. Indeed, Levi's use of ekphrasis is a manifestation of his attempt to shape a language capable of obtaining the same adherence to the object it represents that painting is able to achieve and that peasant language reveals. This identity of sign and signified is, for Levi, the mark of what he calls "realismo contadino." It is a realism that does not aim to reproduce the world as it is, because it gives it reality and life in the act of representation ("Il contadino e l'orologio" 31). As we have seen in the previous discussion of "realismo contadino," Levi anticipates here contemporary views of mimesis as an instrument for producing, rather than representing, reality, as well as cognitive activity (Compagnon 96). In the numerous examples of the *contadini* recognizing in his paintings the existence of faces and places that constitute their everyday reality, Levi proposes painting as a powerful heuristic tool, both for the painter, who, through painting, achieves a deeper understanding of the world of the peasants, and for the viewers of the work of art, who can gain awareness of the existence of this world. In this respect, through his art Levi fulfills the role of the Gramscian intellectual in the education of subaltern classes. The figure of the organic intellectual—able to detach himself from the bourgeois tendencies of Italian culture—represents, in the Gramscian schema, an instrument of radical social transformation. Through education, in fact, the intellectual is able to empower the dispossessed by providing them with the self-awareness necessary to enact positive change.[22]

In *Cristo si è fermato a Eboli*, the educational potential of art emerges in a particularly powerful manner in connection to the children of Gagliano, Levi's most faithful friends. They seek his company, moved at first by their curiosity for his dog, Barone, and then fascinated by his painting. They gladly and proudly pose for him as models, follow him on his painting expeditions, help carry his tools, and even jealously preserve as precious treasures his empty paint tubes and old brushes. A member of this circle of young admirers, Giovanni Fanelli, becomes so enthused about painting that he secretly applies himself to becoming an artist, imitating Levi in all the technical details of the craft, from preparing the canvas to stretching it on the easel. In eight-year-old Giovanni's mind, technique is as essential to art as the act of painting itself, as his bemused teacher observes: "[N]on vidi mai in nessuno quella sua fiducia in una rivelazione che dovesse venire da sola, dal lavoro; quel suo credere nella ripetizione della tecnica come di una infallibile formula magica, o come di un lavoro della terra, che, arata e seminata, porta il suo frutto" ["I have never seen another boy with his faith that a spontaneous revelation would come out of his labor, that the practice of a technique would work like magic, and that his efforts would bear fruit as certainly as a field that has been plowed and sown"] (187, 212). In Levi's description, the boy's pictures have a certain "incanto," thus manifesting the magic quality their author attributes to them. "Incanto," in its multiplicity of meanings, from "magic" to "fascination, charm," is a key word in Levi's description of the children's attitude toward his painting. Indeed, as for the would-be painter Giovanni, for the other young peasants the magic of painting is a source of endless wonder, in its capacity to create reality from nothingness: "[N]on finivano di stupirsi delle immagini che apparivano, come per incanto, sulla tela, e che erano proprio le case, le colline e i visi dei contadini" ["(T)hey never ceased to marvel at the images that appeared, as if by magic, on my canvas, of the houses and hills and faces they knew so well"] (186, 211). Art, thus, proves to be an essential instrument in the construction of the children's consciousness of their own being and of the existence of the world.

Levi's understanding of his painting as an epistemological tool is radically opposed to that of another artist living in Gagliano, Don Trajella, the parish priest who was demoted to the village as a punishment for sexual misconduct. Like the Turinese activist, he is a foreigner in Lucania and an exile. He shares Levi's love for books, and he is also a painter. Nonetheless, the cleric's notion of culture is completely different from Levi's. Trajella sees an unbreacheable chasm between his former intellectual labors and the present of his life in Gagliano. Faced with the peasants' incomprehension and their indifference to the systems of knowledge he is accustomed to, the clergyman condemns them as heathens and heretics. His constant use of Latin emphasizes even more the distance between him and his flock. Thus he becomes a symbol of the aloofness of the educated classes, whether linked to the state or the church, from the people they are called to instruct. Trajella's historiographic oeuvre, a biography of the obscure Spanish saint Calogero, will not change the peasants' lives, nor will they be touched by his polyptychs representing salient episodes of the holy man's life.[23] On the other hand, the split between the priest and the people causes the weakening of his own intellectual energy, deprived of its purpose: his books lie abandoned in a corner of his decaying house, among roosting chickens, while his paintings remain stashed under his bed. Through the tragicomic figure of Trajella, then, Levi deprecates the elitist idea of culture normally proposed by church and state, predicated upon the contemptuous condemnation of other forms of cultural expression and destined to remain profoundly alien to people's lives.

Whereas Trajella and his parishioners will never speak the same language, Levi's painting speaks to the peasants, revealing the world anew. As Levi articulates in theoretical terms in his essay "L'invenzione della verità," the subaltern agrarian society becomes conscious of its own being and the separate existence of reality through the encounter with art. This recognition founds for the peasants the possibility of a creative relationship with society, one in which they will no longer be "strumenti meccanici: braccia, schiene, mani, macchine di lavoro servile" ["mechanical instruments: arms, backs, hands, slavish labor machines"] but rather agents in the construction of their own future ("L'invenzione della verità" 54). In *Cristo si è fermato a Eboli* the capacity of art to open the doors to the world of "potential action and expression, the domain of time, discourse, and history" (Mitchell, *Iconology* 110) belongs to the children. Their discovery of painting as an instrument of knowledge intensifies their desire to understand the world, as Levi writes: "Erano, in generale, molto più intelligenti e precoci dei ragazzi cittadini della loro età: rapidi nell'intuire, pieni di desiderio di apprendere e di ammirazione per le cose ignote del mondo di fuori" ["As a general rule, they were further advanced, both mentally and physically, than city children of the same age. They were gifted with insight, a thirst for learning, and ready appreciation of all the wonders of the outside world"] (*Cristo* 190, 215–16). Made aware, through the visual means of art, of the existence of this "mondo di fuori," the peasant children realize that, in order to negotiate the distance that separates them from it, they must learn to use its language and instruments. Thus they ask Levi to teach them how to write: "Un giorno che mi videro scrivere mi chiesero se avessi potuto insegnarglielo: a scuola non imparavano nulla, col sistema delle bacchette, dei sigari e delle chiacchiere dal balcone, e dei discorsi patriottici. Andavano tutti a scuola, l'istruzione è obbligatoria, ma, con quei maestri, ne uscivano analfabeti. Così presero di loro iniziativa l'abitudine di venire qualche volta la sera a scrivere nella mia cucina" ["One day when a group of them saw me writing they asked me to teach them the art. They learned precious little at school with the inspiration of Don Luigi's cane, cigars, and patriotic speeches; although attendance was obligatory they came out as illiterate as when they went in. Of their own free will some of them came in the evening to practice writing in my kitchen"] (190, *216*). As for Levi painting constitutes the magic key that allows him to enter the universe of the *contadini*, for the children of Gagliano art is the gateway to a broader world. As this episode shows, in fact, painting does not limit the peasants' realm of expression to the irrational domain of art. On the contrary, it establishes here the possibility of an encounter between the marginal civilization of the rural South and the rationalistic positions embraced by the centers of ideological and political power.

For Levi the civilization of southern peasantry, with its resistance to the categories of modernity, history, the state, and binary logic, becomes a critical intellectual position from which to observe the hegemonic North-West axis and assert the necessity of preserving difference in the face of authoritarian models of modernity. The peasants' defiance is the symptom of the confrontation taking place between two different civilizations, neither one of which is able to assimilate the other: "Campagna e città, civiltà precristiana e civiltà non più cristiana, stanno di fronte; e finché la seconda continuerà ad imporre alla prima la sua teocrazia statale, il dissidio continuerà . . . Finché Roma governerà Matera, Matera sarà anarchica e disperata, e Roma disperata e tirannica" ["Country and city, a pre-Christian civilization and one that is no longer Christian, stand face to face. As long as the second imposes its deification of the State upon the first, they will be in conflict . . . Just as long as Rome rules over Matera, Matera will be lawless and despairing, and Rome despairing and tyrannical"] (221, *251*). Levi discusses the opposition between Matera and Rome sporadically throughout *Cristo si è fermato a Eboli* and more at length in the final pages of the text. Only a peasant revolution, leading to a radical redefinition of the state, can result in an inclusive and authentically progressive social and political dynamic, empowering the rural underclass of the Italian South. The new state can correspond neither to the fascist state nor to the liberal or communist regimes, which are different shapes of the same religion of the state. Whereas in these forms of government the individual is subordinate to the interests and objectives of the nation-state, Levi calls for a radical reform, which, according to the implicit laws of solidarity and community of peasant civilization, would involve a dramatic reevaluation of the individual's role in society and of the function of local autonomies. The actual forms of this autonomy would need to be worked out in relation to the circumstances of specific local experiences (222–23).[24]

By trying to give voice to the peasants' own voices through a narrative style that includes the Other of the word, the image—just as the peasants are the internal Other of Fascist Italy—Levi gives legitimacy to Lucania's "southern thought," "as the thinking of southern Europe thinking itself as a subject" (Dainotto 381). Levi's defense of the civilization of southern Italian peasantry against the totalizing modernization imposed by the fascist regime represents, in this sense, a first attempt to "consider the Mediterranean before, between and beyond the self-serving objectifying logic of European humanism, its modernity and its nationalism" (Chambers 68). The South "becomes the site of an ongoing and unfolding critique of the 'progress' which has sought to enclose and explain it over the last five hundred years that constitute 'our' modernity" (Chambers 42). Cassano, the theorizer of this new "southern thought" recognizes how Levi's understanding of the South resonates with his own. When Levi was writing his memoir, the dominant perspective on the South of Italy was (as it continues to be) that of a homogeneously backward area that needed to be transformed according to the model of Northern-European modernity. Levi, however, rejects the notion of the South as a "black hole of barbaric primitiveness" (Cassano, "Cinquantasei anni" 9). Without ignoring the social inequality, hardship, and grief that define life in the southern regions of Italy, Levi challenges the idea that a new, modern society can be built over a *tabula rasa* of old repression and oppression. Levi's project for the South, as he outlines it in *Cristo si è fermato a Eboli*, is to give its people the responsibility of building their own future, in a "civic society that is not controlled by the political class and parties," in a new form of political autonomy (Cassano 11). Levi's political vision for the South is, indeed, prophetic; after the failure of every centralized intervention, crippled by lobbyism, organized crime, and corruption, *today* southern Italy has the opportunity to redefine itself in its own terms, precisely as Levi augured immediately after World War II. This opportunity cannot be squandered by theorizing the South as pure subalternity, as a space to be colonized (Cassano 14). Precisely against this colonizing logic, Levi represents southern Italy as a space that is Other, different, but that despite its history of domination cannot be reduced to a series of negative attributes. It is a world in which the present and the past coexist in collective memory, in which a sense of community protects individuals from pain and death, in which the individual is not lost in the mass but embraced by a choral solidarity. It is a world from which it is possible to resist the uprootedness and isolation of modernity without being lured by the comfort of totalitarian ideologies—a world that offers a framework that "decolonizes the mind" (Cassano 16).

Indeed, while Levi's representation of the South is a protest against modernity, it is also a political act of resistance against the fascist imperialist project, which experiments, within Italy's internal borders, with the very logic of colonial occupation and rule that it aims to impose in Africa. Piedmont had "rehearsed" "the language of colonialism and its civilizing mission" in the annexation of southern Italian regions in 1860–61 (Chambers 145). The liberal governments of postunification Italy, moreover, justified the colonization of Libya and East Africa as a solution to the question of southern poverty and backwardness (*Cristo* 117). Mussolini's concept of an imperial national destiny for Italy simply recast an old ideal of colonial supremacy in the Mediterranean in Roman terms, arguing for the necessity to spread modernity and progress to the parched lands of the Italian South and Africa alike. The colonial enterprise is an important subtext in *Cristo si è fermato a Eboli*, emerging forcefully when, thanks to the conquest of Addis Abeba, an amnesty is declared and Levi can return home. Yet the peasants do not celebrate this as a national victory. They do not feel included in the successes of the fascist state, and the *podestà* shares the Duce's triumphal announcement with an empty square. Once again, the peasants "pensavano che, malgrado le promesse, non ci sarebbe stato posto per loro in quelle terre favolose e male acquistate; e non pensavano all'Africa quando scendevano alle rive dell'Agri" ["in spite of all that was promised . . . saw no openings for themselves in the mythical and ill-gotten new land. The thought of Africa did not even cross their minds as they went down to the banks of the Agri"] (233, 265–66). The basin of the Agri river and Africa are collapsed in Levi's narrative, as different spaces in which the "civilizing mission" of modernity unfolds. In *Cristo si è fermato a Eboli*, Levi asserts the value of this civilization in the face of the colonizing forces of modernity and anticipates the notion of the South as a space of multiplicity, complexity, and hybridity—a privileged space that allows us to think *beyond* modernity.

2

L'Orologio

The Challenge of Time

In the novel *L'Orologio*, published by Einaudi in 1950, Levi develops and expands the critique of totalizing epistemological positions that he had begun in *Cristo si è fermato a Eboli*.[1] He does so through a highly modern style that breaks down traditional narrative structures and dilates the dimension of time toward a sense of Bergsonian *durée*. In this respect, the novel traces its genealogy back to Laurence Sterne's *Tristram Shandy*, which Levi himself recognized as its greatest literary influence. Writing about Sterne's novel, Levi observes that in many ways it anticipated James Joyce's *Ulysses* by embracing a notion of time as "durata, che si sostituisce al tempo, e costringe a una vaga corsa dietro alla sfuggente realtà, e scioglie e distrugge la struttura e il tempo del romanzo" ["durée, which replaces time and forces us to run after an elusive reality and dissolves and destroys the structure and timing of the novel"][2] ("Il Tristram Shandy" 150–51). Linear narrative is broken down by digressions and diversions whose purpose, writes Levi, is to inflate time and exorcise death—whose inexorable advance is marked by the ticking noise of clocks and watches (153). Levi's analysis of *Tristram Shandy* applies equally to *L'Orologio*. At the beginning of the book, the watch that gives the novel its name breaks, signaling in this way the collapse of historical time and the narrator's entrance into an expanded temporal dimension, where memories, prophetic visions, and dreams exist on the same plane as events unfolding in the present. This layered notion of time corresponds to the space where the story takes place, the city of Rome, which, in its palimpsestic nature, contains in its present the living traces of its past.

In representing Rome as a space that challenges the course of progressive temporality Levi relies once again on a poetics of the visual, using the image as a challenge to the flow of time. The dialogue between temporal and spatial dimensions that his pictorial style introduces repeatedly defies the unfolding of consecutive temporality. The objects of the narrator's gaze here are, first of all, architectural spaces and urban trajectories, details of the broader topography of the city that Levi creates in his book. The first result of this visual approach is, indeed, the construction of a verbal map of the city. Like Charles Baudelaire's *flâneur* in Paris, the first-person narrator of *L'Orologio* wanders through the streets of Rome, creating a series of labyrinthine itineraries that reflect spatially the temporal meanderings of his narration, which is constantly shifting between dreams and reality, the present and the memory of the past. But very much like Baudelaire's Paris, Levi's Rome is not a deserted space. At the center of the city's topography pulsates the heart of the Roman people. Levi's narrator revels in the crowds of the streets of Rome just as the *flâneur* enjoys losing himself amid the Parisian masses. Baudelaire describes this experience in entirely visual terms, defining the *flâneur* as "a mirror as vast as the crowd itself ... He is an 'I' with an insatiable appetite for the 'non-I,' at every instant rendering and explaining it in pictures more living than life itself, which is always unstable and fugitive" (9). This emphasis on the visual aspect of the *flâneur*'s relationship to the city is extremely relevant to understanding Levi's project in *L'Orologio*. As we shall see, in this novel Levi successfully attempts to fix in time "Roma fuggitiva"—as he calls it in the title of a later collection of essays—by creating the verbal equivalent of pictures that make present, as Baudelaire suggests, what belongs to the moment and is thus inevitably condemned to disappear. The images of the Roman people are superimposed on the map of the city that Levi designs through his narration, creating a gallery of portraits in which the inexorable advance of time is conquered.

As in *Cristo si è fermato a Eboli*, Levi's aesthetic choices in *L'Orologio* are not an end in themselves. Rather, they must be understood as participating in Levi's ethical and political concerns at the time. As Levi's mouthpiece, Casorin, declares during a very important conversation in the novel, the breakdown of narrative that takes place in *L'Orologio* corresponds to the author's refusal to impose a univocal meaning to the multiplicity of human experience. After Auschwitz, Casorin argues, echoing Theodor Adorno, such totalizing representations of human history are no longer possible. On a more strictly historical level, *L'Orologio* recounts the disillusioned chronicle of the failure of the parties involved in the Resistance truly to renovate the Italian political class. By formally challenging the linear development of time, Levi makes a statement about the lack of historical progress toward social reform and freedom that characterized the Italian political vicissitudes after the fall of Fascism.

L'Orologio is a politically charged autobiographical novel, in which the first-person narrator recounts a series of seemingly banal events taking place in his life over the course of three days, in November 1946. At the beginning of the novel, the protagonist, Carlo, accidentally breaks the gold watch he received from his father upon graduating from university and has to cross the entire city of Rome in order to find somebody who will repair it. After finally leaving the watch with a jeweler, he attends a series of work meetings at the newspaper he directs, runs into a friend who asks him to accompany him in his search for a mysterious woman, and moves to a new apartment in a patrician mansion. He then concludes the evening attending an important press conference at the Viminale. The following day, having worked all night at the press, he hurriedly leaves for Naples, where an uncle lies in critical condition. Having arrived in Naples, after various adventures, at a late hour, he decides to postpone his visit to his uncle until the following morning, reassured about his state of health by a telephone conversation. However, he wakes up on the morning of this third day to find that the uncle has died. He pays a brief visit to the uncle's deathbed but nonetheless must rush back to Rome, where he arrives much more quickly thanks to a car ride offered to him by a high-powered political ally. The novel closes in a circular manner, with the protagonist contemplating the gold watch—identical to the one he had broken earlier—he has received in inheritance from his uncle.

At the center of these apparently unremarkable fictional events lies an actual political occurrence—namely, the fall of the government of the *Partito d'Azione*, headed by Ferruccio Parri. Parri was well-respected as a partisan hero and Resistance leader, but ultimately proved incapable of achieving real political authority. Elected prime minister in June 1945, he held office until November of the same year, when the Liberal Party withdrew its support and, in accord with the Christian Democratic Alcide De Gasperi, forced him to resign. Socialists and Communists also decided not to back Parri, mainly for reasons of political opportunism. His cabinet was eventually replaced by a coalition led by De Gasperi himself (Ward, *Antifascism* 168).[3] Levi followed these events very closely, since at the time he was the editor of *L'Italia Libera*, the Action Party newspaper, in its Roman offices. In the novel, Levi describes the press conference in which Parri announces his resignation, and presents the fall of Parri as an episode of crucial importance in shaping the identity of postwar Italy:

> Sapevamo tutti benissimo, come una verità evidente e ovvia . . . , che quelli erano avvenimenti decisivi, che il futuro dell'Italia, per molti anni, ne sarebbe dipeso; che si trattava di decidere se quello straordinario movimento popolare che si chiamava la Resistenza avrebbe avuto uno sviluppo nei fatti, rinnovando la struttura del paese; o se sarebbe stato respinto tra i ricordi storici, rinnegato come attiva realtà, relegato tutt'al più nel profondo della coscienza individuale, come una esperienza morale senza frutti visibili, piena soltanto delle promesse di un lontano futuro. (50–51)

> We all knew very well . . . that these were decisive events and that they would affect the future of Italy for many years.
>
> The question now was whether that extraordinary popular movement called the Resistance would actually develop further, remolding the shape of the country, or would be pushed back into historical memory, disavowed as active reality, be relegated, at best, to the depths of the individual conscience, like a spiritual experience without visible fruits, filled only with the promises of a distant future. (The Watch 48–49)

The rise to power of the Christian Democratic Party (DC) coincides, for Levi, with the relegation of the Resistance to a myth of the past, bearing no consequences for the present. This represents the culmination of the unavoidable process of corruption and defeat that ideals undergo when they confront the reality of Roman politics. Indeed, when Levi arrives in Rome for the first time in August 1945 after having spent the months of the Nazi occupation hiding in Florence and publishing articles in clandestine papers, he immediately realizes the incongruity between his former political experience and the present situation. In the opening pages of *L'Orologio*, his encounter with the city is described in terms of a cultural shock. He relates his "ansia gioiosa" ["joyous anticipation"] in climbing the stairs that led to the newspaper's offices, but his enthusiasm is immediately tamed in the first meeting with the former head of his newspaper. On this occasion, Levi is faced for the first time with the discrepancy between words and their substance that seems to define Roman life:

> Mi fece i suoi auguri per il mio prossimo lavoro al giornale con parole gentili, oratorie e ricercate: mi parlò della situazione politica con nobiltà e bello sdegno, mi disse dell'organizzazione e dei redattori con sapiente competenza, mi accennò alle difficoltà che aveva incontrato con orgoglioso ritegno. Io lo ascoltavo: a un certo punto della sua allocuzione appoggiai sulla scrivania il bracciuolo del seggiolone che mi era, durante tutto questo tempo, rimasto in mano. Come egli posò gli occhi su quel pezzo di legno, il corso della sua eloquenza si interruppe, e i suoi pensieri e i suoi detti presero un'altra via. – Tu non sai, – disse all'improvviso, con voce mutata, – tu non sai quante umiliazioni, in questo posto. Non si può far nulla. Il giornale non ha mezzi, vedrai. Non c'è un soldo. (37)

> *He wished me luck with future work on the newspaper, in kind, sophisticated, and somewhat oratorical words. Then he spoke of the political situation with nobility and fine scorn, praised the organization and the editorial staff, and confessed with proud reserve to all the difficulties with which he had had to cope. I listened. At one point I put the arm of the chair I'd been holding in my*

hand all this time on the desk. When his eyes fell on it, the flow of his eloquence was interrupted and his thoughts and words turned in another direction.

"*You don't know,*" *he said in an entirely different tone of voice,* "how many humiliations there are in this place! Nothing can be done. The paper has no money, you'll see. There isn't a cent." (35)

The former director's oratorical mastery—brilliantly parodied by Levi's use of clichéd expressions, such as "bello sdegno," "sapiente competenza," "orgoglioso ritegno"—breaks down when confronted with a concrete piece of reality: the armrest of the director's chair, falling into pieces just as the newspaper, the Action Party, and the nation are collapsing under the pressure of political forces urging compromise.

This distrust of language, provoked by the gap between words and things that is typical of Roman politics, runs through the entire novel. In a conversation among former *guerrieri*, disillusioned Resistance leaders from northern Italy who are discussing the causes of the fall of the Action Party and the success of the DC, a Milanese judge bitterly complains, "Qui tutto si impantana, e perde forma, . . . o meglio, prende una forma retorica, e perde la propria sostanza" ["Here everything falls in the mire and loses shape . . . Or rather it takes on a rhetorical form and loses its own substance"] (184, *204*). The word *Roma*, one of his interlocutors confirms, is associated in the popular imagination with the artificiality and ultimate extraneity of the national language, or, worse, with the Latin of imperialism: "Regere imperio populos" has remained the motto of the Roman political class since the times of Tiberius. Even the famous wine from the Castelli, another participant in the discussion comments, turns into poison when tasted by the idealistic outsider: "È l'arma segreta della città di Roma: chi arriva qui pieno di vitalità e di volontà di fare, un po' che ci rimanga, con quel vino, gli passa la voglia, si trova un cantuccio al fresco, ben riparato, si accontenta di un impiego, cade in letargo e diventa romano . . . Qui ti addormentano col Frascati e con le chiacchiere e l'alta politica" ["It's the secret weapon of the city of Rome. The man who comes here full of vitality and a desire for action, after he's been here awhile drinking that wine, loses his energy, finds a cool, sheltered corner, is content with an office job, falls into lethargy, and becomes a Roman . . . In Rome they put a man to sleep with their Frascati and their chatter about high politics"] (186–87, *207*). In other words, concludes the narrator, Rome is the capital of the *Luigini*, the members of the bourgeoisie that "posseggono tutti i segreti di questa virtù che trasforma le cose in parole e si impadronisce delle parole per stravolgerne il senso a piacere" ["possess all the secrets of the ability to transform deeds into words and to subjugate words in order to change their meaning into anything they please"] (187, *208*).

The distinction between *Luigini* and *contadini*, to which the narrator refers here, is critical to an understanding of Levi's ethical and aesthetic project in *L'Orologio*. As a close reading of the passage where this opposition is elaborated reveals, the antagonism between *Luigini* and *contadini* is tantamount to a profoundly different conception and use of language, whose political implications are thus made explicit. In Chapter 8 the narrator recounts how, after attending the press conference during which Parri, "il Presidente," announces his resignation, two of his friends, Andrea Valente (alias Leo Valiani) and Carmine Bianco (who stands for Manlio Rossi Doria), accompany him toward the Traforo Umberto, the tunnel linking via Nazionale and via del Tritone. Both Carmine and Andrea are actively engaged in politics. The latter, a former Communist, has abandoned Marxist orthodoxy in favor of a concrete involvement with social and economic issues, although occasionally the earlier passion for party struggle and organization resurfaces in his speech. The former, though young, has already accumulated a remarkable variety of political and personal experiences, from exile and prison to philosophical and historical studies, from party leadership to captainship in the Resistance struggle in northern Italy. Levi admires both because their thinking is not ideological and preserves a certain freedom from dogmatism, maintaining an uncertainty that, as he writes of Carmine, "gli chiariva le idee, gli impediva di fossilizzarsi in una abitudine mentale, lo conservava vivo e appassionato" ["clarified his ideas, kept him alive and passionate, and prevented him from becoming a fossil in his mental habits"] (155, *171*).

This intellectual independence is the condition for authentic conversation—from the Latin *cumversari*, which means to turn together— among the three friends, which takes place in the symbolically charged space of the *Traforo*. In this "antro di una sibilla, adatto alle parole della profezia" ["sybil's cave, designed for words of prophesy"] (158, *174*), Andrea, in particular, seems to be animated by "spiriti profetici" ["his soothsaying mood"] and his words seem to incite the kind of response elicited by "le cartomanti, le sibille e le pitonesse" ["the reader of cards, the sibyl, or the pythoness"] (161, *178*). Responding to Carmine's critique of the Action Party, which he sees as effective when it needs to support and feed the opposition but paradoxically incapable of constructive action, Andrea also condemns the party leadership for its failure to speak the language of the people, thus contributing to the distance between political classes and common citizenry: "I contadini non capirebbero. È naturale. Come vorreste che capissero queste cose che non poggiano su nulla, che non sono altro che un linguaggio convenzionale che anche noi non capiremmo, se non avessimo un giorno deciso di accettarlo una volta per tutte?" ["The peasants wouldn't understand . . . That's natural. How can you expect them to understand things that are based on nothing, that are nothing but conventional words, that we wouldn't understand either if we hadn't made ourselves decide one day to accept them for good?"] (159, 175). The idiom of politics is made of beautiful formulas and words, which have nothing to do with the concrete lives of actual people. Using imagery that is openly reminiscent of Plato's myth of the cave, Andrea chastises all politicians for following shadows, abstract passions that have no substance. Indeed, there is no difference between "good" and "bad" politicians, as they all assume the empty language of the *Luigini*, as opposed to the language of the *contadini*.

Andrea is here a spokesperson for Levi himself, elaborating further the theory of the two Italies that he had already introduced in *Cristo si è fermato a Eboli* (Ward, "From North to South" 400). For him, *contadini* and *Luigini* are the only appropriate names for the two parties that fight each other in the Italian political arena: "[L]e cose vanno chiamate con i loro nomi: io ho scelto questi, perché sono veri" ["Things have to be called by names, and I've chosen these names because they're true"] (165, *183*). *Contadini* are, first of all, the peasants, with their alternative culture grounded in orality rather than the written word; but this category includes also entrepreneurs, landowners who invest their capital in modernization and land reclamation, and, of course, factory workers: "Sono Contadini tutti quelli che fanno le cose, che le creano, che le amano, che se ne contentano. Sono Contadini anche gli artigiani, i medici, i matematici, i pittori, le donne" ["All men who make things, create them, love them, and are content with them are Contadini. Contadini, too, are artisans, doctors, mathematicians, painters, women"] (166, *184*). Progressive intellectuals are also *contadini*, while those who inhabit the abstract space of literary Arcadia belong to the category of *Luigini*, for whom art and life belong to essentially discrete dimensions. *Luigini* are the majority, in Italy. They include all members of the bourgeoisie: bureaucrats, state employees, bank clerks, lawyers, judges, policemen, college graduates, students, some priests, shopkeepers, industrialists that steal from the state, military men, and even politicians across all parties and positions (167). They live as parasites, sucking their nourishment from the *contadini*, who will never be able to overthrow their power, because, as Andrea explains,

> I Luigini hanno il numero, hanno lo Stato, la Chiesa, i Partiti, il linguaggio politico, l'esercito, la Giustizia e le parole. I Contadini non hanno niente di tutto questo: non sanno neppure di esistere, di avere degli interessi comuni. Sono una grande forza che non si esprime, che non parla. Il problema è tutto qui. La lingua degli altri, il loro Stato, bandiere, partiti, non conviene a loro: non ha senso sulle loro bocche. Devono parlare, ma a modo loro. (167)

The Luigini have the numbers, they have the state, the church, the parties, the political language, the army, the courts, and the press. The Contadini have none of them. They don't know that they exist, that they have any common interest. They are a mighty force that doesn't express itself, that doesn't speak. That's the whole problem. The language of the others, their state, flags, parties, do not suit the Contadini and have no meaning in their mouths. They too must speak, but in their own way. (185–86)

Andrea's discussion of language recalls some of the preoccupations that Antonio Gramsci expounds in his cultural writings, where he identifies, in the gap between the subaltern classes and the *intelligentsia*, the main reason for the ultimate failure of all attempts to reform Italian society, beginning with the Risorgimento. Even the most progressive intellectuals, according to Gramsci, do not speak the same language as the common people, having accepted the idiom of party politics as their own. And in fact, Andrea observes in *L'Orologio*, the Action Party itself, born as a movement of *contadini*, has become infiltrated by *luiginismo* and can only escape its inevitable transformation into an instrument of bourgeois power by disappearing as a political party (168). For Andrea/Levi the problem of the Action Party (and a party system in general) is indeed that its logical and progressive way of thinking and its neat categories resonate more with the *Luigini* than with the *contadini* (Ward, "From North to South" 399). Parri's resignation signals, for Andrea, the unavoidable result of the domestication of the only authentic example of *rivoluzione contadina* in Italian history, the Resistance.

The theme of the defeat of the revolutionary impetus of the Resistance by the *luiginismo* of the party system is a recurring claim in *L'Orologio*. Perhaps one episode more than any other strengthens and illuminates Levi's argument, grounded in the dialectic between Rome and Florence: "Così, per esempio, durante nove mesi, dai giorni drammatici della sua liberazione a quelli della fine della guerra, l'intera città di Firenze, fino all'ultimo artigiano o ragazzo, era stata concorde in una quotidiana battaglia contro Roma, in nome della libertà" ["For example, during the nine months from the dramatic days of its liberation to the end of the war, the entire city of Florence to the last artisan and boy had been united in the name of freedom in a daily battle against Rome"] (188, *209*). Among other initiatives, all parties in the Florentine Comitato di Liberazione agree on drafting a document in which they ask the government to abolish the institution of the *prefetti*, centrally nominated, or at least replace them with individuals chosen by local organizations. Two representatives for each party, for a total of ten persons, are sent to Rome to ask for the government's approval of the proposal. Levi, who participated in the mission, describes the sense of historical consequence the group felt while ascending the steps of the Viminale and presenting themselves proudly to the full cabinet. The ministers, Levi observes, "avrebbero dovuto avere le stesse opinioni dei dieci fiorentini: essi non erano infatti che i capi di quegli stessi partiti a cui i dieci appartenevano" ["should have shared the opinions of the ten Florentines since they were the chiefs of the parties to which the ten belonged"] (189, *210*). Nonetheless, it becomes rapidly clear to the Florentine delegation that there is something dissonant about the Roman politicians, something that Levi refers to, once more, in linguistic terms: "un diverso linguaggio nel quale tutto si modificava" ["a different language that modified everything"] (189, *210*). And in fact, carefully choosing their words and skillfully composing their sentences, the ministers effectively reject the proposal as immature and superfluous. As Levi explains, it was evident that "quel nome di partito aveva un senso completamente diverso a Firenze e a Roma ... Quello che premeva era soltanto la restaurazione di una struttura, di un linguaggio, di un potere che qualunque riforma avrebbe messo in pericolo" ["the name 'party' had an entirely different meaning in Rome than it had in Florence ... What mattered to them was only the restoration of a structure, of a language, of a power that any reform might endanger."] (190, *211–12*). Words, then, do not signify in the same way in Rome and Florence. Whereas in Florence signifiers and signifieds are connected in a poietic way, aimed at the transformation and renewal of society, in Rome words are employed as instruments of power, completely disconnected from reality.

In "L'arte luigina e l'arte contadina," Levi builds on the binary opposition between *Luigini* and *contadini* developed for the first time in *Cristo si è fermato a Eboli*—where the *podestà*, don Luigi, epitomized the bourgeoisie of Aliano in its constant antagonism with the despised peasants—to present an alternative to this empty use of language. Unlike the art of the *Luigini*, peasant art "consiste nel creare le cose nell'atto stesso di rappresentarle, per cui parole o figure vengono a fare, tutte, una sola verità" ["consists of the creation of things in the act of representation, so that words or images all contribute to create one truth"] (48). Poetry, from *poiein*, "making," coincides with "il momento in cui l'espressione coincide, per la prima volta, con la realtà" ["the moment in which the expression for the first time coincides with reality"] (48). In *Cristo si è fermato a Eboli*, Levi attempted to achieve this adherence between sign and meaning through a highly pictorial style, whose main trope is ekphrasis. In *L'Orologio*, his writing is ekphrastic in a broader sense, for his verbal pictures do not correspond to actual paintings, but his visual style turns, as Quintilian recommends, the reading experience into a form of spectatorship (Sholz 81). Levi fully exploits the capacity of the written word to adhere pictorially to visual experience, emphasizing the visionary nature of the narrator's myriad encounters in the city of Rome (Fonti 25).[4] In particular, in the novel he visualizes the urban plan of Rome, of which he reconstructs the complex topography while following his protagonist's wanderings through its busy streets. In his urban meanderings, he evokes the figure of Baudelaire's *flâneur*, quite literally a painter who dives into and depicts the spectacle of the city in images that are more vivid than the reality they represent (Baudelaire 9).

Indeed, like the *flâneur*, the protagonist of *L'Orologio* is, first of all, an observer, a "passionate spectator" of reality, endowed with a unique gift for seeing and an even rarer capacity to express his visual experience. His description of the black market spreading out from Piazza di Spagna offers a vivid example of the verbal pictures of people and environments he draws throughout the book:

> Passavo tra banchi e trespoli carichi di cibi proibiti, allungati lungo i muri, o disposti in disordine sugli angoli e fin in mezzo alle strade. Dappertutto, torri e piramidi di pane bianco si alzavano, come trionfali monumenti alla pace. Era un pane profumato, dorato, di forme diverse, e tutte belle, alcune piccole, rotonde o allungate, altre lunghe come bastoni, o ad anello come focacce; o in nodi, in trecce, in spirali, in forme di conchiglie o di soli raggianti... Su altri tavoli si allineavano sigari avana, sigarette, e monticciuoli di tabacco di vario colore, frutto della paziente raccolta dei mozziconi. La polvere bianca dello zucchero sporgeva dall'imboccatura rovesciata dei sacchetti di tela; e altri sacchetti mostravano il riso, i fagiuoli, i ceci, le lenticchie, i lupini, la pastina, e la farina bianca e quella gialla, queste due chiavi, d'oro e d'argento, del paradiso delle cucine. Un altro oro splendeva, verdastro, nelle bottiglie o nei fiaschi; l'olio... C'era poi ogni altra sorta di cose: dentifrici, saponi, medicine, scatole, caramelle, salami, biscotti, carne, spazzole, occhiali, penne stilografiche, gomme da masticare, vitamine, polli, cioccolato, trippa... La terra era piena di carta sporca, di foglie di cavolo, di avanzi di verdure e di frutta; e bambini e pezzenti frugavano dappertutto, in cerca di qualcosa ancora utilizzabile. Le venditrici gridavano, le donne discutevano, gli oziosi chiacchieravano. (75–76)

> *I walked along between wooden stands and rickety carts that were lined up along the walls, or stood in disorder at the corners and even in the middle of the street. They were all loaded with black-market food. Everywhere towers and pyramids of white bread rose like triumphal monuments to peace. The bread was golden, fragrant, and of different forms, every piece beautiful: some small, round, or elongated, others like canes or made in a ring like cakes, or knots, braids, and spirals, like shells or like radiant suns... On other tables cigars were laid out, cigarettes and little mountains of tobacco, the fruits of a patient harvesting of cigarette butts. The white powder of sugar bulged out from open*

mouths of linen sacks. Other sacks showed rice, beans, dried peas, lentils, noodles, spaghetti, white flour and yellow—those two keys, silver and golden, to the paradise of the kitchen. Another gold shone green in bottles in flasks, as olive oil . . . Besides these, there was every other kind of merchandise: toothpaste, soap, medicines, canned goods, caramel candy, salami, biscuits, meat, brushes, eyeglasses, fountain pens, chewing gum, vitamins, chickens, chocolate, and tripe . . .

The ground was covered with dirty paper, cabbage leaves, and remnants of fruit and vegetables. Children and beggars rummaged everywhere, looking for something they could use. The women vendors shouted, the women customers haggled, loiters chatted. (77–78)

In describing the illegal market scene, Levi draws attention to the visual. He lingers on the visible details of stand after stand, focusing on colors, shapes, and volumes. The monumental piles and pyramids of bread show, for instance, loaves and rolls of all sorts: large and small, round or elongated, braided, ring shaped, knotted, shell shaped. Sugar, pasta, dry legumes, wheat and corn flour are visible from the openings of the rough cloth sacks in which they are held. The golden yellow of the corn is matched by the greenish-gold hue of olive oil. Through the rhetorical trope of the catalogue, which refuses hierarchy, Levi expresses the abundance of visual sensations that the environs of Piazza di Spagna offer. In describing each of the tables that line its streets, Levi paints a series of verbal still lives and genre scenes that recreate for the reader the visual atmosphere of the ancient neighborhood.

In another passage, in which Levi recounts the ride in his friend Marco's Jeep toward the Garbatella,[5] where they hope to find a phantomlike woman with whom Marco is deeply in love, he reproposes the language of spectatorship that Baudelaire associates with the *flâneur*, by comparing himself explicitly to a member of a theater audience: "Stavo seduto, sul sedile di ferro, come uno spettatore capitato a caso in un teatro" ["I sat on the iron seat like a spectator who happens to be in a theater by pure chance"] (110, *119*). And indeed, the streets through which they drive seem to be the background against which the drama of everyday life is played by a never-ending cast of characters:

Personaggi strani apparivano tra la gente comune: una vecchia signora, alta e magra, con un ombrellino di pizzo nero, e un vestito nero lungo fino ai piedi, il vitino sottile, il colletto alto, retto dalle stecche di balena, gli scarpini col tacco Luigi XV, aquilina e nobiliare nell'andatura, anacronisticamente intatta dai tempi della fine del secolo; un uomo con la paglietta e degli enormi baffi, che traversava la strada agitando un bastoncino di giunco; un vecchio con i capelli lunghi sulle spalle e le labbra dipinte; un giocoliere, dal gran torso gonfio e sporgente in una maglia a righe gialle e verdi, sopra le lunghe gambe storte e sottili; due giovani preti magri, nelle loro tonache nere, a passeggio, allegri, in groppa a due cavalli bianchi. (110)

> *Strange characters appear among the common people. Here was a tall and gaunt old lady, with a little black lace parasol and a black dress that came down to her feet, a slender waist, a high whale-boned collar, and shoes with Louis XV heels. Superior and proud in her walk, she was an anachronistic survival of the end of the century. A man with a huge mustache, wearing a straw hat, crossed the street waving a Malacca cane; then an old fellow with painted lips and his hair falling down over his shoulders; and a juggler with a heavy torso, wearing a green-and-yellow striped jersey over a pair of long, skinny bowlegs; and two slender young priests in black cassocks gaily riding by on two white horses.* (119)

With a few brushstrokes, Levi briefly portrays each of these peculiar apparitions, conveying their anachronism and incongruity with the crowd from which they materialize. However odd their subjects are in their outward appearance, Levi's portraits are not caricatures, a source of ridicule or sarcasm. On the contrary, he immediately relates them to the history of the city and the nation, recasting them as symbols of the newly acquired Italian freedom. The elderly gentleman who walks along via del Corso clothed solely in ivy leaves makes this connection explicit by gloriously declaring, "Venti anni ho dovuto aspettare, per vestirmi così . . . ; ora posso morire contento" ["I've waited twenty years to dress myself up like this . . . Now I can die happy"] (110, *120*).

Thus although his detractors often see the visual properties of Levi's writing as a sign of his decadent taste for the picturesque or have accused him of *bozzettismo*,[6] less ideological critics interpret his interest in the visible as an indication of his passion for the reality surrounding him, which he likes to represent, as Italo Calvino observes fondly, "gremita di cose e di persone (e animali, e piante), viste e descritte sempre con grande amore" ["filled with things and people (and animals and plants), always seen and described with great affection"] ("La compresenza" 240). The passage describing the crowd in piazza Margana where he happens to stop on his walk from piazza del Gesù toward the Viminale later in the day, manifests clearly Levi's amorous interest in all forms of human experience:

> Nel centro della piazza era raccolta una folla allegra: ne udivo le risate, e le grida gaie dei ragazzi. In mezzo alla folla si levava un piccolo teatrino di marionette . . . Uomini, donne, vecchi, bambini, operai in abito da lavoro, venditrici di sigarette, raccoglitori di mozziconi, mendicanti, giovanotti con i capelli lucidi, ragazze con le pelliccette corte, vecchie sdentate, soldati, impiegati, guardavano intenti; e tutti i visi erano aperti, senza segreti,

abbandonati a un incanto felice. E anch'io, in mezzo a quel gruppo di uomini sconosciuti, mi sentivo invadere da un senso improvviso di gioia ...
   Rimasi a lungo a guardare lo spettacolo, e mi pareva di dover ringraziare qualcuno di questo bene regalato. (140–41)

In the center of the square a happy crowd was gathered. I could hear the laughter and gay shouting of the children. A little marionette theater was standing in the middle of the crowd ... Men, women, old people, children, laborers in their work clothes, vendors of cigarettes, collectors of cigarette butts, beggars, youngsters with shiny hair, girls with fur jackets, toothless old women, soldiers, clerks—all watched intently, their faces open and without secrets, lost in a happy enchantment. I, too, in this crowd of strangers, felt myself invaded by a sudden sense of joy ...
   I stayed here for a long time watching the spectacle, and it seemed to me that I should thank someone for the gift I had received. (154)

This colorful description of the crowd intent in watching the puppet show, once more confirms Levi's correspondence with Baudelaire's *flâneur*. Like him, Levi here can be compared to "a kaleidoscope gifted with consciousness, responding to each one of its movements and reproducing the multiplicity of life and the flickering grace of all the elements of life;" for him "it is an immense joy to set up house in the heart of the multitude, amid the ebb and flow of movement" (Baudelaire 9).

   The affinity between the *flâneur* and Levi's character is extremely relevant to the writer's ethical and aesthetic concerns in *L'Orologio*, especially in the light of Walter Benjamin's understanding of the Baudelairian figure. Benjamin was fascinated by the unique social function of the *flâneur*, as described by Baudelaire, in the mass societies generated by capitalism. As he explains in a letter to Theodor Adorno, his concern in the essay "On Some Motifs in Baudelaire" is "the theory of the flâneur ... At the core of the text, [resides his] critique of the concept of masses" (Benjamin, *The Correspondence* 589). The importance of the *flâneur* depends on his potential for social critique, as he represents the theoretical opposite to the idea of the mass. As a "man of leisure," the *flâneur* is an individual who wanders through city streets with no concern for time or specific direction, and by his presence he offers a critical counterpoint to the mass.[7] For Benjamin—whose views of the mass in modern society present many parallels with Levi's own analysis in *Paura della libertà*—the mass is the result of the homogenization generated by rationalism, characterized by the positivistic obsession with progress that underlies the development of capitalist societies. Adopting the position of the *flâneur*, in his urban writings Benjamin explores the city as a labyrinthine structure, a space in which lost dreams, hopes, illusions, and remnants of the past coexist alongside new fashions and artifacts.⁸ In this way, he proposes a powerful critique of narrative, problematizing its linear account of historical progress, which for him is a manifestation of the contemporary enslavement to reason (Gregory 233).⁹ Indeed, Benjamin "effectively 'spatialized' time, supplanting the narrative encoding of history through a textual practice that disrupted the historiographic chain in which moments were clipped together like magnets" (Gregory 234). Benjamin's unfinished *Arcades Project* illustrates how he searched for a style that reproduced the city's lack of connections and found it in a verbal form of visual montage. As a painter, Levi finds its equivalent in a visual form of writing that emphasizes spatiality against temporality, coexistence over exclusion, in a subversion of traditional narrative that is as powerful as Benjamin's own.

In *L'Orologio* this critique of conventional narrative emerges explicitly in a discussion between two collaborators of his newspaper, Casorin and Moneta, which resonates deeply with Benjamin's own thought. According to Casorin, the novel is a derivative of the rationalistic philosophy, based on abstraction, which is at the origin of the apocalyptic tragedies of the twentieth century. In an Adornian echo, he asks, "Che romanzi volete che ci siano, dopo Auschwitz e Buchenwald? Avete visto le fotografie di quelle donne che seppelliscono piangendo dei pezzi di sapone fatti col corpo dei loro mariti e dei loro figli?" ["What sort of novel do you want after Auschwitz and Buchenwald? Did you see the photographs of women weeping as they buried pieces of soap made from the bodies of their husbands and their sons?"] (57, 56). Traditional narrative forms are no longer adequate to describe a world that has lost its sense of direction:

> Così è andata a finire la confusione: l'individuo scambiato col tutto. Eccola, la vostra *tranche de vie*: un pezzo di sapone." . . .
> Un pezzo di sapone, – continuava, senza darci il tempo di interromperlo, – che dobbiamo seppellire piangendo; un pezzo di sapone che è il corpo e l'anima di un uomo. Così va a finire l'azione faustiana. Questa è la conclusione, la scadenza dei vostri romanzi, della vostra ragione astratta, che vi obbliga ad agire, a fare qualche cosa, in un tempo astratto e individuale segnato sugli orologi, dove nulla è vero e contemporaneo, a concludere alla fine del libro, con un pezzo di sapone. (57)

> *That's the way the confusion ended. The individual exchanged for the whole . . . There you are! Your* tranche de vie—*a piece of soap . . .*
> *"A piece of soap," he continued, without giving us a chance to interrupt him, "that we must bury with tears. A piece of soap that is the body and soul of man. That's the result of the Faustian action. That's the conclusion, the destination of your novels and of your abstract reasoning. It forces you to act, to do something in the abstract and individual time marked out on watches, where nothing is*

true and contemporary, and it forces you to sum up at the end of the book with a piece of soap." (56)

In this passage, Casorin is evidently a mouthpiece for Levi's own reflections, reelaborating some of the concepts he developed in the earlier philosophical essay, *Paura della libertà*.[10]

As in that essay Levi's analysis concludes with the affirmation of the redeeming power of art, as the *locus* of man's totality (165), so Casorin's critique of narrative is not exhausted in purely negative terms. In fact, he concludes his inflamed speech by proposing an alternative to rationalist abstraction and the alienation of mechanically measured time: the concept of *contemporaneità*:

> Ma noi siamo invece nella contemporaneità. Non c'è un filo d'erba solo in un prato. Non c'è un albero, ma c'è il bosco, dove tutti gli alberi stanno insieme, non prima e poi, ma insieme, grandi e piccoli, con i funghi e i cespugli e le rocce e le foglie secche e le fragole e i mirtilli e gli uccelli e gli animali selvatici, e magari anche le fate e le ninfe e i cinghiali, e i cacciatori di frodo e i viandanti smarriti, e chissà quante altre cose ancora. C'è la foresta. (57–58)

> *We, on the other hand, are rooted in an awareness of things around us. There isn't just one blade of grass in a meadow, there is not one tree but a forest where all trees stay together, not one in front of the other but merged, big and small, along with mushrooms, bushes and rocks, dry leaves, strawberries, myrtle berries, birds, wild animals, and perhaps fairies and nymphs and boars and poachers, and wanderers who have lost their way, and who knows how many more things... There is the forest.* (56–57)

To the abstract exaltation of the individual and its power, Casorin opposes the recognition of the existence of the Other as participating in the connectedness of all things. He defines this coexistence of self and other in terms that complicate the distinction between space and time, describing contemporaneity in spatial terms. The image of the forest, presented as the synthetic embodiment of the concept of *contemporaneità*, functions thus as a veritable chronotope, to adopt Bakhtin's productive notion: in the chronotope "time, as it were, takes on flesh, becomes artistically visible; likewise, space becomes charged and responsive to the movements of time, plot and history" (Bakhtin, "Forms of Time" 84).

Casorin's metaphor also recuperates the characterization of Rome as a forest that runs through *L'Orologio*, thus suggesting that the city itself is a concrete place of *contemporaneità*. Indeed, Levi often compares the capital to a forest or the woods. He describes its streets as paths, the stones of its buildings as mossy trunks of trees, and equates its *piazzas* to natural clearings (212). The analogy is established in the very opening lines, where, with an unusual privileging of auditory experience, the narrator observes, "La notte, a Roma, par di sentire ruggire leoni" ["At night in Rome one seems to hear lions roaring"] (3, 1). Gazing at the rooftops and cupolas of the city from his apartment, he continues, "mi pareva di non aver nulla alle spalle se non il vuoto, e di affacciarmi, altissimo, su una foresta misteriosa" ["it seemed to me that there was nothing but emptiness behind me, and that I was leaning out from a great height over a mysterious forest"] (7, 6). The images of the roaring lions, the nocturnal desert, and the forest seem strangely at odds with the traditional representation of one of the most significant urban centers of Western civilizations. (Indeed, the few pictorial representations of the Roman landscape by Levi are profoundly urban). But the forest is also a "metaphor for the narrative text, not only for the text of fairy tales but for any narrative text" (Eco 6). In the narrative woods "you go for a walk. If you're not forced to leave it in a hurry to get away from the wolf or the ogre, it is lovely to linger, to watch the beams of sunlight play among the trees and fleck the glades, to examine the moss, the mushrooms, the plants in the undergrowth" (Eco 50). Thus, by adopting the metaphor of the forest, Levi seems to invite the reader to abandon his search for a direction and to allow himself to "get lost," following the narrator's meanderings in the suspended temporal and spatial dimensions of his textual Rome.

Moreover, in psychoanalytic theory, with which Levi was fascinated, the forest is a powerful image for the unconscious, a theme that he never ceased to explore in his work.[11] In this respect, the association of Rome with a forest also echoes the analogy that Sigmund Freud explicitly draws between the Eternal City and the layered nature of the human mind in *Civilization and Its Discontents*. After observing how much of ancient Rome remains buried under the ground or covered by buildings of more recent construction, Freud goes on to imagine a different kind of palimpsestic urban space, in which traces of successive epochs coexist simultaneously in space and annihilate historical distance (18). This psychic construction reflects the Freudian notion of the unconscious as an entity that "knows no time, contains all times, annihilates the distinction (in time) between desire and fulfillment, is eternal" (J. P. Russo, qtd. in Harding 3). In his text, Levi depicts Rome as an analogous space where time is dilated into an entirely subjective dimension, occupied by memories, desires, and oneiric visions, defying the forward movement of the story and questioning the progress of the history that constitutes its background.

In its particular temporal dimension Rome is really a noncity, opposed not only to Florence but also to Naples and Turin in the pages of *L'Orologio*.

Thus in the chapter devoted to the long political discussion in the Traforo, Levi describes how the unexpected conversation with his friends transports him to another city and another time, "nell'antica e unica città dell'adolescenza, a Torino, dove le idee e l'amicizia sono dei beni esaltanti, e i corsi alberati sono così lunghi e vasti e deserti, che le parole pare vi possano correre, e allargarsi senza inciampi" ["in that old and only town of my adolescence, Turin, where ideas and friendship are exalted possessions, and the tree-lined avenues are so long and vast and deserted that words can race and scatter along them without hindrance"] (157, *173*). For Levi, this kind of intellectual exchange is unusual in Rome, where the spectacle of the city offers constant distractions to the eye, and, above all, where the presence of the past seemed to petrify the forward movement of the mind (157). On the contrary, Turin is fully involved in the progress of time: Turin "era la capitale di uno Stato autocratico e militare, di uno stato secondo ragione, che poteva brillare agli occhi di un grande spirito come Joseph de Maistre, e manifestava la sua natura nella dirittura delle strade e nella nitidezza delle architetture" ["was the capital of an autocratic and military State, a rational state, which could shine in the opinion of a great spirit like Joseph de Maistre, and which showed its nature in the straight lines of its streets and the sharpness of its architecture"] (19). Once it lost its role as capital, it was able to recreate itself as an industrial capital, becoming the vibrant city of an inventive bourgeoisie and a modern proletariat, able to adapt to the changing times. Thus while in Turin words are used in a productive relationship with reality, Rome's history seems to charge them with a multiplicity of significations that makes them ambiguous and ultimately meaningless. Both in *L'Orologio* and in his later essays, Levi draws a direct relation between the configuration of urban space and the temporal dimension that seems to dominate the city. In this respect, Turin and Rome are profoundly opposed chronotopes. With its long, straight streets and the symmetrical order of its architecture, Turin presents itself as a space linked to progress and the future, whereas Rome shows a palimpsestic structure that hinders the linear development of time.

As *Paura della libertà* shows, after the experience of European totalitarianism between the two world conflicts and the tragedy of the war, Levi's attitude toward the Turinese faith in human reason that manifests itself in its urbanistic organization is qualified by a certain distrust and ambiguity. In his article "Crisi di civiltà," published in 1944 in *La Nazione del popolo*, Levi explains nazism and fascism precisely as "una rivolta interna delle forze irrazionali compresse in questo mondo sclerosato" ["the internal revolt of irrational powers trampled in this rigid world"] (53), as the sudden explosion of the unconscious drives that the modern cult of rationality had violently repressed. In *Cristo si è fermato a Eboli*, Levi chronicled his discovery of the mythical imagination of the Lucanian peasants as a revelation of the limitations of rationalism in making sense of the world. In *L'Orologio*, this awareness is deepened in the exploration of the urban space of Rome. In its bringing together different epochs, in its juxtaposition of incongruent sites—such as the ancient Forum and the monument to Victor Emmanuel II, or the black market and the regal architectural space of Piazza di Spagna—the city as object of representation allows Levi to shape a textual practice that contests the idea of history as progress, the "progressive optimism" of rationalism.

Indeed, in *L'Orologio* the concern for time is as persistent as the preoccupation with language, as the title itself suggests. In the first pages of the novel, Levi explicitly discusses the distinction between time as measured by the watch—the time of adulthood—and the seemingly infinite time of childhood, preserved to some degree in the unconscious. After taking his gold Omega watch off and placing it on his dresser, as he usually does before going to bed, Levi reflects on the meaning of time: "Sentivo il suo ticchettío regolare, e pensavo che il tempo dell'orologio è del tutto l'opposto di quel tempo vero che stava dentro e attorno a me. È un tempo senza esitazioni, un tempo matematico, continuo moto materiale senza riposo e senza angoscia. Non fluisce, ma scatta in una serie di atti successivi, sempre uguali e monotoni" ["I could hear its regular ticking and thought that the time of a watch is the exact opposite of the real time inside and around me. A watch has a time without hesitation, a mathematical time, continuous material motion without rest and without anxiety; it does now flow, but jerks in a series of successive actions, always alike and monotonous"] (11, 9). The time of the watch, then, is an inexorably moving force, whereas, as Levi observes longingly, "[C]om'erano lunghi, senza fine, i giorni dell'infanzia! Un'ora era un universo, un'epoca intera, che un semplice gioco riempiva, come dieci dinastie. La storia era ferma, stagnava in quel gioco eterno" ["How long, how endless were the days of childhood! An hour was a universe; an entire epoch could be filled by a mere game, as if it were ten dynasties. History was motionless, stagnating in that eternal game"] (12, *11*).

For Levi, *real* time is the everlasting moment experienced in youth, an inner temporal dimension that is entirely subjective, whereas mechanically measured time is an expression of the Law of the Father.[12] The watch itself, argues Levi, is a symbol of a person's submission to this law:

> Tutti questi orologi da tasca, grandi, pesanti, in un certo modo solenni, e un poco antiquati . . . , tutti questi orologi hanno una loro storia, familiare e paterna. È raro che se ne faccia acquisto per il proprio uso. Essi sono quasi sempre un regalo, e un regalo importante, del Padre, o del Nonno,

o dello Zio, in una occasione importante, nel momento più decisivo della vita, quello in cui il giovane entra nel mondo, acquista la sua autonomia, si stacca dal passato, dalla sicurezza indistinta del tepido clan familiare, per cominciare a percorrere il proprio tempo personale. È allora che si riceve dal Padre l'orologio che ci seguirà per sempre . . . Così, la catena d'oro che teneva legato l'innocente orologio, diventa la catena che ci lega e ci trascina, ed è la piccola macchina del taschino che tiene ormai dal suo capo, come un padrone, la catena ben salda, e ci mena alla cavezza, come buoi da sgozzare, sempre più in fretta, sempre più in fretta, chissà dove. (11–12)

> *These pocket watches are huge, heavy, somehow solemn and slightly antiquated . . . All such watches have a story of their own, a family and paternal history. One rarely buys them for one's own use. They are almost always a gift, and an important gift, from father, grandfather, or uncle on an important occasion at the most decisive moment of life, when a young man enters the world, acquires his autonomy, detaches himself from his past, from the uncertain security of the tepid family clan to start walking through his own personal time. It is then that we receive from our father the watch that will follow us always . . . Thus the gold chain that once tied down the innocent watch becomes the chain that binds us and drags us. And it is this small pocket machine that by now masterfully holds the end of the firmly tied chain, and faster and faster leads us by the bit like bulls to be slaughtered, who knows where. (10–11)*

The gift of a watch intends to mark the passage to adulthood, to the possibility of giving a personal direction to the time of one's life. But this freedom, Levi suggests, is deceiving and is soon revealed to be a form of servitude. Real freedom lies in the time of childhood, "lunghissimo, fermo, pieno di cose, di ogni cosa del mondo, e, in un certo modo, quasi eterno, come quello del Paradiso Terrestre, che è insieme un mito dell'infanzia e dell'eternità" ["long, . . . still, and . . . filled with things, with everything in the world, and was somehow almost eternal, as it was in the Garden of Eden, a myth of both childhood and eternity"] (14, *12*).

Although permanently exiled from the Earthly Paradise, humanity can recover its timeless dimension in dreams. Following his bedtime reflections on time, Levi falls asleep and dreams of his watch being stolen from him, of a trial—presided by Benedetto Croce—taking place to establish his ownership of the lost object, and of his fortuitous retrieval of the watch, albeit broken. When Levi wakes up, his dream is partially realized when the watch drops from his hands, apparently of its own volition—"più che cadermi di mano, fece un salto, come una ranocchia che si buttasse nell'acqua" ["rather than falling, it jumped like a frog into water"] (22, *19*)—and is badly damaged. As the watch escapes from Levi's grip, so does time from the reader's grasp. From this moment onward, the plot seems to move not in linear fashion but according to a spiral motion, shifting from one temporal plane to the other without transitionary breaks. The peculiar temporality introduced by the breaking of the watch is connected to a precise space, the city of Rome, with its labyrinthine structure. The need to find a goldsmith who will repair his watch, in fact, prompts Levi to enter the depths of the Roman urban space.

This first walk, which leads Levi from via Gregoriana, where he has been temporarily lodging, circuitously to via del Vantaggio, where his newspaper's offices are located, is only the first of a series of strolls through central Rome, which he explicitly associates with the notion of *contemporaneità*, as exemplified in the paragraph that describes part of his walk toward the Viminale:

> Era l'ora del tramonto: un'aria piena di colori mutevoli avvolgeva le case, tra la luce e l'ombra: e pareva che ogni cosa brillasse di una sua luce interna e propria, e lanciasse sulle altre i suoi raggi, in un tessuto infinito e impalpabile. Passavo in strade strette e piccole piazze, in vicoli, tra mura continuamente variate di archi, di colonne, di cornici, di ornamenti, di arcani rapporti di spazi, *come un linguaggio sensibile della contemporaneità dei tempi, in un passato armoniosamente presente*, fra scale, botteghe, campanili, terrazze, finestre abitate da figure silenziose, e il passaggio continuo della gente, dei loro visi brillanti nella penombra, dei loro occhi neri, del bianco acceso delle carni, fra l'onda delle voci, dei sussurri, dei richiami. L'ultimo sole batteva sulla cima delle facciate, e le tingeva di un color di rosa, umano come quello delle nuvole, contro il verde e il violetto del cielo. (140, emphasis mine)

> *It was the hour of sunset; the air full of changing colors enveloped the houses between light and shadow. Everything seemed to glow with a true light of its own, and threw its rays on others in an infinite and impalpable tissue. I went through narrow streets and small squares into alleys between walls constantly varied by arches, columns, embellishments, ornaments, and by mysterious relationships of space, like a language that contains all of the past, and yet in its contemporaneousness is proof of the oneness of time; among stairs, shops, bell towers, terraces, windows inhabited by silent figures, and the passage of people with their faces bright in the dusk, their eyes black, the radiant white of their flesh among the wave of voices, whispers, and calls. The last sunlight struck the tops of the facades and tinged them with a rosy color, human like that of the clouds against the green and violet of the sky.* (153, emphasis mine)

Here, Levi foregrounds the visual aspect of his experience of the city. He underscores the chromatic richness of the urban landscape at sunset, the balance of volumes, the constant variation of architectural shapes, suggesting that these elements contribute to the construction of a language of *contemporaneità*. And in fact, if the palimpsestic structure of the city renders the past "armoniosamente presente," at the same time the writer can render verbally the timelessness in which this urban architecture seems to exist, by lingering on the visual description of each of its elements and thus stopping time and thwarting the advancement of the narration. Thus in *L'Orologio*, Levi's poetics of *contemporaneità* is inextricably linked to what I call his "visual writing," which allows the writer to constantly impede the development of the plot through descriptive digressions depicting the city, with its streets, squares, and patrician *palazzi*, as well as the people that populate it. The focus on the spatial dimension instituted by his pictorial technique reinforces his challenge to the notion of time as progress by obstructing the unfolding of consecutive temporality that defines narrativity.

Levi's visual writing becomes overtly ekphrastic in the pages devoted to his first arrival at Palazzo Altieri, into one of whose apartments he moves after the first day of his peripatetic narration.[13] This baroque palace—explicitly compared to a city in the text[14]—represents a symbolic microcosm of Roman life, mirroring it closely both in its architectural structure and in the *varia umanità* that takes refuge within its walls. Moreover, as Rome reflects the complexities of the human mind in its assimilation of different temporal dimensions in the present, so Palazzo Altieri is treated as a space of great "powers of integration for . . . thoughts, memories and dream" (Bachelard 6) in which present, past, and future constantly interact with each other. The detailed ekphrastic passage in which the writer first describes the imposing simplicity of the façade, dominating piazza del Gesù, immediately calls attention to the interaction between its baroque design and the busy passage of the contemporary crowd, between its ancient construction and the present life of the city:

> Le colonne, sui loro basamenti di pietra lisa, sporgevano sul marciapiede, obbligando i passanti a farsi da parte; diritte come due guardiani, fermi sulla piazza da chissà quanto tempo. In alto, reggevano, come un architrave, un balcone di parata, con l'asta di ferro della bandiera, e un grande stemma di travertino, tutto pieno di lune e di comete. Sotto il balcone stava rannicchiata, nella chiave dell'arco, una donna, o meglio una sfinge o un angelo. Aveva soltanto la testa e il petto: ai lati della testa spuntavano due ali, che parevano enormi orecchie, da cui pendevano festoni di frutta e di foglie. L'angelo aveva gli occhi socchiusi, e pareva guardasse fra le ciglia, da quel suo nascondiglio di pipistrello, con l'aria insieme sensuale e melensa di una dama del Seicento. Un sole obliquo batteva sulla facciata, percorsa dalle lunghe ombre delle cornici delle finestre e delle altissime mensole sul tetto. Il portone era chiuso. (124)

> The columns on their worn, stone bases jutted out over the sidewalk, forcing passersby to step aside, erect like two guards who had stood on the square for endless years. They supported a ceremonial balcony like an architrave with an iron flagstaff set in it, and a stone coat of arms covered with moons and comets. Under the balcony the figure of a woman, or better a sphinx or an angel, crouched in the keystone of the arch. She had only a head and breasts, and wings sprang out from both sides of her like enormous ears with festoons of leaves and fruits hanging down from them. The angel's eyes were half closed and she seemed to peer out through her lashes from that hiding place of bats with the sensual and foolish air of a lady of the seventeenth century. The sunlight beat obliquely across the facade, crossing it with long shadows from the windows, the cornices, and the high, overhanging roofs. The big house-door was closed. (135)

In this paragraph, Levi's style tends to assume the characteristics of the *prosa d'arte*, in which, as Giorgio Patrizi writes of the great master of twentieth-century Italian art criticism Roberto Longhi, the epistemological drive of critical discourse aims to represent "the complexity of the artistic text with the complexity—the excess—of the discourse discussing it" (107). The detailed description of the angelic creature sculpted under the balcony reproduces, in its linguistic surplus, the late baroque aesthetic that dominates the building. This discursive excess successfully recreates the complex layout of the interior courtyards, with their apparently infinite multiplication of architectural elements:

> Mi trovai in un atrio, selciato a grossi lastroni, con una doppia guida di granito per le ruote delle carrozze. Era diviso in tre ampi passaggi da due file di pilastri, le cui basi erano circondate da alti sedili di pietra. Nella penombra dell'ingresso si intravvedevano, ai lati, sotto gli archi, delle porte, alcune chiuse, altre aperte, che portavano forse a dei magazzini o a delle scale. L'atrio sboccava su un portico, che circondava un grande cortile, e dava, a destra, su un secondo cortile, vasto come una piazza, di dove giungeva un rumore continuo, come di pioggia fitta, dell'acqua di una fontana. Dall'ingresso ... vedevo, contro il muro illuminato della parete di fondo del primo cortile, una fila oscura di pilastri e, sopra di essi, le linee delle costole delle arcate che si perdevano nelle volte buie. (124–25)

> *I found myself in a vestibule paved with great flagstones that had a double rut in them for carriage wheels. This vestibule was divided into three ample passageways by two rows of pillars with high stone seats around their bases. In the faint light I could make out at the sides under the arches a number of doors, some closed and some open, leading perhaps to storerooms or to other stairways. The vestibule opened into an arcade that circled a huge courtyard, and at the right was a second courtyard as vast as a piazza, from which came the continuous splashing of a fountain, like pouring rain.*

> *Pausing at the entrance . . . , I saw against the sunlit far wall of the first courtyard a dark row of pillars, and above them, outlines of the ribs of arches disappearing among dark vaults overhead. (136)*

The courtyards of the palace foreshadow the labyrinthine quality of the interior building, faithfully guarded by the Charon-like *portiere*, a giant whose dimensions reflected the immensity of the architecture (125). After having reluctantly been shown the way to his apartment by the doorman, Levi begins his ascent to the upper floors, which he describes again in great detail, lingering on the massive proportions of the architectural elements and on the ancient statues that decorate staircases and hallways:

> Seguii il porticato, fino ad uno dei suoi estremi, verso lo scalone. Salii qualche largo gradino di pietra, e mi trovai in un vastissimo ambiente, dalla volta oscura come quella di una grotta, e dalle pareti ingombre di statue antiche. In faccia, biancastro sul muro grigio, un enorme guerriero Gallo stava cadendo, ferito, sulle ginocchia avvolte nelle pieghe minute delle mutande barbare. A destra, due uomini nudi si fronteggiavano dai loro piedistalli: uno era un giovane efebo: al corpo dell'altro era stata sovrapposta la testa di un vecchio barbuto, strana per la sua grandezza su quel corpo esile e quelle gambe sottili. A sinistra, si apriva la prima rampa dello scalone, così largo che dieci persone avrebbero potuto salirlo insieme, tenendosi per mano . . . Era quasi piuttosto una cordonata che una scala: si svolgeva, voltando su se stessa, tra archi rampanti e volte altissime, balaustre a pilastrini obliqui, cornici sporgenti, e giganteschi finestroni, come un immenso nicchio traforato. Statue sorgevano qua e là, vecchi abitatori di quella solenne cavità di pietra. Alla prima svolta, due torsi femminili, due dee, stavano ai lati della vetrata che dava sul secondo cortile, dove vedevo delle donne lavare i panni alla fontana, e degli operai, piccoli nella distanza, limare un loro pezzo di ferro davanti alla porta di un'officina. (126)

> *I followed the arcade to the stairway at the rear. I climbed some wide stone steps and found myself in a vast, vaulted space as dark as a cave. Its walls were crowded with antique statues. In front of me, whitish against the gray wall, an enormous Gallic warrior fell wounded to his knees, wrapped in the narrow pleats of his barbaric shorts. On the right two naked men faced one another on their pedestals. One was a young ephebus; on the other was superimposed the bearded head of an old man, strange in its bigness on that lithe body with its slender legs. On the left was the first flight of steps. They were so broad that ten people holding hands could have climbed up together . . . It was almost a stone-ribbed slope rather than a stairway; it turned on itself among rampant arches and lofty vaults, balustrades of slanting pillars, jutting cornices, and gigantic windows like immense opened-out shelves. Statues rose here and there, ancient inhabitants of this solemn stone hollow.*

> At first turn stood two female torsos, two goddesses alongside the wide glass window that looked out on the second courtyard. I could see from here women washing clothes in the fountain and some workmen, small in the distance, filing pieces of iron outside their workshop door. (137–38)

The structure of the Palazzo reflects the composite quality of Roman urban space, with its baroque elements coexisting alongside classical remnants and neoclassical reconstructions, in a coincidence of temporal planes that Levi's style tries to reproduce, very much in the same way as the *prosa d'arte* is the attempt to reduce the gap between the synchronic nature of the work of art and the diachronic quality of discourse, by eliminating the temporal dimension and placing all the elements of the description on the same plane in order to achieve the illusion of presence (Patrizi 106). Thus rather than recounting his entrance into the new apartment—ostensibly the most significant personal event of the day—through a series of verbs in the *passato remoto*, which would emphasize progress and sequentiality, Levi chooses to render it mainly in the *imperfetto* of his ekphrastic descriptions, establishing in the text a temporality of simultaneity, which once more hinders narrative development.

The synchronic dimension that defines Palazzo Altieri from an architectural perspective is extended by Levi to its inhabitants. In fact, its statuesque "vecchi abitatori" share their immense rooms with a new population of displaced people, in a microcosmic reflection of the coexistence of different worlds that defines life the capital immediately after the war. Levi compares this space to a *corte dei miracoli*, but while the myth of the Parisian Court of Miracles was generated in order to confine illegality symbolically within a limited and peripheral space, making it easier to recognize and thus exorcise from society (Moretti 103),[15] in *L'Orologio* this image seems to be linked, rather, to the idea of *contemporaneità*. In the Court of Miracles of Palazzo Altieri cohabit the world of power and wealth, signified by its monumental architecture, and the world of the marginalized that have taken possession of its grandiose and empty spaces. In this respect, the ancient Palazzo anticipates the real *corte dei miracoli* that Levi will discover in Naples: it is a carnivalesque kingdom where the poor and the dispossessed have the power, a subversive counterstate that explicitly opposes the rule of Roman politics.

Levi needs to leave for Naples because his uncle, whom he considers a father, is dying. Having fortuitously found a rental car in Piazza San Giovanni, Levi joins its passengers, who represent a variety of social types, from a cowardly priest involved in the black market to a Calabrese peasant who survived the Nazi concentration camps, from a spoiled child of the petite-bourgeoisie to a prosperous madam to a poor widow whose eldest son joined the infamous *Decima Mas*. Thus the road proves to be another privileged textual space of *contemporaneità*, or a chronotope in which "the spatial and temporal paths of the most varied people—representatives of all social classes, estates, religions, nationalities, ages—intersect at one spatial and temporal point. People who are normally kept separate by social and spatial distance can accidentally meet; any contrast may crop up, the most varied fates may collide and interweave with one another" (Bakhtin, "Forms of Time" 243). For Levi these casual and unexpected encounters are a direct reflection of the possibilities granted to the new Italian nation. Recuperating the topos of the body politic, in fact, the writer compares the frenetic movement of the immediate postwar period to the current of blood cells transporting oxygen to the various body parts: "Il corpo dell'Italia, pestato dalle bombe e dagli eserciti, dissanguato dalla guerra, tornava a respirare; un sangue nuovo e imprevedibile circolava, in milioni di corpuscoli che trascinavano dappertutto, nei modi più loschi e illeciti, un ossigeno necessario. Non si era mai viaggiato tanto, quando tutto era in pace e in ordine" ["Italy's body, pounded by bombs and by armies, bloodless from war, was breathing once again. New and unforeseen blood was circulating in millions of corpuscles, carried everywhere in the most dubious and illicit ways, supplying oxygen. People had never traveled as much when everything had been at peace and in order"] (249, *279*).[16]

To the world of peace and order maintained by the Fascist regime, Levi directly opposes the epic *gesta* of the Neapolitan people in their daily struggle to survive. In this underground world, the rules and values of conventional society are subverted, in a revolutionary appropriation of power by the powerless. Their ruler is the self-proclaimed and universally loved *Re di Poggioreale*, Giuseppe I Biscaglia, a real figure who has acquired mythical proportions in the public's imagination.[17] Born a ragman, he promised his higher-born wife to make a queen of her, and he maintained his promise thanks to his ingenuity:

> Venne la guerra; don Giuseppe cominciò a trafficare, prima in piccolo, poi sempre più in grande. Fece lavorare tutti, i poveri, i pezzenti, i camorristi, i sensali, i lenoni, le ragazze, gli scaricatori del porto, i borsaioli, la gente senz'arte e senza professione, i sinistrati, quelli che non avevano più casa, gli ingegnosi, i miserabili, tutti i cristiani che avevano bisogno di vivere e nessuno che li aiutasse. Onoratamente lavoravano, con i soldati, con i mercanti, con gli speculatori: nelle piazze, sui mercati, sulle strade, nel porto, di giorno e di notte: la città era mezza distrutta, le fabbriche chiuse; e così si campò. Don Giuseppe divenne Re, e sua moglie la Regina. (283)

The war came. Don Giuseppe started in to trade, first in a small way, then larger and larger. He found work for everyone: the poor, beggars, gangsters, fencers, pimps, prostitutes, stevedores, pickpockets, people without skill or profession, those who'd been bombed out of their homes, the resourceful, and the miserable, all those human beings who needed a living and had no one to help them. They worked honorably with soldiers, merchants, and speculators. They worked in the squares, the markets, the streets, and the port, by night and by day. The town was half destroyed, the factories closed, but they got on.

Don Giuseppe became king and his wife queen. (318)

Although an absolute monarch, don Giuseppe is loved and respected by his subjects because of his legendary generosity, which appears as a corrective to the indifference of Roman politics to the real social problems, from low-cost housing to health care, from unemployment to the administration of justice, which are instead are solved immediately and efficiently by the carnivalesque sovereign. But his truly revolutionary power resides in his willingness and ability to eliminate the distance between the Naples made of opulent villas and luxurious gardens, where—as the ancient Greek etymology of Posillipo suggests—all grief is suspended, and the city of the infamous *bassi*, in which life is defined by poverty and illness, which Matilde Serao denounces in *Il ventre di Napoli*.[18]

It is in this very *ventre* that Levi introduces himself in his stroll from the hotel near the train station to his uncle Luca's house, mapping an urban itinerary that resembles yet differs radically from his Roman wanderings. In his passage from periphery to center, in fact, Levi gradually moves from the bright vivacity of the street market of Porta Capuana to the gloomy and suffocating atmosphere of the *bassi*, thus reversing the opposition between the central quarters of Rome and its popular *borgate*. While the sites of power in the capital occupy the heart of the city, in the belly of Naples live the poor and the destitute among its people. But in this first return to the South after his Lucanian exile, the autobiographical narrator discovers in Naples one of the "real" places in the world (301), which validates the intuition, poetically expressed in *Cristo si è fermato a Eboli*, of the peasant world as a more authentic human dimension, eternal because, as childhood, it is extraneous to history and progress. And indeed, his descriptions of the Neapolitan populace echo very closely some of the depictions of Lucanian peasants in the earlier memoir, similarly emphasizing the ageless quality of their appearance by comparing them to ancient artifacts, in which time has been stopped:

Quei visi, quegli atti avevano una bellezza antica, come di statue affinate del tempo, parevano uscire da pitture ed encausti nascosti per secoli sotto terra, con i loro profili nitidi, i grandi occhi neri: l'ovale del volto delle donne sotto le ciocche dei capelli spettinati, classico insieme e familiare, aveva la naturalezza superba delle dee, coperta della naturalezza modesta dei poveri, velata di sentimenti quotidiani come un marmo incrostato di muschi; . . . e anche i vecchi e le vecchie portavano i segni della loro età come Dèi viandanti, travestiti, per non essere riconosciuti, sotto spoglie tremule e cadenti. (294–95)

And they had an ancient beauty like statues, refined by time, that seemed to have come out of paintings and encaustics hidden for centuries under the earth, with their clear-cut profiles and big black eyes. The ovals of the women's faces, at the same time classical and unfamiliar, under their locks of untended hair, had the proud naturalness of goddesses, covered by the modest naturalness of the poor, and were veiled like a marble image . . . And the old men and women too carried the signs of their age like vagabond gods, hiding under this trembling and feeble disguise so they would not be recognized. (333–34)

The aura of antiquity that emanates from the people he encounters seems to derive, for Levi, from their rootedness in the circular temporality of myth, from the awareness that behind their existence "ci fosse un altro mondo, già tutto vissuto in una sua regola eterna e immutabile di semplice dolore" ["there was another world that had already lived out its time in its own eternal and unchangeable law of simple sorrow"] (295, *334*).[19] But this consciousness does not make the Neapolitan people resigned or passive. On the contrary, to Levi they appear to be passionately engaged in their daily lives, "liberi e attenti in quel presente imprevedibile, fuggitivo come una voce nell'aria" ["free and diligent in the unpredictable present that is a fugitive as a voice in the air"] (299, *338*). Levi conveys the paradoxical contrast between the ephemeral quality of the instant and the presence of a "tempo immutabile" in the pages devoted to his long Neapolitan *passeggiata*, proving to be, once again as Baudelaire's *flâneur*, "the painter of the passing moment and of all the suggestions of eternity that it contains" (Baudelaire 5).

And in fact, Levi's strategy to "distil the eternal from the transitory," as Baudelaire puts it (12), is to stress once more the visual aspect of his experience as an urban wanderer, thus conquering the passing of time and giving permanence to the moment. The chromatic vividness of the Neapolitan landscape, with its uniquely deep blue sky and bright sun, seems to encourage the pictorial tendencies of Levi's narration, which, following the protagonist's long walk through old Naples, is constantly delayed by the wealth of visual details attracting his attention, from the ragged children at play to the different varieties of bread on sale, to the immaculate bed linens put out to dry and waving in the wind. Particularly striking is the passage describing the spectacle of the meat market in one of the city's inner streets:

> Dai due lati della strada, su banchi o nelle vetrine, erano esposti animali squartati, pecore, agnelli, capre, dal corpo aperto e spalancato; interiora d'ogni genere, cuori, polmoni, fegati, coratelle; e anche pesci, polipi, conchiglie; ma soprattutto trippe d'ogni specie. Stavano appoggiate in fila sul piano dei carretti, o attaccate davanti ai negozi; bianche come la neve, o giallastre, grigie, marroni, a forma di rotolo, di libro, di nodo, di treccia, di ricciolo; alcune come grandi fogli di carta punteggiati, altre tagliate in lunghe strisce come corde; ventricoli, intestini, stomaci, budella: e insieme pezzi di cotenna, musi schiacciati di bestie: ... tutta la strada ne era coperta e tappezzata. (300–301)

> *On both sides of the street, on stands or in shop windows hung quartered animals on display: sheep, calves, goats. Their bodies were split and opened wide, with entrails of all kinds: hearts, lungs, livers, brains. There were fish, polyps, and shells also, but mostly tripe of every variety. The tripe was lined up on the shelves of the pushcarts, or hung up in front of the shops, white as snow or yellowish, gray, or brown, shaped like a roll, a book, a knot, a braid, a curl. Some of the pieces were large sheets of paper with holes punched in them, others were cut in long bands like ropes: gizzards, intestines, stomachs, bowels. And along with them lay pieces of head meat and the flattened out muzzles of animals . . . The whole street was covered and papered with them. (339–40)*

The detailed description of the variety of colors and shapes of the animal entrails is aimed at recreating, in its linguistic excess, the sensorial experience of walking among the stands and shops of the market. Although linked to the contingency of Levi's casual passage through that street, this experience is immediately transferred onto the metahistorical plane of the Biblical tale of Jonah, thus bridging the gap between the transient nature of his visual impressions of the city and their potential for eternity:

> Mi pareva di camminare nell'interno di un enorme animale, che la strada stessa fosse un gigantesco budello carnoso, lo stomaco di un grande pesce, pronto a discendere alle radici dei monti; e che io, per tre giorni e tre notti, come l'antico profeta, l'avrei percorso, e seguito nel suo viaggio nell'abisso. Ma pensavo che non avrei chiesto di uscirne, di essere sputato fuori sulla terra asciutta ... Sentivo che ero in un luogo vero: in uno dei luoghi veri del mondo. (301)

> *I seemed to be walking inside an enormous animal, that the street was a gigantic, fleshy bowel, the stomach of a huge fish, ready to dive down to the roots of the mountains, and I, for three days and three nights, like the ancient prophet,*

> would stay in the fish's belly, and traverse it and follow it in its voyage to the abyss.
>
> I thought, however, that had I been Jonah I would not have asked the Lord to release me, to be spewed out on the dry land ... I felt that I was in a true place, in one of the true places of the world. (340)

The connection between the Neapolitan parenthesis in *L'Orologio* and the world of myth is further established in the last stop in the narrator's wanderings. In fact, he accidentally discovers a house where the philosopher Vico—whose theories of historical *corsi* and *ricorsi* and on the poetic origins of language exert an evident impact on Levi's thought—used to give private lessons. Vico's mythical philosophy is immediately opposed to the dialectic thinking of the present occupier of the house, Benedetto Croce, "il maestro dei nostri saggi" ["the master of our sages"] (301, 340), as Levi calls him in an ironic Dantean echo. In fact, although he recognizes Croce's authority, he does not hesitate to criticize him by comparing him to the mythical figure of Cola Pesce, the male siren who seduces mariners into throwing themselves into the abyss to devour them (301–2). Such a harsh indictment of the influential philosopher derives primarily from Levi's (and Gobetti's) conviction that Croce's view of fascism as a temporary illness of an otherwise healthy Italian nation was fundamentally erroneous and dangerous, as it failed to recognize the responsibility of liberalism in creating the premises for Mussolini's raise to power (Ward, *Antifascisms* 185–88). This suggestion of failure reinforces the idea, proposed earlier in *L'Orologio*, of the inadequacy of positivist philosophy to either prevent or make sense of the European tragedies of the twentieth century and of the need for an inclusive intellectual approach that would not censure the irrational aspect of human experience. Thus, very much according to Vico's notion of *ricorsi*, Levi brings to conclusion the main philosophical argument of his novel in a circular manner, returning to the terms of the discussion on narrative that opened it.

The circularity of the structure is made manifest in the last Neapolitan episode, when Levi, finally aware of the passing of time and of the urgency to see his uncle, abandons his wanderings and arrives at his house only to find that he has died during the night. While contemplating the old man's face, now existing outside of time like a statue, a work of art, Levi is brought back to his father's death and the bitter sense of freedom from bonds and ultimately of solitude he experienced then. On the contrary, his uncle has not left him alone but has invested him with the responsibility to gather and order his life's research and has left him his watch: "un orologio d'oro, da medico, col contasecondi; uno splendido vecchio Omega, in tutto simile a quello che mi aveva regalato mio padre" ["a gold watch, a doctor's watch, with a hand that counts the seconds, a splendid old Omega, in every way like the one my father had given me"] (304, *344*). The recovery of the watch marks the restoration of a linear temporality of action and movement that the narrator had abandoned at the beginning of the book, when his father's watch had broken. From this point, the plot advances quite rapidly to its conclusion, as if its development were determined by the inexorable march of the clock's hands. Thanks to a fortuitous coincidence, Levi finds a ride back to Rome in the government vehicle of a Communist minister who happens to be in Naples. With them travels also a member of the cabinet who belongs to the rival party, allowing Levi to stage a dialogue that reinforces the notion of the tremendous distance between the political class—the *Luigini*—and the common people—the *contadini*. While the Action Party's program was aimed at bridging this gap, the conversation between the two ministers makes clear that both the Communist and the conservative leadership have a different vision for the new Italy: "In fondo, e su questo si dicevano del tutto d'accordo, non c'era ora che un problema: restaurare l'autorità dello Stato. Bisognava liberarsi di certi residui anacronistici della Resistenza, sfondare quello che non corrispondeva più alla congiuntura internazionale, e serbare a tutti i costi l'unità, per realizzare quella necessaria Restaurazione" ["Basically there was only one problem, as they both agreed: to restore the authority of the state. One had to free oneself of certain anachronistic holdovers from the Resistance, to suppress everything that no longer fell in with the international situation, to preserve unity at all costs, in order to accomplish that necessary Restoration"] (308, *348*, translation modified.) Here Levi returns to the earlier theme of the Resistance as the only historical attempt at an Italian *rivoluzione contadina* and of its inevitable defeat by the hands of the *Luigini* of any political color. To the *Luigini*, in fact, ultimately belongs the state machine, which functions precisely like a watch (307), attached to the golden chain that binds and pulls us (12).

For Levi, the only alternative to the political and existential alienation symbolized by the watch is the affirmation of *contemporaneità* as a rejection of abstract rationalism and its faith in the progressive movement of time. Adapting to Levi the characterization that Casorin proposes of Leo Tolstoy in the literary discussion that grounds the novel's aesthetics, in *L'Orologio* Levi is "il poeta di un istante unico, che non può durare, né ripetersi, né mutare . . . È un impressionista: è come i grandi pittori impressionisti. Come gli impressionisti, non ha bisogno di raccontare, di fare i quadri storici. Soltanto, fermare una volta per tutte un momento che non tornerà più" ["the poet of the unique instant, which cannot last nor repeat itself nor change . . . He's an impressionist. He's like the great impressionistic painters. And like the impressionists, he doesn't need to tell a story or paint historical pictures. All he needs to do is to catch, once and for all, an instant that will never come back"] (56, *54–55*). The reference to painting in this crucial discussion confirms the importance of the pictorial imagination in determining the stylistics of *L'Orologio*. Through a highly ekphrastic style, which emphasizes spatiality and visuality over temporality, Levi introduces in the text the equivalent, on the level of language, to the challenge to the notion of time as progress that he voices throughout the novel. In this manner, Levi offers a scathing critique of the Italian political situation after the end of the war, denouncing its failure to move toward authentic social reform and political transformation. But perhaps more important, by proposing a visual mode of approaching and knowing reality, Levi calls into question logocentrism, traditionally associated with the law, and advances an alternative epistemology, where word and image are seen as equal partners in the process of knowledge. Thus his text realizes the revolution that the Resistance was unable to bring to completion, blurring the boundaries between art and life, literature and politics, according to his profound conviction that "vi può essere qualche rapporto tra la letteratura e la vita, tra la poesia e la verità" ["there can be a relationship between literature and life, between poetry and truth"] (Levi, "Il contadino e l'orologio" 35).

3

Portraits of the South in *Le parole sono pietre* and *Tutto il miele è finito*

The topos of the journey is fundamental in Levi's literary work and determines not only its imagery but also the very narrative edifice of his books, leading many scholars to consider Levi's oeuvre in its entirety as travel writing.¹ Gigliola De Donato identifies two major thematic veins in Levi's literary journeys: the psychological return to the memorial places of childhood and the *indistinto originario*, and the physical journey of discovery ("Il viaggio in Carlo Levi" 14). *Cristo si è fermato a Eboli* and *L'Orologio* place themselves in the latter category, for they document Levi's factual travels, in Lucania and through Rome on to Naples respectively. *Quaderno a cancelli*—the object of the next chapter—is instead a psychological journey, chronicling Levi's descent into the darkness of blindness and the mysteries of his own soul.

Levi traveled extensively during his life. After living in France for most of the 1930s, during the postwar period he visited England and Germany. In 1947, he traveled to the United States on the occasion of the American translation of *Cristo si è fermato a Eboli*. His visit also coincided with an exhibition of his paintings at the Wildenstein Gallery in Manhattan.² An official political trip to the Soviet Union in 1955 was followed by visits to India (1957) and China (1959). In Italy, he traveled to Sicily and Sardinia on several occasions to document the work of the local *movimento contadino*. While traveling, Levi took ample notes and kept diaries, which served as the basis for various reportages he published in the Turin newspaper, *La Stampa*, as well as in other media outlets.³ Each of these trips constituted for him an opportunity to continue the exploration of cultural difference that he had begun in Lucania and expressed in *Cristo si è fermato a Eboli*, engaging in an intertextual dialogue of great complexity that, as Vanna Zaccaro observes, embraces "codici espressivi diversi quali la pittura, la poesia e la prosa; ma anche tra gli stessi testi, con un andare e ritornare di Levi su riflessioni, espressioni, immagini, riconducibili certo alla sua 'biblioteca mentale,' ma soprattutto al bisogno di 'ritorni'" ["different codes of expression, such as painting, poetry, and prose; but also (travels) between the texts, with Levi's returning upon reflections, expressions, images, which are certainly traceable back to his 'mental library,' but above all to his need for 'returns'"] ("Il viaggio di Carlo Levi" 105).[4]

In this chapter, I focus in particular on Levi's "returns" to the South of Italy and how his relationship with the South develops after *Cristo si è fermato a Eboli*. The two travel accounts from Sicily, *Le parole sono pietre*, and from Sardinia, *Tutto il miele è finito*, as well as his friendship with the mayor of the Lucanian town of Tricarico, Rocco Scotellaro, and the numerous paintings that he devoted to the most important figures of southern social history of his time, all testify to Levi's lifelong concern with the South, in both cultural and political terms. Beginning with *Cristo si è fermato a Eboli*, Levi's goal in writing about the South was not simply to celebrate its difference but, more important, to empower it with agency over its own history. Levi's artistic, political, and literary activity in the 1950s and 1960s thus concentrates on the new role of the South in Italian society as an active political and social agent, rather than the passive colonial possession of an indifferent state. Particularly important are *Le parole sono pietre* and *Tutto il miele è finito*, where Levi explores the revolutionary promise of the peasant movement in the South during the years following the agrarian reform.[5] As Vincenzo Consolo writes in his preface to the second edition of *Le parole sono pietre*, Levi's reportage from Sicily demonstrates a renewed attention to the historical and political dimensions of southern Italy. A sense of the urgency of civic engagement permeates the book. Words become weighty—to echo Levi's own phrase in the title—because they have an impact on the reader's political consciousness. Analogously, Levi describes *Tutto il miele è finito* as a chapter in the history that is being built and written everywhere in the South (7). The book takes his title from the words of a traditional funerary lament, in which the dead child is compared to the honey that the house mistress can no longer offer her guests. With this explicit reference to folkloric poetry, which also closes the book, Levi revisits the concept of peasant poetry as revealing that which "permane nella sua verità, come una parola detta, una forma formata, il carattere di una cosa, un segno" ["endures in its truth, like a spoken word, a formed shape, like the character of an object, a sign"] (58). Both in *Tutto il miele è finito* and in *Le parole sono pietre*, the titles recast in new terms the meditation on the role of art and creativity that Levi pursues in all his work, beginning with *Paura della libertà*, and confirm his belief in the transformative power of artistic creation upon reality.

In *Cristo si è fermato a Eboli*, Levi had explored the potentialities of painting as a source of words and poetry: the memorial reconstruction of his exile was based mostly on his paintings of the time (*Cristo* xix). Painting was also an epistemological instrument, introducing the peasants of Aliano to self-awareness through representation. Levi repeatedly describes the villagers' surprise in recognizing themselves and their own existence in his paintings, as a first step in the process of self-differentiation from the original communion with primordial chaos, which is a condition for historical self-realization. In *Cristo si è fermato a Eboli*, the power of painting is both a thematic line and a stylistic tool, for Levi grounds his writing in visual experience, using ekphrasis as the main trope of his narrative prose, both literally—as when he verbally reproduces his own paintings—and as a tendency to privilege vision and description over narrative dynamism.

Twenty years later, in *Tutto il miele è finito* and *Le parole sono pietre*, Levi returns to this poetics of the visual through the form of the portrait—the genre that is for him the most authentic form of painting. As we have seen, for Levi all painting is portrait insofar as it establishes and expresses a relationship, based on equality and reciprocity, between the painter and his subject ("I ritratti" 21). The portrait thus can serve as a means of self-discovery for both sitter and painter, who are engaged in an act of mutual recognition (14). Levi's pictorial production during the 1950s testifies to the renewed importance of the portrait as a visual means of exploring the same concerns that he examines in his books. Particularly the portraits of Rocco Scotellaro and Danilo Dolci that Levi painted between 1952 and 1956 "significano il faticoso passaggio, in quegli anni, da una situazione umana di 'senza storia,' alla nuova consapevolezza conquistata mediante le lotte sindacali e contro la mafia" ["signify the labored passage, in those years, from a human situation 'without history,' to a new awareness, conquered through union and antimafia struggles"] (Pauletto 14). In his "Avvertenza al lettore" in *Tutto il miele è finito*, Levi further authorizes the overlap between painting and writing, when he describes the book as "un ritratto, . . . un tentativo, soltanto accennato e parziale, di ritratto di una persona conosciuta nel tempo, il cui viso racconta e comprende, oggi, i diversi momenti della sua storia" ["a portrait, . . . an attempt to make a portrait, albeit only partially sketched, of a person known in time, whose face recounts and includes, today, the different moments of his life"] (7).[6]

The literary portraits of Sicily and Sardinia, as well as the actual paintings of Scotellaro and Dolci, participate in Levi's lifelong concern with the *questione meridionale*, which can be traced back to his years in the intellectual circles of *Rivoluzione liberale* and, later, his involvement in Carlo Rosselli's *Giustizia e Libertà* (Russo 21, Doria 68). Levi's thinking about the South developed especially in dialogue with Gobetti, from whom he gained an earlier understanding of the urgency of the southern questions, while also realizing the need to think about the South in its own terms, beyond the categories of Enlightenment thought that guided Gobetti's philosophy.

In his 1922 "Manifesto della Rivoluzione Liberale" Piero Gobetti identified the main cause of the contemporary Italian political crisis in a crisis of unity—according to his analysis, "l'incapacità dell'Italia a costituirsi in organismo unitario è essenzialmente incapacità nei cittadini di formarsi una coscienza dello Stato e di recare alla realtà vivente dell'organizzazione sociale la loro pratica adesione" ["Italy's inability to achieve organic unity is essentially the inability of its citizens to form a consciousness of the state and to make their own practical contribution to the living reality of organized society"] (1, "Our Liberalism" *110*). For Gobetti, as for his contemporary Antonio Gramsci, the Risorgimento failed to achieve the unification of the Italian peninsula because its architects wanted to impose the Piedmontese paradigm even in those areas where this model was not applicable (Ward, *Antifascisms* 159). This was the main reason for the absence of a leading political class in Italy, the lack of a modern industrial economy with an advanced class of entrepreneurs and skilled technical workers, and, finally, the lack of political consciousness and freedom (Gobetti, "Manifesto" 1). Levi's analysis of the southern situation in *Cristo si è fermato a Eboli* echoes directly Gobetti's diagnosis. In his memoir, Levi talks about the presence of two Italies within the same nation, two inimical Italies, whose opposition has been exacerbated by fascism and its middle-class ideology (221–22).[7] As it was for Gobetti, for Levi the only possible answer is a radical reconceptualization of the state: "Bisogna che noi ci rendiamo capaci di pensare e di creare un nuovo Stato, che non può più essere né quello fascista, né quello liberale, né quello comunista, forme tutte diverse e sostanzialmente identiche della stessa religione statale" ["We must make ourselves capable of inventing a new form of government, neither Fascist, nor Communist, nor even Liberal, for all three of these are forms of the religion of the State"] (223, *253*). As Gobetti advocated an organic conception of the state, one in which the individual would realize his potential ("Manifesto" 2), so Levi calls for a solution that would fill in the gap between state and individual, beyond the dialectic between fascism and antifascism—both fundamentally reducible to forms of idolatry of the state (*Cristo* 219, 233). His proposition is based on the concept of autonomy, which he adopts, once again, from Gobetti.

In his manifesto, Gobetti described the value and necessity of grassroots political movements, explaining how the uniqueness of Rivoluzione Liberale was its embracing of "tutte le esperienze di autonomia, proponendosi di chiarire, aiutare, rinnovare secondo la logica dello sviluppo empirico il movimento di redenzione del popolo" ["all the experiments in autonomy, (becoming) a practice and assigning itself the tasks of clarifying, assisting, and renewing the movement for the redemption of the people, following the logic of empirical development"] ("Manifesto" 2, *120*). Levi expands on Gobetti's concept of autonomy in *Cristo si è fermato a Eboli*: "Lo Stato non può essere che l'insieme di infinite autonomie, una organica federazione. Per i contadini, la cellula dello Stato, quella sola per cui essi potranno partecipare alla molteplice vita collettiva, non può essere che il comune rurale autonomo" ["The State can only be a group of autonomies, an organic federation. The unit or cell through which the peasants can take part in the complex life of the nation must be the autonomous or self-governing rural community"] (223, *254*). Here, the adjective *organic* is particularly important, for it implicitly responds to Gobetti's critique of federalism as an outdated political concept in "Manifesto." Levi's idea of federalism requires a rethinking of the function of the state, whose structures would be built "from the bottom up" (Ward, *Antifascisms* 172). According to Levi, this is the only form of statehood that would allow for the coexistence of the two civilizations of Italy, without one oppressing or burdening the other, "e che infine, attraverso l'abolizione di ogni potere e funzione sia dei grandi proprietari che della piccola borghesia locale, consenta al popolo contadino di vivere, per sé e per tutti" ["and which, finally, by the abolition of the powers and functions of the landowners and the local middle class, can assure the peasants a life of their own, for the benefit of all"] (*Cristo* 223, *254*). For Levi, as for Gobetti before him, this autonomy does not concern one class or one area of Italy only: "[L]'autonomia del comune rurale non potrà esistere senza l'autonomia delle fabbriche, delle scuole, delle città, di tutte le forme della vita sociale" ["(T)he autonomy or self-government of the community cannot exist without the autonomy of the factory, the school, and the city, of every form of social life"] (*Cristo* 223, *254*). Thus the idea of autonomy is connected to the notion of class awareness and class struggle, whose potential both Gobetti and Levi had appreciated in Antonio Gramsci's work with the factory councils in Turin. The use of the word *organic* in Levi's description of autonomy is a reminder of the closeness he felt—despite their political divergences—to Gramsci's sensitivity for the subaltern classes.

The concept of autonomy is not only political but also connected to the principle of creativity, which, as David Ward has pointed out, represents the cornerstone of Levi's philosophy and emerges, once again, from his intellectual dialogue with Gobetti (*Antifascisms* 160). As discussed in the introduction, Levi first developed his theories of history and creativity in his "poema filosofico" *Paura della libertà*, written in 1939, and returned to them often during the course of his life. In *Paura della libertà*, Levi reads fascism as a direct result of the crisis of Western civilization, deriving in turn from humanity's fear of its own powers of creation. Creativity generates fear because it draws man's rationality back toward the chaos of the *indistinto originario*, the formless original state from which each human being has emerged through a process of self-individuation. For Levi, through creative activity the person can both affirm herself as an individual and maintain a connection with the original chaos. In preserving this connection, humanity can avoid the excesses of rationality that have produced twentieth-century totalitarianisms.[8] For Levi all creative activity is poetry, in its etymological sense of poiesis, making ("L'invenzione" 51). And all poets are, in some way, *contadini*—a term that refers to the Lucanian peasants and manifests the enormous impact of his southern exile on Levi's thinking. As he described in *Cristo si è fermato a Eboli*, peasant culture had maintained its connection with the *indistinto originario*, but political autonomy within a reconceptualized Italian state would allow the peasants to also acquire the self-differentiation they still lacked. Within the pages of the book it was Levi's painting—as a metonymy for poetry and creativity—that allowed for the self-discovery necessary for the peasants to emerge from the original chaos and become active players in their own history.[9] Thus invested with agency, southern peasant civilization had for Levi the potential to offer a real alternative to the dictatorship of reason that afflicted modern Europe.[10]

No one incarnated the potential of the South as clearly as the young mayor of Tricarico (Basilicata), Rocco Scotellaro, whom Levi and Manlio Rossi Doria met in 1946. The friendship with the Socialist Scotellaro influenced Levi's view of *meridionalismo* in a progressive sense. As an *intellettuale contadino*,[11] Scotellaro embodied the Gramscian ideal of the organic intellectual, who possesses the historical awareness of the class from which he originated and devotes himself to its political representation (Torriglia 125). Scotellaro's political activism did not translate into a rejection of his agrarian origins, which reemerged as the subject matter of his poetry and prose. For example, in *Contadini del sud*, which was conceived as a vast anthro-sociological inquiry into the lives of the rural classes in Basilicata, Scotellaro gathered the first-person narratives of five agricultural laborers and craftsmen from his town and strived to maintain the rhythm and style of the local language in his written narrative. As Levi wrote in the preface to the 1964 edition of *L'uva puttanella and Contadini del sud*, these stories were meant to be more than an ethnographic document; they aimed to compose "una storia generale poetica del mezzogiorno" ["a general poetic history of the mezzogiorno"] (228). Scotellaro's literary activity and political engagement inspired Levi to elaborate further his idea that historical agency did not require a rejection of peasant culture but could coexist in a creative *linguaggio contadino*. This language is, for Levi, fundamentally poetic, as he writes in "Il contadino e l'orologio": "Se la poesia . . . non è che l'invenzione della verità, il mondo contadino è tutto immerso in una atmosfera di poesia" ["If poetry . . . is but the invention of truth, the peasant world is all immersed in an atmosphere of poetry"] (27). According to Levi, whereas peasant civilization maintains its connection with the *indistinto originario*, modern culture has relegated it to unconscious memory, from which it must be recuperated in order to preserve freedom and creativity (27). In the trajectory of Rocco Scotellaro's life and work, he recognized the possibility of such poetic politics and political poetry, as he suggests in the 1955 preface to *L'uva puttanella:*"Questa [attività politica] fu la forma pratica della sua poesia, come la sua poesia, e il libro dell'Uva puttanella, sono la forma poetica della sua attività politica" ["This (political activity) was the practical form of his poetry, just like poetry and the *Uva puttanella* book are the poetic form of his political activity"] (rpt. in Bronzini, *Il viaggio antropologico* 182).

Levi identifies in Scotellaro's arrest on false corruption charges a turning point in his political and personal trajectory. In the prison in which he spent 45 days, before being cleared of all allegations, the mayor of Tricarico was moved to reconsider the meaning and effectiveness of his political actions in the *mezzogiorno*, to reevaluate "la vanità di un certo tipo di azione politica astratta, mossa da macchine amiche, ma anch'esse esterne, come quella tradizionale e nemica dello Stato" ["the vanity of a certain kind of abstract political action, moved by machines that are friendly, but also external, like the traditional and inimical State machine"] (Levi, rpt. in Bronzini, *Il viaggio antropologico* 167). This reflection generated in Scotellaro the awareness of "la necessità di impostare sul piano nazionale la lotta contadina, e di formarsi in modo da essere capace di condurre efficacemente questa lotta più larga e complessa per la libertà" ["the necessity to establish the peasant struggle at the national level, and to educate himself in order to lead this broader and complex struggle for freedom"] (169). Levi interprets Scotellaro's subsequent decision to leave the South and become involved in *meridionalismo* on a national scale as "un momento esemplare dello sviluppo del mondo contadino: il momento più difficile, quello del contatto con l'altra civiltà, con dei fini diversi, con dei modi diversi; il momento in cui l'autonomia deve cimentarsi con un mondo più vasto, spesso indifferente ed ostile, ma con cui essa deve entrare in rapporto e iniziare una lotta e una collaborazione" ["an exemplary moment in the development of the peasant world: the most difficult moment, the moment of the contact with the other civilization, with different goals and different methods. The moment in which its autonomy must confront a broader world, often indifferent and hostile, but with which it must establish a relationship and begin a struggle and collaboration"] (169). Scotellaro's view of the South does not, then, stop at Eboli, but expresses his trust in the southern capacity for autonomy in dialogue and collaboration with the progressive forces of the rest of the nation (174).[12] What distinguishes Scotellaro from Guido Dorso or Giustino Fortunato, the fathers of classic *meridionalismo*, is, for Levi, his understanding that

> [i]l problema del nuovo meridionalismo è di storicizzare, di portare alla storia il mondo contadino nel suo complesso, nel suo completo divenire, così come esso è e si va formando e modificando, e quest'opera deve essere fatta dal mondo contadino stesso *per opera propria* e con propri mezzi originali. Non si tratta, cioè, di imporgli, per il suo bene, una storia esterna o di servirsene, anche per il suo bene, come di un ausiliario. (175)[13]
>
> *the problem of the new meridionalismo is to historicize, to bring into history the peasant world in its complex and complete becoming, as it is and is shaping and changing itself, and this work must be accomplished by the peasant world by itself and by its own original means. In other words, this is not about imposing upon it an external history for its own good, or using it for its own good as an auxiliary force.*

In other words, for Levi the new *meridionalismo* must respect the autonomy of the peasant world, intended as its cultural and historical difference.[14] In a brief poem, Scotellaro foregrounds and legitimates the particular historicity of the southern peasants as they appear on the national scene of class struggle: "È fatto giorno, siamo entrati in giuoco anche noi / con i panni e le scarpe e le facce che avevamo" ["Day has dawned, we have joined the game as well / with our usual clothes and faces and shoes"] (qtd. in Bronzini 179, qtd. in Moloney, Italian Novels, 30).

Scotellaro's own face is at the center of several of Levi's paintings. The 1952 portrait, now exhibited in the National Museum of Medieval and Modern art of Basilicata, in Matera (Figure 7), displays Levi's characteristic wavy (Levi's own word) brushstrokes, which infuse the painting with dynamism and give strength to its powers of expression. As is typical of Levi's earlier paintings of the South, there is virtually no contrast between Scotellaro's face and the landscape behind him. His complexion is the same color as the earth—the light ochres and browns that dominate the canvas—evoking the profound relationship between the man and his land. What distinguishes him from the background are his dark eyes and his intense gaze, which transmit the self-awareness and sense of purpose that marked Scotellaro's political and social action. Scotellaro's left shoulder is slightly higher than his right one, as though he was caught while walking forward. This dynamic posture, as well as the vigorous brushstrokes, convey a sense of energetic movement, suggesting, in Levi's terms, Scotellaro's

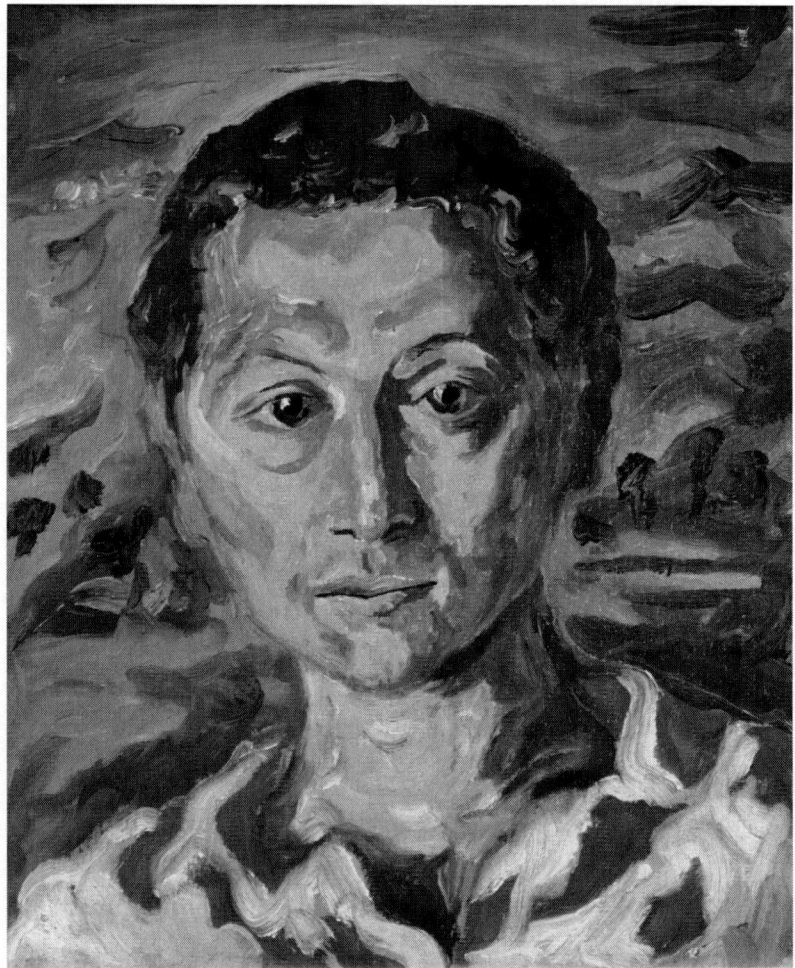

Figure 7. Carlo Levi, *Ritratto di Rocco Scotellaro* (1952)

© 2012 Artists Rights Society (ARS), New York / SIAE, Rome;
Photo Soprintendenza per i Beni Storici, Artistici ed
Etnoantropologici della Basilicata—Matera

emergence from the original indistinction and his entrance into the realm of history and action.

If this first portrait conveys a sense of possibility and faith in the future, very different is *Lamento per Rocco Scotellaro* (1953), which he painted after Scotellaro's premature death (Figure 8). Scotellaro lies on his deathbed, surrounded by a crowd of women in dark clothes. At the center stands Scotellaro's mother, her face and hair equally ashen in her pain. She is shown while she prepares to cover her head with her shawl, as the other women have already done, as a sign of mourning. The women's expressions and gestures suggest a dignified resignation in front of Scotellaro's death. There seems to be no desperation in their actions, but rather the consciousness of the ineluctability of death. Among the mourners on the right side of the painting, three men are distinguishable: a young boy, whose grief-stricken features remind the viewer of Levi's Lucanian pictures; another young man seen from behind; and, finally, Levi himself. His unmistakable profile faces directly, in a diagonal line, Scotellaro's face, indicating the intellectual and affective connection between the two friends. The darkness of the colors chosen for this canvas contrasts dramatically with the lightness of the earlier portrait of Scotellaro. Markedly different is also the style of this painting, where Levi seems to present the viewer with a condensed history of his art. The smoothness of his self-portrait and of Scotellaro's face, for instance, reminds the viewer of his early Turinese years; the two women on his right demonstrate the expressionistic quality of his Lucanian paintings, with their dramatic brushstrokes. In the other figures, Levi gives prominence to the lines, creating an overall effect of sculpted rigidity, again in contrast with the dynamic energy of the first portrait.[15] Absent is the natural scenery, leaving in its stead a landscape of faces. The immobility of the composition powerfully conveys the gravity of the moment, the weight that Scotellaro's life and death have had in advocating the rights of southern people.

Scotellaro's death does not end his influence over Levi's thinking about the South. Perhaps most significantly, Levi reproposes Scotellaro's poetry in a lecture on Antonio Gramsci and the South that he gave in 1967 and that was later published in the journal *Basilicata*. Levi first knew Gramsci through Gobetti, who had met him and valued his work among Turinese industrial workers.[16] Levi identified in the essay "La questione meridionale" the most important contribution that Gramsci gave to *meridionalismo*. In this 1926 essay, the Marxian thinker analyzed the southern question as a national question, as "la questione in cui il problema dei rapporti tra operai e contadini si pone non soltanto come un problema di rapporto di classe, ma anche e specialmente come un problema territoriale, cioè come uno degli aspetti della questione nazionale" ["the question that poses the

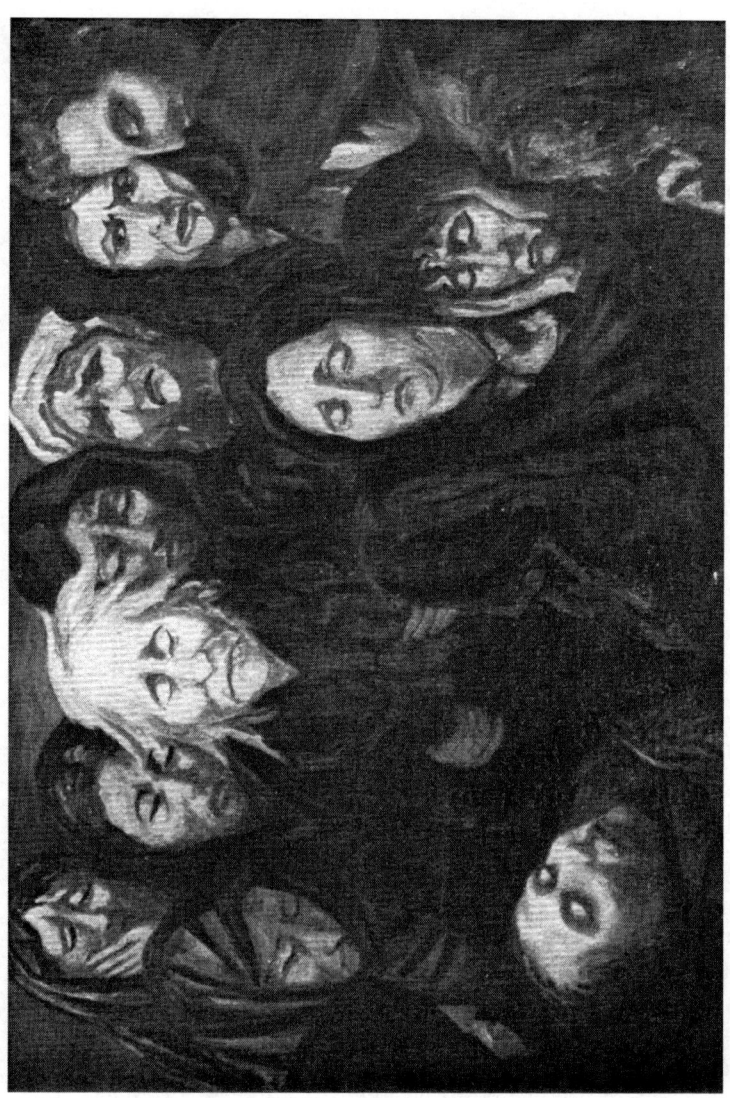

Figure 8. Carlo Levi, *Lamento per Rocco Scotellaro* (1953)
© 2012 Artists Rights Society (ARS), New York / SIAE, Rome

problem of the relationship between workers and peasants not only as a problem of class, but also, and especially, as a problem of territory, as one of the characteristics of the national question"] (Gramsci, *Questione meridionale* 20, *Southern Question* 75). For Gramsci, the problem of southern peasants could only be resolved through a pact of solidarity between northern industrial workers and rural classes, which he saw as the axis of the proletarian revolution (9). But in order to achieve this union between North and South, between city and countryside, it was necessary, Gramsci argued, for the peasants to acquire class consciousness and to engage in systematic and organized action to overthrow oppressive social relations (6).[17] Levi reinterprets the Gramscian lesson to emphasize its similarities with his own thinking about the South and plays down Gramsci's belief that the northern workers needed to assume a leadership role in the class struggle—a position that, as a convinced supporter of southern autonomy, he could not embrace. Here, he prefers to attribute to Gramsci a "senso continuo dell'autonomia e della storicità," where autonomy, he continues, means the kind of freedom that enables hegemony and the reappropriation of one's own place in history (Levi, "Gramsci" 4). Levi places this need to reclaim the subaltern's historical agency at the root of the affinity between Gramsci's thought and his own project in *Cristo si è fermato a Eboli*. Including Gramsci in the first person plural, he concludes, "se abbiamo narrato quel mondo immobile era perché si muovesse" ["if we told about that motionless world it was in order for it to move"] (6).

Levi's reportage from Sicily, *Le parole sono pietre*, focuses specifically on this movement, as he explains in the "Avvertenza al lettore" from the 1955 edition:

> La Sicilia, come tutto il Mezzogiorno, ma in modi propri e particolari, si muove; e le azioni, le parole, i sentimenti, le lotte, le attese, le morti . . . sono momenti del suo sviluppo . . . Si accontenti dunque, per ora, l'amico lettore, di quel poco che oggi gli offro qui, e che non è che una prima, rapida immagine di un mondo che va, giorno per giorno, modificandosi, e prendendo coraggiosamente coscienza di esistere. (31)

> *Sicily, like all the South of Italy, is moving, but in its own particular ways; and the actions, the words, the emotions, the struggles, the expectations, and the deaths . . . are moments in its development . . . But for now, I hope that my friend the reader will be satisfied with what little I can offer here, and understand that it is nothing more than a first glancing image of a world that, day by day, is changing, and courageously gaining an awareness of its own existence. (Words are Stones, 162)*

The structure of the book reflects this progressive movement and advances from the mythical to the historical dimension of life in Sicily. The narrative is divided into three parts, corresponding, in chronological order, to three different journeys to Sicily in 1951, 1952, and 1955. The first part opens with an account of the mayor of New York City Vincent Impellitteri's visit to his native village, Isnello, in 1951. Levi's depiction of Impellitteri's arrival and brief stay in Isnello contains open references to the gospels, and the illustrious guest is associated closely with the Christ. In describing the aura surrounding Impellitteri, Levi explains, "Come in quella di Omero, di Cristoforo Colombo (o, più precisamente, di Gesù Cristo), c'era qualcosa di misterioso nella sua nascita, e qualche cosa di miracoloso nel suo ritorno, nella sua prossima epifania" ["As in the birth of Homer or Christopher Columbus (or, more to the point, Jesus Christ), there was a mystery in the circumstances of his birth, and something miraculous about his return, his imminent epiphany"] (42, *11*). "Impy" was born, a local woman tells him, "in una camera piena di paglia e fieno, come Gesù Bambino" ["in a room full of straw and hay, just like Baby Jesus"] (43, *12*). His return, "dopo la fuga in Egitto avvenuta cinquanta anni fa, era l'ingresso di Cristo a Gerusalemme" ["after the Flight into Egypt that took place fifty years ago, this was the entry of Christ into Jerusalem"] (47, *15*), is reenacted, as during the holy week, in a sort of secular passion play. "Egli era come Cristo, un Dio-Uomo" ["He was like Christ, a Man-God"] (51, *19*), so much so that a priest leading a procession, having spotted Impellitteri's car, abandons the Holy Sacrament to see the mayor up close.

Levi's evangelical echoes in these pages, as well as the placing of this episode at the beginning of the book, situate *Le parole sono pietre* in direct dialogue with *Cristo si è fermato a Eboli*. Whereas the *contadini* Levi met during his exile considered themselves as fundamentally excluded from the message of historical purposefulness of Christianity, here he shows how Christ has finally gone beyond Eboli, to include in the forward movement of history the *contadini* and laborers of Sicily. The citizens of Isnello see in the Christlike Impellitteri a reflection of their own selves; as Levi writes, "il paese di Isnello festeggiava se stesso; ciascuno, in Impellitteri, riconosceva se stesso" ["the town of Isnello was celebrating itself; everyone recognised themselves in Impellitteri"] (51, *19*). In identifying with him, the people of Isnello experience the hope in the future that the Lucanian peasants did not know. Here, the man-god speaks the language of the local people, no longer a foreign presence but a familiar one. However, the Biblical subtext tempers the villagers' optimism with an element of irony, for they are clearly mistaken in placing their hopes for change in Impellitteri's visit, whose generosity can be fruitful only in the short term. As Joseph Farrell has observed, Levi's reconstruction of Impellitteri's day-trip to Isnello according to the evangelical plotline effectively places it in the realm of myth, thus exposing the illusory nature of the peasants' trust in a salvation coming from outside (135). The *isnellesi* should not wait for the coming of a Christlike figure but claim for themselves a place in history through political and social action. Impellitteri's visit can bring about change only insofar as his fellow citizens recognize in him the possibilities that an active engagement with history offers.

If Levi still highlights the mythical dimension of Sicilian mentality in reporting from Isnello, it is in Lercara that he encounters a movement with true political and social self-awareness. In Lercara, he writes, "[e]ro venuto per visitare, da semplice curioso, una vecchia zolfara, in uno dei mille paesi della immobilità contadina; e mi trovavo invece in un centro vivo, in pieno movimento e cambiamento, dove tutti i sentimenti sono nuovi, le azioni appassionate, le volontà tese e violente, e qualche cosa che prima non esisteva nasce nel cuore degli uomini" ["I had come, out of simple curiosity, to visit an old sulphur mine in one of the thousands of villages of rural stagnation; and instead I found myself in a place in ferment, in a state of flux and change, filled with new emotions, impassioned actions and focused, violent determination, where something that had previously not existed was burgeoning in the hearts of the people"] (71, 36). In this passage, Levi candidly acknowledges the prejudice with which, after his experience in Lucania (and, as, we have seen, in Isnello) he approached the South—expecting it to conform, so to speak, to his own image of it. This was exactly the criticism that leftist reviewers, such as Carlo Muscetta, had moved against *Cristo si è fermato a Eboli*, accusing him of forging a portrait of an imaginary world, whose existence was justified by poetic reasons: "[Q]uello era il mondo sognato dalla sua poetica, un mondo senza Storia, un mondo chiuso alla Libertà e alla Ragione" ["That was the world dreamed in his poetics, a world without History, a world that excluded Freedom and Reason"] (Muscetta, qtd. in De Donato and D'Amaro 178). By admitting his bias, here Levi accomplishes two goals: he obliquely responds to Muscetta's criticism and continues to play the reality of the new Sicily against his account of Lucania.

Indeed, the echoes of the earlier memoir continue throughout this first part of *Le parole sono pietre*, in which Levi chronicles the strike of the Lercara miners against unsafe working conditions and the exploitation of which they are victims. After an accident in which a 17-year-old boy died, the owners of the mine took half a day out of his paycheck, since he had not completed his workday; similarly, the *padroni* subtracted the equivalent of an hour of work from the other miners' salary, because they had used this hour to remove his body from the mine. In the face of such injustice, writes Levi, "il senso antico della giustizia fu toccato, la disperazione secolare trovò, in quel fatto, un simbolo visibile, e lo sciopero cominciò" ["(a)n ancient sense of justice was triggered, an age-old desperation found, in this occurrence, a visible symbol, and the strike began"] (73, *38*). The miners on strike and their families seem, to Levi, elated by the possibilities that their gesture opens up for them. They feel a collective sense of ownership of their own lives, the power of agency within their own history: "[I]l piacere che essi hanno di sentirsi vivere, e la sicurezza di vincere, è l'ineffabile, inconsapevole senso di essere entrati, come attori, in una vicenda vera, nel mobile fiume della storia" ["And the pleasure that they experience in sensing that they are alive, and the certainty that they will win, is the ineffable, unconscious sense of having stepped, as actors, into an actual story, into the flowing river of history"] (81, *46*). In describing these events, Levi employs language that is reminiscent of *Cristo si è fermato a Eboli*: he writes of the miners' "discovery" of themselves and their historical situation for the first time, just as in *Cristo si è fermato a Eboli* he had described the peasants recognizing themselves and their landscape in his paintings. Here, too, the moment of self-discovery is directly connected to an act of visual representation: "Volevano tutti essere fotografati: avevano trovato il coraggio di esistere, non erano più nemici della propria immagine" ["They all wanted to have their pictures taken: they had found the courage to live, they were no longer enemies of their own image"] (82, *47*). Whereas the *contadini* of Lucania systematically refused to be portrayed, and Levi resorted to violence in order to persuade his housekeeper to model for him, the Sicilian workers he meets in Lercara are eager for B. (the photographer who accompanies Levi in his journey) to take photographs of them. The writer foregrounds, here, the symbolic power of images, and of portraiture in particular, which runs as a constant theme in his work. For Levi, the self-portrait manifests the moment of self-discovery as a distinct individual, separate from the primordial chaos of creation. One's ability to shape a visual image of herself corresponds thus to her entrance into the flow of history. In highlighting the miners' desire to be photographed, Levi indicates the sense of hopefulness and optimism toward history that the workers' movement was able to generate in the South after the end of the war. It is important, moreover, to notice how the workers are motivated here by their pride in the strike—an action they organized independently—and not by Levi's initiative or idea, marking a significant difference with the portraits of Lucanian peasants he took during his exile.

Directly in contrast with the workers' willingness to be portrayed stands the reticence of the owner of the mine, whose face was so peculiar that, Levi writes, it would have deserved a painting, or at least a photograph. Levi laments the inability of his words to represent his visage:

Nell'ingresso stava seduto un vecchio, un uomo gigantesco, pesante, grosso, con un collo corto e robusto, una camicia aperta e un grigio abito trasandato; con una testa dalla pelle come un cuoio, dalle enormi mascelle, una bocca piena di denti, e degli occhi sottili, sfuggenti, dietro le spesse lenti di un paio di occhiali di ferro. Era il signor N., il gabellotto e padrone delle miniere. Ma come descriverlo? Forse soltanto la pittura potrebbe rendere l'aria di quel volto, l'atmosfera che lo avvolgeva, il modo inusitato dei suoi movimenti. Era un viso impassibile e impenetrabile, ma nello stesso tempo mosso in smorfie espressive di sentimenti diversi da quelli che siamo abituati a comprendere: un misto di astuzia, di diffidenza estrema, di sicurezza e di paura mescolate, di alterigia e violenza e forse, chissà, anche di una certa arguzia: ma tutte queste cose parevano fuse in quel volto in un modo per noi lontano ed estraneo, come se il tono dei sentimenti, e l'aspetto stesso del viso appartenessero a un altro tempo, di cui serbiamo soltanto un arcaico ricordo ereditario. (74)

Sitting in the lobby was an old man, huge, heavy, massive, with a short powerful neck, an open-necked shirt and a shabby grey suit; a head covered with leathery skin, with enormous jaws, a mouth bristling with teeth, and small, evasive eyes behind the thick lenses of a pair of metal glasses. This was Signor N., the subcontractor and foreman of the mines. How can I describe him? Perhaps only a painting could adequately render the aura of that face, the atmosphere that enveloped it, the uncommon manner of his gestures. His face was impassive and inscrutable, and yet at the same time it was enlivened by grimaces expressing feelings different from those we are accustomed to perceiving: a mixture of cunning, extreme mistrust, mingled confidence and fear, arrogance and violence and even, perhaps, a certain wit: and yet all these elements seemed to be fused in that face in a way that was distant and alien to us, as if the tone of the emotions, and the very appearance of the face belonged to another era, of which we have nothing more than an archaic, hereditary recollection. (39)

But when Levi mentions the possibility of taking a picture, N. resolutely denies the photographer the opportunity to come close: "A me, una fotografia? – esclamò. – È proibito, assolutamente proibito. Nessuno me ne ha mai fatte né me ne farà mai. Me l'ha proibito il dottore." ["'Of me, a photograph?' he exclaimed. 'No, that's prohibited, absolutely forbidden. No one has ever taken my picture, and no one ever will. My doctor forbids it.'"] (75, *40*). With his refusal to be portrayed, then, N. places himself decisively among those who reject change and progress at all costs. While the miners' faces "erano facce nuove, facce di oggi, occhi vedevano oggi le cose, fino a ieri nascoste, che vedevano se stessi" ["were new faces, faces of today, eyes that today could see the things that until yesterday had been hidden, eyes that saw themselves"] (81, *45–46*), Mr. N.'s face is that of a feudal master, firmly lodged in an unchanging mentality that cannot envision an alternative way of life (81).

If Mr. N. refuses to engage in the dialogue that a portrait establishes between a painter and the subject of representation, completely different is the attitude of Francesca Serio, the mother of a Sicilian union organizer, Salvatore Carnevale, who was killed by the mafia. Levi describes her vividly in the text, before actually representing her in painting:

> È una donna di cinquant'anni, ancora giovanile nel corpo snello e nell'aspetto, ancora bella nei neri occhi acuti, nel bianco-bruno colore della pelle, nei neri capelli, nelle bianche labbra sottili, nei denti minuti e taglienti, nelle lunghe mani espressive e parlanti: di una bellezza dura, asciugata, violenta, opaca come una pietra, spietata, apparentemente disumana. (169)

> *She is a woman of about fifty, still young in appearance, in her slim body and her face, still beautiful in her intelligent dark eyes, in the light-dusky hue of her skin, her black hair, her thin white lips, her small sharp teeth, her long expressive and eloquent hands: it is a hard beauty, dry, violent, as opaque as a stone, pitiless, apparently inhuman. (126)*

Francesca Serio returns in the painting, *Le parole sono pietre* (Figure 9),[18] where she occupies the lower corner on the right side. She sits isolated from the other figures, who populate the picture and who also incarnate the Sicilian struggle against criminal corruption. In the opposite corner stands Danilo Dolci, the sociologist and reformer who defended the rights of Sicilian agricultural laborers. Francesca Serio wears the black veil of mourning, but her expression is not one of resignation or passivity. Her look is full of determination, and her right hand is raised in a gesture that suggests resistance and refusal. Indeed, in Levi's verbal portrayal of Carnevale's mother, she rejects the logic of violence that the mafia imposes on Sicily. The other characters of the painting share Francesca Serio's strong features, emphasized by Levi's use of thick black lines, and her look of serious determination. Levi abandons, here, the organic and fluid brushstrokes that we have seen in his Lucanian paintings from the 1930s and in Scotellaro's first portrait. The human figures no longer emerge from the landscape through the movement of the paintbrush but are set against it, clearly distinct from it, signifying their full belonging to history. Among them appear some figures from Levi's Lucanian work, who transmit a sense of continuity in the painter's art. As Antonio Del Guercio once wrote, indeed, Levi saw each of his paintings not as a poetic fragment, but as a moment in a continuous narration (72).

It is as part of this continuous narration that Francesca Serio and Dolci had appeared together in another painting, a portrait of Dolci that echoes his pose in *Le parole sono pietre* (Figure 10). In the portrait, Dolci

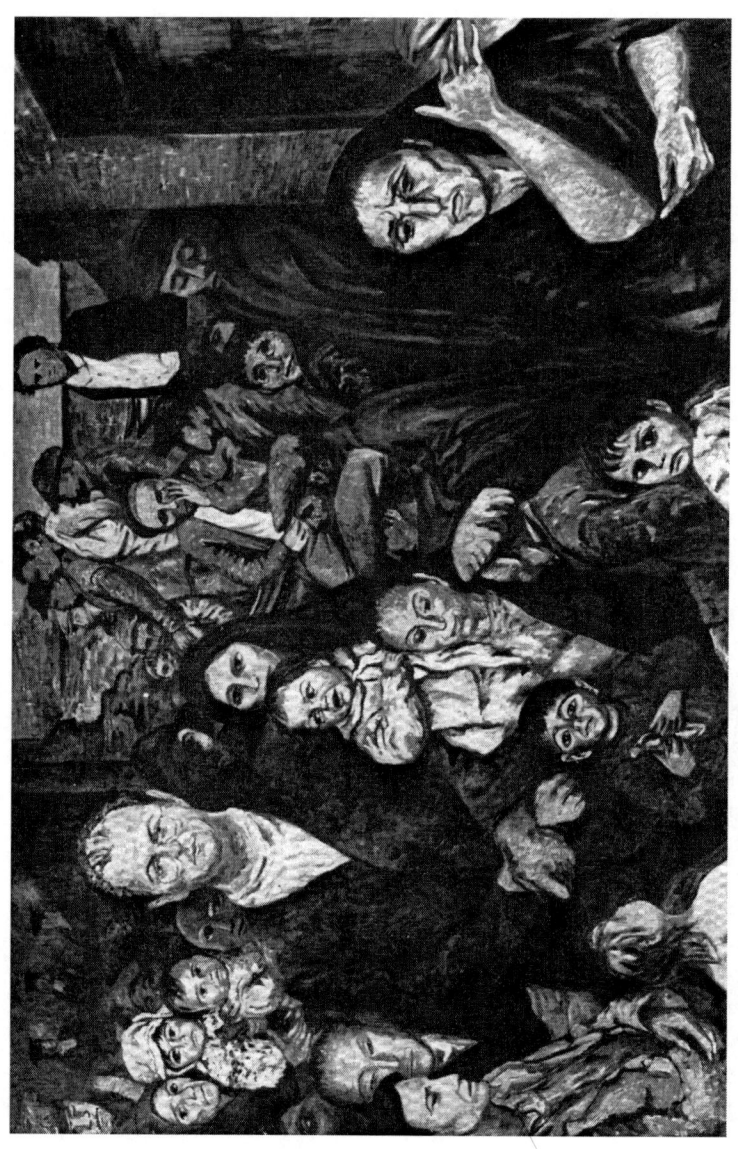

Figure 9. Carlo Levi, *Le parole sono pietre* (1955)
© 2012 Artists Rights Society (ARS), New York / SIAE, Rome

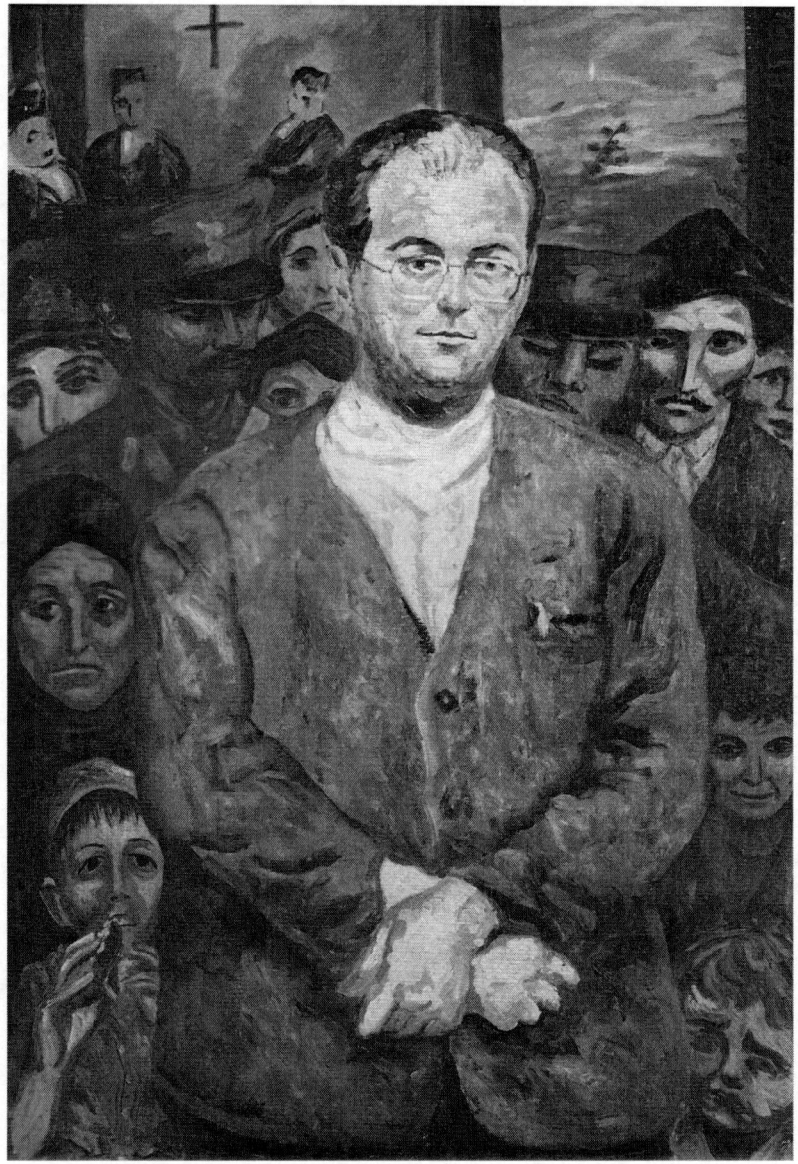

Figure 10. Carlo Levi, *Ritratto di Danilo Dolci* (1956)
© 2012 Artists Rights Society (ARS), New York / SIAE, Rome

is depicted in the courtroom where, in 1956, he stood trial for unauthorized occupation of public soil, after organizing two hundred unemployed men to repair the main road in the town of Partinico. Dolci stands erect in the foreground, looking directly into the eyes of the viewer. His hands are cuffed, and behind him are two Carabinieri, who are leading him out of the courtroom. All around him appear the faces of the people whose plea he has embraced. Some of them are recognizable from other paintings: on the bottom right corner is the child whose portrait Levi called "La porta del sud" (1953, Figure 11); around the child are boys that remind the viewer of Levi's many portraits of Lucanian youngsters. Behind Dolci's right arm is Francesca Serio's tragic face, enveloped in the black veil of mourning. At the far back are visible the three faceless judges that, under the authority granted to them by the state and, ironically, the crucifix that hangs in all Italian courtrooms, have condemned Dolci for his Christlike dedication to the poor.[19] Opposite the judges, at the top right corner, a window opens onto the barren Sicilian landscape, depicted in the yellow and light purple brushstrokes that Levi recognized as characteristic of his first southern paintings.[20] The faces of the Sicilian townsfolk, as well as the Carabinieri, are marked by strong lines, in a *grafismo*, as Alberto Moravia puts it, that evokes the seventeenth-century Counter-Reformation (26). Their complexion, their eyes, their clothes are dark, of that color that evokes the darkness of the soil and death. Dolci's face is, in contrast, softer and wider and brightened as if by an interior light. His countenance is serious but serene—an expression of his trust in the righteousness of his mission. As Levi recognizes in "Le ragioni di Danilo Dolci," the Christian activist stands as a representative of the individual and collective destinies of the Sicilians behind him. Levi praises Dolci's efforts to advocate for the Sicilian underclasses from within their world, choosing to share their poverty and embracing their mode of life. As one of them, he has helped them to find their own voice in the social and political struggle: "I mezzi del movimento, le forme del suo agire, saranno dunque quelle che nascono direttamente dai suoi bisogni fondamentali, dai problemi reali, dalla necessità della sua vita, che, rovesciandosi e invertendosi di segno, diventano libertà, metodo liberatorio" ["The tools of the movement, the forms of its activity, will therefore be those that are directly born from the movement's fundamental needs, its real problems, the necessities of its life that, in a reversal, become freedom and liberating strategy"] (11).

The Christological references seen in Dolci's portrait return in Levi's account of his first meeting with Francesca Serio. He reverses the meaning of these references, however, for he narrates the death, rather than the nativity, of Salvatore (the savior). Salvatore Carnevale, like Jesus, has given his life for his people: "Chi uccide me uccide Gesù Cristo, – ripete Francesca"

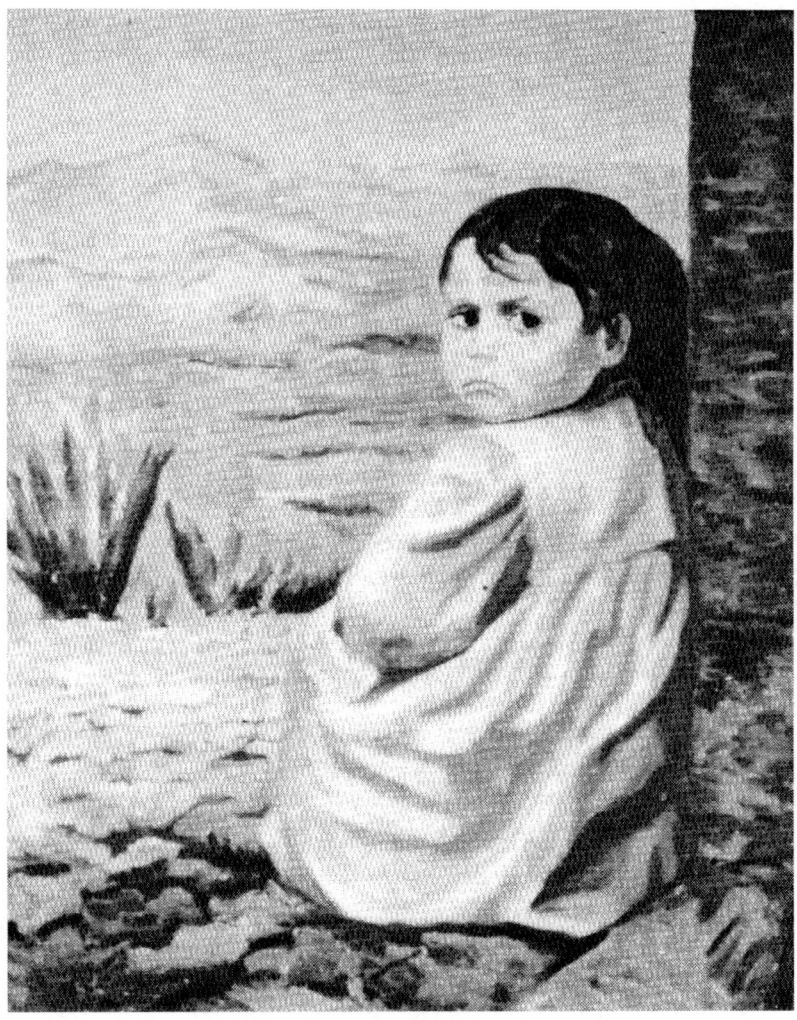

Figure 11. Carlo Levi, *La porta del sud* (1953)
© 2012 Artists Rights Society (ARS), New York / SIAE, Rome

["'He who kills me, kills Jesus Christ,' Francesca repeated"] (*Le parole sono pietre* 175, *131*). Like for Christ, Carnevale's death has not been useless, for "la sua Chiesa è in piedi tuttavia" ["his Church still stands"] (175, *131*).[21] It is Carnevale's mother, Francesca Serio, who sustains the structure of this church through words that weigh like stones, as Levi writes. He describes the mourning woman as entirely defined by her act of speech: "Niente altro esiste di lei e per lei, se non questo processo che essa istruisce e svolge da sola, seduta sulla sedia di fianco al letto . . . Essa stessa si identifica totalmente con il suo processo . . . Così questa donna si è fatta, in un giorno: le lacrime non sono più lacrime ma parole, e le parole sono pietre" ["Nothing else exists of her and for her, other than this trial, which she has assembled and carried out on her own, sitting in her chair by the side of the bed. . . . She identifies wholly with her trial. . . . And so this woman created herself, in the course of a day: tears are no longer tears, they are words now, and words are stones"] (169–70, *126–27*). Indeed, Francesca's words are stones because they are accusations that she throws in the face of the mafia bosses that have killed her son. Through her words, she has broken the wall of *omertà* that has always protected the mafiosi from justice and has thus continued her son's work. Francesca's words are the manifestation of a new political and social awareness, an awareness that, for Levi, is based on "un potere nemico del potere: il Partito" ["a power that is opposed to power: the party"] (171, *128*). The party has given Francesca the language she needs to mourn her son:

> Non è il linguaggio poetico della madre lucana che racconta la vita del figlio morto: è un linguaggio di rivendicazione, di oratoria, di discussione, un atto di accusa, è un linguaggio di partito. . . . Ma nella sua bocca, davanti alla morte, questo linguaggio, questo convenzionale e monotono linguaggio di partito, diventa un linguaggio eroico, come il primo modo di affermare la propria esistenza, l'arido canto di una furia che esiste per il primo giorno in un mondo nuovo. (175)

> *It is not the poetic language of a Lucanian mother who tells the story of her dead son's life: it is a language of demands, of oratory, of debate, an act of accusation, it is a language of the party . . . But in her mouth, in the face of death, this language, this conventional and droning language of the party becomes a language of heroism, as if it were the first way to affirm one's own existence, the arid chant of a Fury who exists for the first day in a new world. (131–32)*

There is a qualitative difference between Francesca's chronicle of her son's tragic end and the poetic forms of the funerary laments. The customary lamentation expresses human impotence and passivity in the face of death, as Levi recounts in *Cristo si è fermato a Eboli*. When a sick man he was unable to treat dies, the women of his family perform a traditional mourning ceremony, tearing their clothes and scratching their faces: "Era una nota lunga, identica, monotona, straziante. Era impossibile ascoltarla senza essere invasi da un senso di angoscia fisica irresistibile: quel grido faceva venire un groppo alla gola, pareva entrasse nelle viscere" ["This single note was long drawn-out, repetitious and agonizing. It was impossible to listen to it without being overcome by an irresistible feeling of physical anguish; it brought a lump to the throat of the hearer and made its way straight to the pit of his stomach"] (*Cristo* 199, *226*). Francesca's lament, on the contrary, is heroic, because it calls for justice ("un atto di accusa") and affirms the survivors' right to continue Carnevale's work ("il primo modo di affermare la propria esistenza") (*Le parole sono pietre* 175). The acquisition of the vocabulary of progressive politics gives Francesca the power of speech; but her recontextualization of it in her own cultural forms gives it a concreteness and substance that conventional political discourse misses.

As we have seen, Levi devotes several pages of *L'Orologio* to a scathing critique of Italian politicians' distorted use of language. For Levi, in Italian politics words are emptied of meaning because they refer not to reality but to abstractions, which have no relationship with the lives of common people, from factory workers to agricultural laborers or teachers. Therefore, the language of politics has thus far belonged exclusively to the *Luigini*, whereas the *contadini* (the term with which Levi indicates all social forces that are capable of creativity), have always rejected it. In a crucial dialogue of *L'Orologio*, Levi's spokesperson, Andrea, explains that the mistake of progressive politicians has been to adopt the conventional idiom of politics, a language that the *contadini* cannot understand, for it is based on vain abstractions. Levi's preoccupation with the sterility of political speech echoes, once again, Gramsci's own analysis of the *questione della lingua* as a fundamentally political question.[22] For Gramsci, the project of one national language in Italy is directly connected to the emergence of a particular hegemonic class. Standard Italian is not an organic language that emerges from the people's relationship with its own history but rather the expression of a bourgeois ideology that excludes and marginalizes the working classes. Gramsci's thesis had a vast influence over the intellectuals of Levi's generation. Pier Paolo Pasolini, for example, denounced the expansion of a language dominated by neocapitalist interests in "Nuove questioni linguistiche," later published in *Empirismo Eretico*: "Voglio dire che mentre la grande e piccola borghesia di tipo paleoindustriale e commerciale non è mai riuscita a *identificare se stessa con l'intera società italiana*, e ha fatto semplicemente dell'italiano letterario la propria lingua di classe imponendolo dall'alto, la nascente tecnocrazia del Nord si identifica egemonicamente con l'intera nazione, ed elabora quindi un nuovo tipo di cultura e di lingua effettivamente nazionali" ["I mean that while the upper and lower bourgeoisie of the paleoindustrial and commercial type has never succeeded in identifying itself with the entire Italian society, and has simply made literary Italian into its own class language, imposing it from above, the nascent technocracy of the North has identified itself hegemonically with the entire country and is therefore developing a new type of culture and language that are actually national"] (*Empirismo Eretico* 20, *Heretical Empiricism* 17).

Pasolini exposes this language as excessively instrumental—aimed at communication without taking into account the need for expressivity that "minor" vernaculars maintain (*Empirismo eretico* 19). Levi shared Pasolini's concern with the poetic power of language, as his characterizations of Scotellaro's literary work and Francesca Serio's mourning chant show. As we have seen, he admired Scotellaro precisely because in his work as a *poeta contadino* he was able to negotiate the gap between political discourse and poetry. Like Scotellaro, Francesca Serio takes ownership of the vocabulary of politics and, in adapting it to the reality of her plea, she redeems it from its abstraction. She understands why her son and his friends "studiavano il vocabolario. Là ci sono le parole, le parole che hanno scoperto e che solo adesso sono diventate necessarie" ["would study the dictionary. In it were words, the words that they had discovered and which have only now become necessary"] (*Le parole sono pietre* 184, *140*). Serio is thus a symbol of the new Sicily, which, as Levi writes in opening the book, "va ... prendendo coraggiosamente coscienza di esistere" ["is ... courageously gaining an awareness of its own existence"] (31, *162*) on the historical plane and shapes a new language to express its own existence.

Le parole sono pietre shows, indeed, a renewed interest in history on Levi's part. Even in its structure, the book is defined by a narrative dynamism that is unusual in Levi's writings. The writer follows the chronology of his journeys to Sicily, and his account is dominated by a storytelling impulse that overcomes the lyrical and descriptive moments of the text. If "every story is a travel story—a spatial practice" (de Certeau 115), in Levi's Sicilian travel journals his movement in space coincides with the advancement of the narrative flow. Each place visited corresponds to a different episode in Sicilian present and past history. Levi discusses Sicily's past and includes folkloric elements in his account,[23] but he does not indulge in nostalgia—his emphasis is on the future, on the potential for change that the present holds. Levi's gaze is focused ahead, and his diaries testify to a certain hurry to move forward, which is both literal ("Mi affrettai in automobile," "mi vestii in fretta, e fuggii," "correvamo nella notte" 45, 57, 82) and an index of the drive toward the future he witnesses in the

Sicilian labor movement. Despite this emphasis on movement, in *Le parole sono pietre* the written word retains its power to evoke visual experience, through its focusing on the human figures and faces that incarnate Sicily's historical destiny. In this respect, Levi's prose presents many analogies with Luchino Visconti's idea of anthropomorphic cinema. Visconti writes, "[I]l peso dell'essere umano, la sua presenza, è la sola 'cosa' che veramente colmi il fotogramma, che l'ambiente è da lui creato, dalla sua vivente presenza, e che dalle passioni che lo agitano questo acquista verità e rilievo; mentre anche la sua momentanea assenza dal rettangolo luminoso ricondurrà ogni cosa a un aspetto di non animata natura" ["(T)he heft of a human being, his presence, is the only thing which really fills the frame; that he creates the atmosphere with his living presence. He acquires truth and character thanks to the emotion he undergoes, while his temporary absence from the screen will cause things to return to the state of non-animated nature"] ("Il cinema antropomorfico"n. pag., *"Antropomorphic Cinema"* 84). Similarly, Levi pays special attention to the human face in the gallery of portraits he offers his readers.

The reference to Visconti is particularly appropriate here, for Levi refers explicitly to his work in the second part of *Le parole sono pietre*, in which he describes a visit to Aci Trezza. These pages are replete with explicit literary and artistic references, from Visconti to Giovanni Verga and Homer, and the structure itself of the account is modeled upon Verga's short story "Fantasticheria." As in "Fantasticheria," the male narrator engages in a dialogue with a foreign woman, who is attracted by the savage beauty of the coastal village. In Levi, the "foreign lady" describes the villagers in a language that is heavily reminiscent of *Cristo si è fermato a Eboli*:

> Non mi sembrano uomini, donne, bambini di oggi, ma alberi di una foresta, o esseri antichi come gli Dèi. I loro sguardi, i loro gesti sono come quelli delle statue: i pescatori, giovani e vecchi, hanno il collo delle statue. Mi pare che qui tutto debba sempre esssere stato così e che sempre sarà così . . . La morte è sempre presente, con questo vulcano e col mare, ma è come se non ci fosse, perché il destino di quelli che rimarranno vivi sarà uguale a quello dei morti: avranno gli stessi gesti, lo stesso modo di accettare le cose, lo stesso modo di avvolgersi nello scialle e di camminare con la grazia degli animali o dei principi. Per questo, questo piccolo paese mi sembra eterno e bellissimo. (120)

> *I don't see them as men, women, children of today, but trees in a forest, or ancient beings like the Gods. Their looks, their gestures are like those of statues: the fisherman, young and old, have the necks of statues. It seems that here everything must have always been this way and that it will always be this way . . . Death is always present, with this volcano and this sea, but it is as if it weren't there, because the destiny of those that remain alive will be the same*

> as that of the dead: they will have the same gestures, the same way of accepting things, the same manner of wrapping themselves in their shawls and walking with the grace of animals or princes. That is why this small town seems eternal and beautiful to me. (82)

With these words, the foreigner recasts in the Sicilian context some images that Levi had used in representing the Lucanian peasants: the monumentality of their figures, their mythical sense of time, the coexistence of animal and human nature in each individual. In representing 1950s Aci Trezza in the same terms as Aliano in 1936, Levi implicitly laments the failure of postwar Italy to help Sicily join the rest of Italy. Despite the interest generated by Visconti's *La terra trema* with its progressive message, for example, the lives of local fishermen have not changed: "I temi del film erano ormai lontani, e i sogni e le strane speranze che ne erano nate; la vita aveva ripreso a scorrere come sempre" ["The days of the film were now far in the past, and with them the dreams and strange hopes that had sprung up; life had resumed its eternal flow"] (117, 80).

Levi's own perspective on the villagers of Aci Trezza is influenced by Visconti, whose vision he contrasts with Verga's. He describes *I Malavoglia* as a fundamentally nocturnal novel, in which the blackness of night envelops places and characters. Verga's standpoint is, according to Levi, an entirely internal one. The author identifies with the world of his characters so deeply that he does not feel the need to describe them or their surroundings and lets the atmosphere be dominated by a darkness that obfuscates the physical details of their existence. Visconti, on the contrary, "partecipa alle cose e le comprende senza immedesimarvisi, ed è perciò tutto occhi, visione e immagine" ["participated in things and understood them without immersing himself in them, and is therefore all eyes, vision and image"] (122, 83). Indeed, Visconti's film adaptation of *I Malavoglia* privileges visuality over dialogue, and it does so not only through the painterly aesthetics that is a constant feature of the director's style but also by using the local vernacular, incomprehensible to most of the audience. It is thus on the image that falls the burden of carrying the meaning and message of the film, and Levi sees Visconti's filmic image as the fundamental signifier of a modern epic that aims to bring the lives of the fishermen of Aci Trezza into the realm of history. However, Levi's companion comment on the immobility of time and mores in the village seems to suggest that Visconti's project has failed, very much in the same way that Isnello will not be changed by Impellitteri's visit: change cannot be imposed from above but must be generated from within local reality, or it will remain in the realm of myth. In contrast with Visconti's mythmaking cinema, Levi's trajectory in *Le parole sono pietre* moves from myth toward history: "With Francesca Serio, the contadini of Sicily develop full consciousness of their situation, and make the step from myth to history. Christ had moved south of Eboli" (Farrell 146).

Unlike other progressive thinkers of his time, who did not believe the peasant classes to be capable of autonomous activism, and faithful to Gobetti's notion of *autonomia*, Levi insists that the new historical consciousness of the South must not be severed from local tradition but, on the contrary, be rooted in it. In this respect, *Le parole sono pietre* is a book filled with ideas about the rebirth and rediscovery of civilization (Falaschi 15), a civilization that can accommodate in itself both a thrust toward the future and a reverence toward its past. For Levi, this coexistence of different temporal planes finds its synthesis in the notion of *contemporaneità dei tempi*, which he elaborates explicitly in *L'Orologio* and to which he returns especially in his Sardinian travel journals.

The *contemporaneità dei tempi* exists both literally and symbolically in *Tutto il miele è finito*. The book gathers Levi's notes and observations from two separate trips to Sardinia, taken at a distance of ten years, but the writer moves freely from one journey to the other in his recollections. For example, after the disappearance of his pet crow, Orune, Levi goes back in his memory to the time when he acquired the bird during his first visit to Sardinia. This mental movement in time corresponds immediately to a reconstruction of the physical itinerary that he followed to Orune, the small town, home to an ancient tradition of popular poetry, whose name he then gave the crow (38). That first visit overlaps, in Levi's reminiscence, with the account of the current visit, ten years later, and the two memories remain indistinct: Orune, he writes, "è dunque per me una immagine, una forma, un nome che unisce una realtà molteplice di animali e di pietre nell'immobile ondulare delle greggi del tempo" ["for me is an image, a shape, a name that unifies, in the wavy stillness of the sheep herds of time, the multifarious reality of animals and rocks"] (97).

This "wavy stillness" corresponds, in an interartistic dialogue within Levi's work, to the dynamic undulation of his brushstrokes in the paintings from the South, which help express the idea of the coexistence of different layers of time and human experience. This interartistic dialogue with painting, moreover, exists within the book itself, because in Levi's pages about Sardinia we find a strong presence of the visual. Whereas in *Le parole sono pietre* the dominant visual mode was that of human portraiture, which found exact correspondence in a series of actual portraits, in *Tutto il miele è finito* Levi privileges vast landscapes. In the opening pages of the book, the writer lingers on a depiction of the rocky countryside:

> Sulla terra, sparsa di rocce biancastre, si levano a perdita d'occhio i gigli selvaggi, e, diritti sui gambi leggeri, i fiori degli asfodeli. Sulle costiere lontane

dei monti, le greggi sembrano pietre, sotto il cielo mutevole, che insensibilmente si muovono, scivolando silenziose per i pendii solitari. Altre pecore meriggiano, in cerchio, sotto una quercia, bianchi anelli attorno al tronco scortecciato. Pietre, rocce, pecore, asfodeli, hanno lo stesso colore, lo stesso biancastro leggero, appena un po' viola e un po' grigio: il colore dei soli trapassati da secoli, delle ossa antiche calcinate sotto il sole ...

Nessun altro segno di vita, né voce di uomini, né geometria di case, né fumo di focolari, appare, da qualunque parte l'occhio si volga, nella larghissima distesa dei monti verdi e azzurri, fino a quelli ultimi, laggiù, quasi trasparenti per la distanza. Su una piccola altura, alla mia sinistra, sorge una torre di pietra. È un nuraghe. (13)

On the land, dotted with whitish rocks, appear, as far as the eye can see, wild lilies and, straight on their light stems, the asphodels. On the distant mountainsides, the herds look like rocks that move imperceptibly, silently gliding along the deserted inclines, under an ever-changing sky. Other sheep rest in a circle under an oak tree, like white rings around the stripped trunk. Stones, rocks, sheep, asphodels, all have the same color, the same light white, with just a little violet and grey: the color of the suns that have been gone for centuries, or the ancient bones calcified under the sun.

No other sign of life appears wherever the eye can reach over the wide expanse of green and blue mountains, up to the last ones, over there, almost transparent in the distance: no human voice, no geometry of human abode, no smoke from a hearth. On a small boulder, on the left, a stone tower stands. It is a nuraghe.

In this long description of the landscape, Levi adopts a lyrical tone, with poetic accents that testify to the influence of his rich literary culture on his writing. Particularly evident, in the alliteration of the *r*, but also of the *s* and *t*, is the presence of the Dantean *rime petrose* as an appropriate model for a prose that—as Levi repeatedly claims[24]—wants to adhere to the reality it represents. The passage emphasizes color, from the whiteness of the rocks that punctuate the mountainous terrain—a whiteness that sheep and flowers also display, with a suggestion of violet and grey in it—to the green of the hills, which becomes almost blue as it slopes toward the horizon and the mountains become indistinguishable from the sky in the distance. In this rocky scenery, even a *nuraghe*, the stony building typical of Sardinia, does not interrupt the natural landscape but seems to be an integral component of it, as a sign of the prehistoric indistinction between man and nature. In another passage, the *nuraghe* is explicitly cast as a space apart, a sort of maternal womb, where Levi reestablishes a connection with the memories that precede his childhood (25). In this sense, the *nuraghe* is the symbol of the experience of the *compresenza dei tempi*, a marker of the presence of times past in the experience of contemporaneity.

For Levi the collapsing of temporal boundaries is not only circumstantial (due to the confusion of memorial planes) but also appropriate to the nature of Sardinian culture: "Qui, nella contemporaneità, dove secoli senza misura sono passati, e dieci anni, anche ricchi di mutamenti e di uomini nuovi e veri, non sono che un istante . . . si sono mescolate le carte, le immagini doppie di viaggi diversi sulle stesse strade ripercorse. Qui, nell'isola dei sardi, ogni andare è un ritornare. Nella presenza dell'arcaico ogni conoscenza è riconoscenza" ["Here, in contemporaneity, where infinite centuries have passed, and ten years, even when full of changes and new and true men, are but an instant, . . . all the cards have been shuffled, double images of different journeys taken on the same roads. Here, in the island of the Sardinians, every going is a coming back. In the presence of the archaic every knowledge is recognition"] (11). The island is the quintessential locus of *contemporaneità*, a unique temporal dimension in which present and past exist at the same time. Levi returns to this concept in another description of the landscape of Gallura, which resembles, he writes,

> un enorme geroglifico che racconta una storia finita di vivere: un luogo di forme parlanti un linguaggio non più inteso, simili a greggi, animali, giganti. Non sono le pietre su cui è passata la mano della storia, le *perdas fittas*, fissate, collocate, in qualche modo, dalla ragione o dalla religione. Sono simboli e parole della natura: intoccate, silenziose parabole, dove la pietra contiene ogni aspetto di una esistenza indifferenziata: ognuna come una persona che vada cercando la propria espressione per uscire fuori dalla caotica identità, e sia rimasta pietrificata nel corso di questo sforzo, contenendo in sé mescolate tutte le immagini possibili. Questo cimitero smisurato di parole non dette, di immobili possibilità, si stende tra pascoli radi, una vegetazione cupa e fitta di lecci, di querce di macchia compatta, coni di monti, creste e alture isolate su cui salgono le greggi di pietra. In questa terra si direbbe che gli uomini non fossero vissuti mai: unici abitatori possibili i radi pastori solitari, che passano e non lasciano tracce. (116)

> *an enormous hieroglyph that tells a story that has ended: a place with forms that speak a language that is no longer understood, similar to herds, to animals, to giants. These are not stones on which the hand of history has passed, the* perdas fittas *that reason or religion have fixed and placed. These are symbols and words of nature. They are untouched, silent parables in which each stone contains every aspect of an undifferentiated existence. Each stone as though it were a person who, while seeking her own form of expression to emerge from the chaos of identity, remained petrified in the process, and kept, confused within herself, all possible images. This immense cemetery of unsaid words, of motionless possibilities, extends itself among thin pastures, a thick and dark scrub of oaks, mountain tops, ridges and isolated mounds which the rocky herds climb.*

> It seems like men never inhabited this land; the only possible inhabitants are the scarce solitary shepherds, who pass by and leave no trace.

In this landscape, he continues,

> [t]utto era stato occhi, continua visione degli aspetti di uno spazio di intatta natura, forme di un tempo perduto, non viste da altri sguardi che quelli attoniti del pastore, o delle molteplici rosse guardate dei greggi; di un vocabolario di granito che conosce soltanto le parole del vento e del sole, che lentissimi lo mutano nel corso delle epoche, e che è lí, gremito di immagini immobili e silenziose, da un passato così lontano che l'immaginazione vi si smarrisce. (118)

> [e]verything was eyes, constant vision of the elements of a space of unspoiled nature, forms of a lost time, which only the surprised gaze of the shepherd, of the red looks of the sheep herds; a space of a granite vocabulary that only knows the words of wind and sun, which modify it, slowly, during the course of the epochs and that remains, filled with motionless and silent images, with a past that is so far that the imagination loses itself in it.

In both these passages, Levi returns to the identity of words and stones that gives its title to the Sicilian travel journals. But here the scattered rocks are words that have not been said yet—words that are waiting for people to pronounce them and exist in the realm of possibility rather than reality. Levi's book aims precisely to turn the immobility of these stones into words that have poetic, constructive power.

It is clear, then, that the notion of the coexistence of different temporal planes for Levi does not imply a fossilization into the past. On the contrary, he repeatedly speaks of "new men" and of change taking place in Sardinia. The constant presence of antiquity does not mean that Sardinians cannot escape it: on the contrary, his fascination with the island is connected precisely with its people's ability to take an active role in history. Despite its geographical isolation, "una civiltà di pastori si trasforma in parte in una civiltà contadina, tra lotte interne e ambivalenze drammatiche, e già la società contadina si dissolve pel mondo, e sorgono centri operai, come querce solitarie, e se ne sente il peso e l'influsso sul costume" ["a civilization of shepherds transforms itself in part into a peasant civilization, between internal struggles and dramatic ambivalences, and already peasant society dissolves itself into the world, and workers' centers emerge, like solitary oaks, and their influence and weight shape customs"] (14). Again, as in *Le parole sono pietre*, Levi's concern has to do with political and social agency.

Levi encounters the most progressive experiences in Carbonia, the city that Mussolini built from nothing in order to house workers from the nearby coal mines. Carbonia is a "viril inferno" (33), where a modern proletariat with a strong class consciousness has nonetheless emerged. It is a hybrid working class, disparate in geographical origins, both rural and industrial, but equally defined by a desire for freedom and self-affirmation *in the present*, in contrast with the feudal immobility of characters like the landowner, *signora* Efisia (24). In Carbonia, miners confront the unique problems that define industrial modernity and that have to do with technology, adaptability, and social strife. It is in facing these issues together that the very diverse mass of workers, coming from all over the country, have created "una città, un popolo, un proletariato, . . . che ha già come valore comune una propria tradizione recente, e la tenacia e la speranza" ["a city, a people, a proletariat that already has, as a common value, its own recent tradition, and its own tenacity and hope"] (33). This tradition, Levi points out, has moved beyond the mythical dimension of *nuraghi* and shepherds—it is a culture rooted in the present and directed toward the future.

The coal miners and industrial workers are not the only Sardinians that have moved into the realm of history. The rural classes have also begun to claim a historical position for themselves. These people "hanno percorso in pochi anni il cammino dei secoli: pastori e operai che risolvono in sé, per propria forza, il contrasto di civiltà opposte come venti di un ciclone" ["in a few years have completed a centuries-long journey: shepherds and laborers that resolve within themselves, with their own strength, the contrast between civilizations that are opposed like the winds within a cyclone"] (76). For Levi, the powerful novelty of the peasant movement of Sardinia lies exactly in its ability to reconcile the differences between the two Italies that he described in "Il contadino e l'orologio:" one whose capital city is Turin and is fully engaged in the forward-looking processes of modernity and one whose ideal capital is Matera and is attached to an agrarian culture and economy and rooted in its ancient past (19).[25] In his journey to Sardinia, Levi recognizes the same attachment to the archaic element of human experience that he had seen in Lucania twenty years earlier:

> Ma nelle terre dove oggi andiamo, questi elementi arcaici non sono soltanto una componente necessaria della persona, che affiora talvolta da un remoto passato, ma il senso stesso dominante della vita di ogni giorno, la qualità di una struttura sociale che permane pressoché immutata dal profondo dei secoli, che nasce dalla persistenza di un mondo pastorale, in luoghi mai domati da nessuno degli stranieri conquistatori che venivano di là del mare, nel corso uguale dei tempi, punici, romani, pisani, spagnoli, piemontesi;

in popoli mai realmente compresi dallo Stato e nello Stato moderno, ma sempre più chiusi in esso, circondati, segregati, con il loro codice di vita, di giustizia e di vendetta, col loro inviolabile mestiere di pastori, la comunanza e quasi l'identificazione con gli animali e le pietre; la coscienza, nel modo di vita, nella famiglia, nella morale, nel costume, di una comunità originaria: come un tesoro nascosto, una miniera segreta nelle montagne, apparentemente intatta. (*Tutto il miele è finito* 75–76)

But in the land where we are going today, these archaic elements are not only a necessary element of a person, which sometimes emerges from a remote past, but they determine the meaning of everyday life, the quality of a social structure that has remained basically unchanged for centuries and that derives from the persistence of a pastoral world in places that were never mastered by the foreign conquerors from across the sea, in the identical course of the ages: the Punics, the Romans, the Pisans, the Spaniards, the Piedmontese. [These elements persist] in populations that were never really understood by and included in the modern State but were increasingly closed within it, surrounded, segregated, with their social codes of justice and revenge, with their unassailable work as shepherds, their community and almost identification with animals and stones, their awareness, in their way of life, families, morals, customs, of an original community like a hidden treasure, a secret mine in the mountains, apparently untouched.

Although speaking primarily of Sardinians, in this long passage from *Tutto il miele è finito* Levi refers to all peoples that have been treated like colonial conquests in their history of subalternity, and his language is evocative of his earlier representations of Lucanian *contadini*. In Sardinia—like in Lucania—local civilization has preserved its connection with the *indistinto originario*, its sense of communion with all beings, whether living or inorganic ("animali" and "pietre"). For Levi, this bond must be treasured, for it represents an alternative to the fragmentation and massification of modernity but is not tantamount to a refusal of or self-exclusion from history. In *Cristo si è fermato a Eboli*, the peasants remained alien to the historical forces that could generate effective change, because, as Levi puts it in *L'Orologio*, they could not understand their language. In *Tutto il miele è finito*, as well as in *Le parole sono pietre*, a radical shift has occurred, for the southern working classes have appropriated the language of politics and given substance to its vocabulary of abstract ideas, as we have seen in Francesca Serio's weighty indictment of her son's murderers. This has not meant, for Levi, a rejection of local culture. As he shows especially in the Sardinian travel journals, in the consciousness of the rural classes the mythical dimension of their ancient civilization and the creative vision of a better future coexist in a productive synthesis.

After Lucania, Levi fully realizes the difficulty of maintaining a balance between the respect for past cultural tradition and a desire for a progressive future. He thus describes Sardinia as a tragic land, playing out the "tragedia dei tempi diversi, fatta di chiusura orgogliosa, di incomprensione, di violenza e di speranza, nel difficile coesistere di due ritmi opposti: quello ondulante del gregge e della luna, e quello matematico dell'orologio" ["tragedy of different times, a tragedy comprised of proud close-mindedness, of violence and hope, in the difficult coexistence of two opposite rhythms: the wavy rhythm of the sheep herd and the moon and the mathematical rhythm of the clock"] (120). In Lucania, he wrote in *Cristo si è fermato a Eboli*, he had lost touch with the forward-looking, historical time of his native Turin and experienced the circularity of mythical time. He expressed this notion through the metaphor of the broken watch—to which he returned, naturally, in the novel *L'Orologio*—"Il mio orologio si era fermato, e nessun rintocco di fuori poteva giungermi e indicarmi il passare del tempo, dove il tempo non scorre. Così finì in un momento indeterminato, l'anno 1935 . . . e cominciò il 1936, identico al precedente e a tutti quelli che sono venuti prima e che verranno poi" ["My clock had stopped and no bells rang in the new year in the land where time did not pass. Thus, at an indeterminate moment, ended the truly tiresome year of 1935, and 1936, its successor, started to repeat the familiar, impersonal indifferent cycle of things past and things to come"] (*Cristo 182, 207*). In *Cristo si è fermato a Eboli*, the two temporal dimensions remain mutually exclusive, and *civiltà contadina* and northern industrial Italy do not relate to each other. As he explains in reacting to his sister's anxious desire to *do* something about the poverty and abandonment she has witnessed in Matera, "capivo ad un tratto come questi due tempi fossero, fra loro, incomunicabili, come queste due civiltà non potessero avere nessun rapporto se non miracoloso" ["(a)ll at once I understood how it was that these two periods were hermetically shut off from one another, that these two civilizations could have no communication except by a miracle"] (*Cristo 72, 81–82*). In "Il contadino e l'orologio," Levi reinterprets the concept of *civiltà contadina* in psychological terms. The South inhabits our beings, "è un elemento della nostra stessa vita, un elemento fondamentale non eliminabile, costituito fin dal principio, un elemento senza il quale non esisteremmo" ["is an element of our own life, a fundamental and indispensable element, constituted from the very beginning and without which we could not exist"] (18). He thus overcomes the earlier opposition between historical and prehistorical thinking by proposing coexistence as a solution that moves beyond dialectical synthesis: "Io uso dire, in modo paradossale, che l'Italia ha due capitali e che una è Torino e l'altra è Matera. Queste due capitali così opposte e lontane, l'una tutta ragione e storia, e l'altra fuori della ragione e della storia, sono necessarie l'una all'altra e si possono intendere benissimo fra di loro" ["I usually say, paradoxically, that Italy has two capitals: one is Turin and the other one is Matera. These two capitals, so opposed and distant, one entirely reason and history, and the other outside of reason and history, are necessary the one to the other and can understand each other very well"] (19). The tension between these two civilizations can have tragic results, for the mutual suspicion with which the two cultures can consider each other generates the fear that, as Levi writes in *Paura della libertà*, is the matrix of totalitarianism. The exceptionality of the workers' movement in Sardinia coincides, then, with its ability to conquer fear and resolve the contrast between myth and history, respecting the multiplicity and complexity of reality:

> Come la realtà è molteplice; come, in ogni cosa, in ciascuno di noi, coesistono tempi diversi e lontanissimi! E quanto più viva, reale e complessa è una persona, quando in lei questa contemporaneità di condizioni e di situazioni diverse, come strati geologici, questa eternità della storia e della preistoria, è presente: e quando gli elementi arcaici non sono relegati o totalmente nascosti in un oscuro subcosciente dove possono parere dimenticati e del tutto inoperanti, ma affiorano alla superficie, e diventano contenuti di poesia, energia vitale, capacità di comprensione universale . . . ! (*Tutto il miele è finito* 75)

> *So manifold is reality! How, in every thing, in each of us, different and distant epochs coexist! And how much more alive, real, and complex a person is, when in her is present this coexistence of different conditions and situations, this eternity of history and prehistory, like geographical strata. And when the archaic elements are not relegated or completely hidden in a dark subconscious where they appear forgotten or completely inoperative, but, on the contrary, they emerge to the surface and become poetic content, vital energy, a capacity for universal understanding . . . !*

Levi here expresses his sense of wonder and respect for the Sardinians' grassroots effort to embrace history and take an active role in it.[26] Without their investment, the agrarian reform, the *Piano di rinascita* sponsored by the government would be doomed to fail as yet another paternalistic imposition coming from a foreign state (120). If, on the contrary, it is supported and sustained at the local level by the people, this plan could generate a radical reorganization of Sardinian society. The emphasis must remain on local and autonomous forms of ingenuity: "Si tenta, in modo autonomo, da tutte le forze vive e popolari della Sardegna, di cercare il fondo dei problemi, di interessare tutti a questa ricerca" ["All the popular and living powers of Sardinia are trying to get to the bottom of problems in independent ways, to encourage everybody's interest in this search"] (63).

Levi's interest in the experiences of the reform movements in southern Italy continues beyond the 1950s and finds its synthetic visual expression in a 1961 canvas he painted on the occasion of the celebrations for the centenary of Italian unity. Mario Soldati, who designed the *Mostra delle Regioni* at the great Turin Expo, asked Levi to participate as a representative for Lucania. Levi produced a large painting, *Lucania '61*, which measured 10.5 by 60.7 feet and offered a comprehensive review of themes and characters that he had been exploring in words and images for the previous 25 years (Figure 12).

The painting, constituted of five panels, is a "pictorial poem" constructed around the epic figure of Rocco Scotellaro. Its narrative moves chronologically from right to left, beginning with young Scotellaro addressing the people of Tricarico in the town square. The fathers of *meridionalismo* and other important figures in the political history of Lucania, from Giustino Fortunato to Vincenzo Nitti, Giuseppe Zanardelli, and Guido Dorso, witness the scene from a short distance but without entering the intent crowd of listeners. This detachment was, for Levi, the real issue in early political and social views of the South, as they remained at the level of abstraction and did not concretely touch the lives of the people. On the opposite side of the painting, the viewer sees a reproduction of Levi's earlier *Lamento per Rocco Scotellaro*, with the addition of Carlo Levi's own mother, but also of Danilo Dolci, Manlio Rossi Doria, Carlo Muscetta, Michele Parrella, Rocco Mazzarone, and even Umberto Saba (Russo 15). These intellectuals, writers, and activists are compositionally and ideologically opposed to the group of Fortunato and the others, for they are *contadini* in the broadest sense that Levi attributes to the word—they are capable of an affective relationship with all aspects of human experience. This is the reason that people with such disparate backgrounds and histories are gathered together to mourn Scotellaro—in his poetry and social action they see a reflection of their own creative impetus and its potential for productive change. At the center of the canvas are scenes of ordinary life in Lucania: villagers completing their daily tasks, peasants traveling to the fields, mothers carrying their children.[27] Each of these scenes is molded on a picture taken by photographer Mario Carbone during a 1960 trip through Lucania.

As Carbone explained in an interview, it was Levi himself who, in preparation for the centennial exhibition, wanted to collect visual material for his projected painting. Knowing Carbone's work as a documentarist, Levi had invited him to join him on his preparatory journey to Lucania.[28] Thus many of the images in *Lucania '61* are recognizable as reproductions of Carbone's photographs: the mother and child, for example, correspond to the picture in Figure 13. The woman traveling through the countryside on a donkey reproduces Carbone's photo in Figure 14.

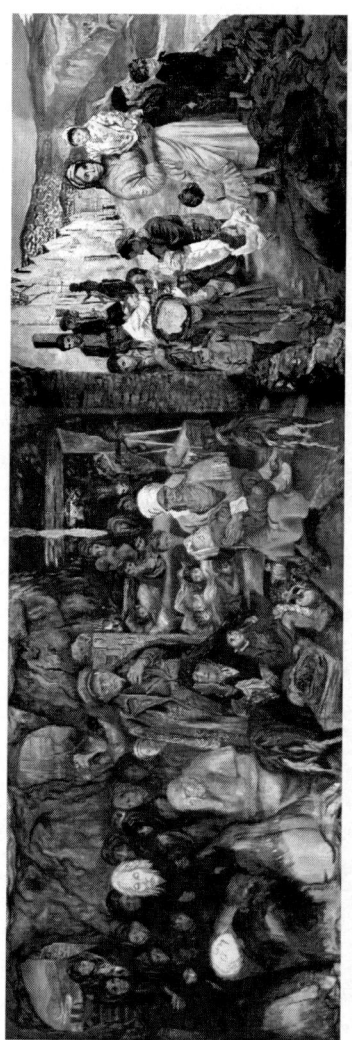 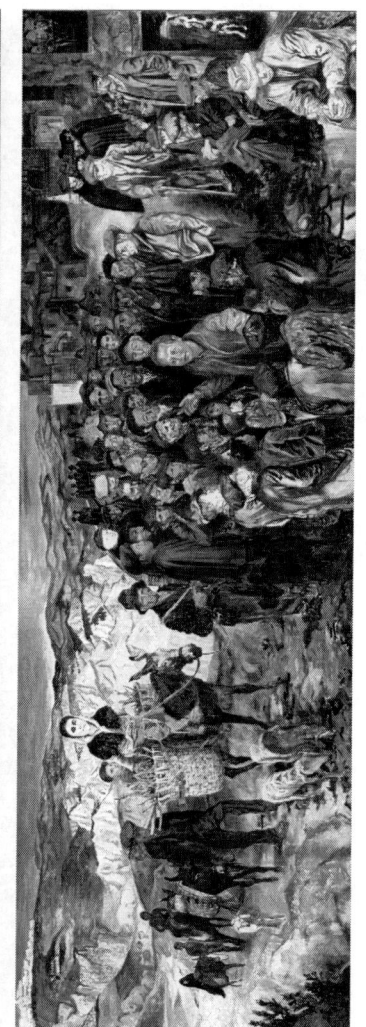

Figure 12. Carlo Levi, *Lucania '61* (1961)

© 2012 Artists Rights Society (ARS), New York / SIAE, Rome; Photo Soprintendenza per i Beni Storici Artistici ed Etnoantropologici della Basilicata—Matera

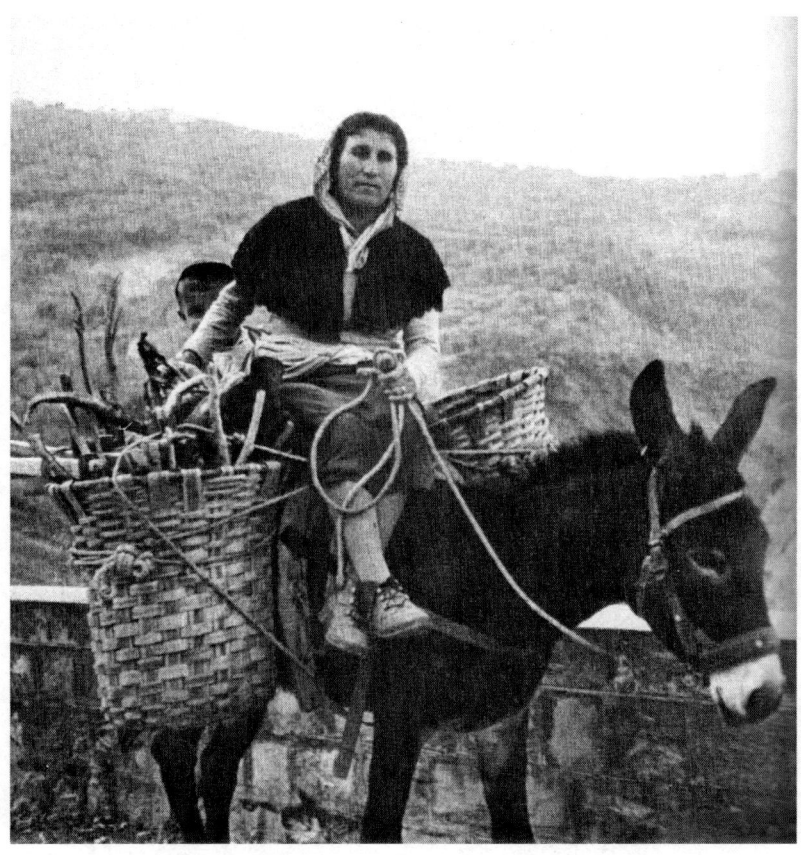

Figure 13. Mario Carbone, Lucanian woman on a donkey (1961)
Courtesy of Archivio Mario Carbone, Rignano Flaminio (Rome).

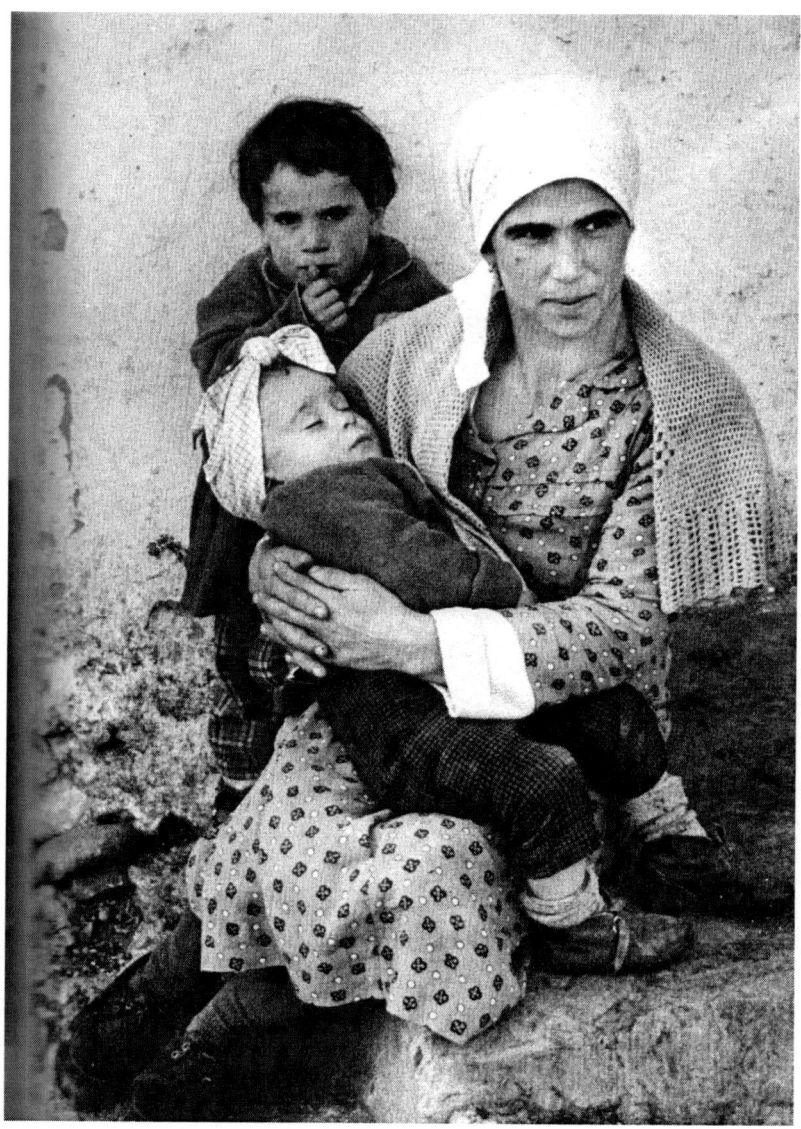

Figure 14. Mario Carbone, Lucanian woman with two children (1961)
Courtesy of Archivio Mario Carbone, Rignano Flaminio (Rome).

Levi's understanding of photography was not, however, just an instrumental one. As he wrote in a brief essay, "Consiglio a un fotografo," photography's relationship with painting is not simply a source of material; it can furnish inspiration, by proposing a formal reelaboration of visual data (71). Just as he criticizes the emptiness of naturalism in literature or painting, he views as a mistake the approach of those photographers who believe in the possibility of catching the truth of reality through candid shots. These mediocre practitioners do not understand that, in posing for a picture, its subjects express the way that they understand themselves and their own position in the world, thus communicating a deeper truth than the one the photographer can catch in a moment of unawareness (73–74). Indeed, among Carbone's pictures there are only a few in which the characters are not conscious of being photographed; in most of them, they look directly into the camera eye. Thus Carbone's photos can be considered portraits, in that they emerge from a free and voluntary relationship between artist and subject, as Levi would put it.

Another visual source of *Lucania '61* is, of course, Levi's own work on Lucania. In addition to the *Lamento per Rocco Scotellaro*, he reelaborates the painting *Grassano come Gerusalemme*, which dated back to his exile, in which Grassano appears to dominate, from the height of a faraway hill, the horizon (Figure 1). Grassano is at the center of the great *Lucania '61* painting, suggesting the centrality of Levi's exile in his overall vision of the South. That first encounter with the human and geographic landscape of Lucania determined Levi's subsequent destiny as a painter, a writer, and a political thinker and activist. It is only right, then, that his last great representation of the South in visual terms should move from an image of Grassano, as a symbol of the mythic immobility of time in the Lucania of the 1930s, to the progressive engagement with social and political issues that Scotellaro incarnated.[29] Lucania in 1961, Levi seems to suggest with the purposefulness of his brushstrokes and the strength of his lines, is no longer fixed in the indeterminateness of prehistoric times. Thanks to the work of people like Scotellaro, who have found creative and autonomous forms of political and social action, Lucania has claimed its own place in the flow of history. But Lucania is for Levi a symbol of the entire South— the painting thus represents a visual synthesis of the movement he has witnessed in Sardinia and Sicily and evoked in the vivid prose of *Tutto il miele è finito* and *Le parole sono pietre*.

4

Quaderno a cancelli

The Space of Memory

Quando la dura sentenza del medico mi rovesciò nel buio . . . dalla prima ansia confusa risorse il bisogno di esprimere, di significare.

When the doctor's harsh decree plunged me into darkness . . . from my first confused anxiety arose once more the need to express, to signify.

—Gabriele D'Annunzio, Notturno

In 1973, during a period of temporary blindness caused by the detachment of his retina, Levi found comfort in listening to his nurse read *Notturno*, the diary Gabriele D'Annunzio kept while similarly confined to darkness by a war wound (*Quaderno* 15). D'Annunzio's blindness had not weakened the urgency of his "need to signify." Forbidden to speak or write, he ingeniously eluded his doctor's strict orders by writing, in total obscurity, single lines of text on narrow strips of paper attached to a wooden tablet. *Notturno* collects these fragmentary thoughts in a visionary text in which the *vate* gives free expression to "a forge of dreams" that, he writes, "[his] will could neither direct nor interrupt. The optic nerve drew on all the strata of [his] culture and [his] previous life, projecting on [his] vision innumerable figures with a rapidity of transition far beyond the more daring lyricism" (qtd. in Rosenthal 6). The same lyric excess defines Carlo Levi's *Quaderno a cancelli* ("Notebook with Bars"), the posthumous volume collecting the dreams and mental figures that came to substitute the external images of the world during his own blindness. Perhaps inspired by D'Annunzio, Levi devised a special mechanism—which he named *quaderno a cancelli*—that would allow him to continue writing. The device consisted of a double wooden frame, closed at the bottom, into which he could slip a sheet of paper. Fine metal wires ran from side to side across the top frame, creating straight lines that he could follow with his pen while writing.[1] His sense of sight was thus replaced by the tactile potential of his hands. With the help of this system, Levi was able to record his inner life during his illness, seemingly abandoning the realist impulse that characterized his previous writing in favor of a quasi-surrealist exploration of his own unconscious being.

This shift away from traditional forms of realism occurs also in Levi's art from the period, which, as we shall see, appears to be entirely new in terms of both style and subjects. Overcoming the physical limitations imposed on him by his illness, with the help of a devoted disciple, Gian Paolo Berto, Levi was able to draw and eventually to paint in total darkness. But as the words he writes in *Quaderno a cancelli* seem to belong to the innermost dimension of his psyche, so the images and themes of his drawings emerge from the landscape of his soul. Some of his pictures seem to be situated on the verge of abstraction, while others explore, almost obsessively, *Quaderno a cancelli*'s recurring textual images of the owl, the lovers, Narcissus, or the Burmese warrior. In this sense I propose—against those critics who argue that it should have never been published—that the book's value emerges from the constant dialogue between the imagistic and verbal dimensions of Levi's art, aimed at exploring the author's own self, now excluded from seeing the world. Levi's journal of illness must be understood in the context of this ongoing interartistic dialogue, which is conducted within a memorial dimension that not only involves his contemporary work but also invites a reconsideration of his entire pictorial production. As *Quaderno a cancelli*'s intertexts include virtually all Levi's books, from *Cristo si è fermato a Eboli* to his later travel reportages, so I suggest that the images that appear in his drawings and paintings from the period virtually represent a *summa* of the most significant symbols explored in the course of his lifelong artistic quest.

In a 1935 letter from the Roman prison of Regina Coeli, Levi wrote to his family that he was planning to write a book on modern painting, conceived as a pictorial autobiography, based on personal memory, and enriched by images and poetry (*È questo il carcer tetro?* 125). Levi's project eventually became "Paura della pittura," but the unsystematic quality of the projected volume, as well as its hybrid literary genre and its reliance upon the visuality of drawing, seems in many ways prophetic of *Quaderno a cancelli*. Indeed, in this "dramatic and excruciating conversation with himself, his subconscious, his memory" (De Donato and D'Amaro, *Un torinese del sud* 327), Levi recuperates the great themes that he began to explore in his paintings from the 1930s and subsequently theorized in his *poema filosofico*, *Paura della libertà*, before developing them in narrative form in the epic pages of *Cristo si è fermato a Eboli* and in the novel *L'Orologio* (*Cristo* xix). In *Quaderno a cancelli* all these forms of representation find coherence and are unified within the mythical dimension of memory, which closes the circle of Levi's lifelong artistic and philosophical search. In the brief personal testimony that serves as the introduction to *Quaderno a cancelli*, Linuccia Saba—Levi's companion until his death and the editor of the book for its first Einaudi edition of 1979—describes the work as an intimate confession generated in the writer by "quello stretto rapporto con se stesso quando scriveva ricordando e dipingeva guardando dentro e non fuori di sé" ["the close relationship he established with himself when he wrote while remembering and painted while looking inside, not outside, himself"] (x).[2] Its pages grew out of a constant flow of memories, images, inventions, and intuitions that existed in his imagination (ix), just as his daily drawings showed "dapprima in bianco e nero, presto a colori, delle cose bellissime, misteriose e leggibili" ["some magnificent, mysterious, and readable things, initially in black and white, and soon in color,"] which belonged to the mental universe of his memory and dreams (x). For Levi, this exclusively interior landscape does not constitute a restriction to his field of vision, but as he writes in the first of the poems that are interspersed with the prose of *Quaderno a cancelli*, "il Quaderno a cancelli / vede fuori dalla prigione" ["the Notebook with bars / can see outside of its prison"] (8). Through the verbal and visual exploration of his inner experience made possible by the *quaderno*, in other words, Levi overcomes the limitations of his situation and secures for himself a privileged perspective on the human condition. His blindness coincides, then, with a view of the world from the inside; it is a form of vision "liberatoria creativa dissacrante demitizzante vitale agente operante e ottica informale" ["liberating, creative, desecrating, demystifying, vital, operating agent and informal optics"] (8–9).

Such a vision generates an equally innovative and defamiliarizing prose, in which the boundaries between dreams and factual reality are constantly confused, distant and close memories overlap and coincide, and words seem to acquire, at times, an existence of their own, independent of their signified. The opening passage of *Quaderno a cancelli* offers an illuminating example of Levi's nonreferential use of language:

> Qui si può scrivere un libro, un libro intero, anche lunghissimo e sterminato: altrettanto lungo e sterminato forse il cerchio del tempo e lo spazio dell'impedimento. Si può anche girarvi attorno, anche con ozio, o per puro divertimento, anche per parentesi e follie, o assonanze o rime o somiglianze o ricordi o estri o capovolgimenti o capriole o ruzzoloni o salti mortali o giri di fianco o numeri di destrezza o veroniche o federiche o gertrudi o tori picassiani e altri più flacos come dovrebbero essere i tori di un eroe cervantesco le cui corna non fossero in verità che temibili attaccapanni a cui appendere idee così vetuste da parere ed essere nuove, e i suoi garretti dusseldorfiani cotti in pentole sigillate servissero da porzioni per tre,

per otto o dodici RR. fra ricordi napoleonici eroici all'andata e antieroici al ritorno o viceversa. (3)

> *Here one could write a book, a whole book, lengthy and immense: as long and immense as the circle of time and the space of one's limitation. One might also circle around it, lazily, or just for fun, or even with parentheses and follies, assonances or rhymes or similarities or memories or whims or turnovers or somersaults or tumbles or flips or juggling routines or veronicas or gertrudes or Picassian bulls and others, more flacos, the way bulls should be for a Cervantean hero, a bull whose horns are really just lethal coat racks to hang ideas that are so antiquated that they appear and are new, and its Dusseldorf gambrels, cooked in sealed pots, could serve portions for three, eight, or twelve RR, between heroic Napoleonic memories on the way in, and antiheroic ones on the way back and vice versa.*

Here Levi projects his potential book as a linguistic *divertissement*, a proliferation *ad infinitum* of words, based on "assonances or rhymes or similarities," with no attachment to the concreteness of the visual reality, from which he is radically excluded by blindness. At the same time, the writer's segregation from normal spatio-temporal coordinates opens his experience up to an infinite time and space, where there is no before or after and opposites coincide, dominated by the oneiric and mnemonic dimensions. Levi calls this special site "il luogo della futilità," "the place of futility," introducing, thus, one of the most important philosophical categories of the book.

Characteristically, the definition of *futilità* remains elusive in *Quaderno a cancelli*, where Levi uses the term with a multiplicity of meanings and connotations.[3] *Futilità* is the place where "le cose senza avvenire avvengono," "le cose che non hanno alcuna storia, o meglio alcuna forma" ["things without a future happen," "things that have no history, or, better, have no shape"] (11). It also coincides with *probabilità* (probability), which in turn is contrasted with *realtà* (reality) as that which is already realized as being (110). Within this dimension there is no dialectic tension, no strength or weakness, no wisdom or foolishness, no temperance or intemperance, no justice or injustice; in it each entity confronts and paradoxically coexists with its reverse (31). In its inclusiveness *futilità* is opposed to the idea of possession and property, hence to God, history, culture, war, and peace, as is powerfully encapsulated in one of Levi's poems: "ma la Futilità / non è utile né inutile / non appartiene e non possiede" ["But futility / Is neither useful nor useless / It neither belongs nor owns"] (25). *Futilità* does not admit the possibility of a God, Levi further explains—recuperating the terms of his antitheological philosophy of *Paura della libertà*—because gods require the establishment of a relationship of authority and symbolic possession over mankind (18); it does not pertain to history and culture, he continues, for it is extraneous to the ideas of property and appropriation: "La Storia, essendo tutta Storia di proprietà, di appropriamenti, di appropriazioni, sta completamente fuori dalla Futilità. E così quella che si usa chiamare cultura: e che è un far proprio, impadronirsi di una nozione o di un metodo mentale, un possedere, un baalizzare certe idee, e quindi cercare di imporle agli altri come le sole vere" ["History, since it is all about property and appropriation, is completely outside Futility. And so is that which we normally call culture, which coincides with appropriating a notion or a mental method, possessing, baalizing certain ideas and then imposing them on others as the only truth"] (21).[4]

To the Western notion of culture, Levi opposes the civilization of the Ronga people of Mozambique, whose language he proposes as an example of *futilità*, because it lacks possessive adjectives and pronouns: "Nella lingua Ronga / non puoi dire mio" ["In the Ronga language / You may not say mine"] (22). The language of the Ronga people resists influence, magic power, the idea of possession, and the appropriation of things and people, thus preserving the space of futility (21). While the notion of ownership and possession underlies the culture of Portuguese imperialism, in Ronga society "si rispettano le cose con le parole" ["with words they respect things"] (22), and humanity's innocence is shielded from the "original sins" that enslave humanity to both religion and colonialism. The Ronga civilization is in this respect tantamount to the peasant culture of Lucania, which returns in *Quaderno a cancelli* as the space beyond Eboli that Christ could not "baalize"—that is, civilize or possess (71). Lucania is not merely a geographical space but also an inner dimension that preserves the innocence of life before the Fall, of that childhood state in which man was akin to all other beings (73).[5]

Repeatedly, Levi's discussion of *futilità* foregrounds his persistent preoccupation with language. In *Quaderno a cancelli*, as in his earlier works, Levi manifests a deep ambivalence toward the word, which can be either an instrument of violence, of authoritarian possession over the world—as shown in the contrast between the Ronga idiom and the language of the Portuguese colonizers—or a powerful means to discover the infinite multiplicity of reality: "Se le spolveri, [le parole] splendono come diamanti sfaccettati, che mandano e rimandano e richiamano e riflettono all'infinito la luce, sì da avere, ciascuna, tutti i sensi possibili, sì da essere ciascuna, in qualche modo, onnidicente. O almeno, così connessa, con infiniti fili, a ogni altra, da contenere in sé, come un segno magico, tutto il pensiero possibile e tutto il potere di tutto il pensiero" ["If you dust them, (words) sparkle like multifaceted diamonds, which reflect again and again and recall and refract light infinitely, so that each word has every possible sense, so that each word is, in some way, all-saying. Or at least, connected to every other word by infinite threads, it contains within itself, like a magical sign, all possible thoughts and all the powers of every thought"] (70). When language is freed from the opaque patina of usage, then, it uncovers the original interconnectedness of all things and becomes poetry, *poesia*: "La parola, la poesia, non è che scoperta: togliere quello che copre, e quindi inventare, trovare quello che era coperto, vederlo per la prima volta, nominarlo, crearne un modo nuovo di realtà" ["The word, poetry, is simply a discovery: unveiling that which covers and thus inventing, discovering what was covered, seeing it for the first time, giving it a name, creating a new manner of reality for it"] (71).[6] Poetry shapes a privileged space in which separate things and experiences can be contemplated together in the fundamental unity that, according to Levi, is the authentic nature of things (71). This poetic dimension, embodied concretely in the marginal civilizations of Lucania's peasants and the Rongas of Mozambique, is for Levi a form of resistance to the hegemonic cultural and social categories: "[I]l mondo subalterno si difende tuttavia nella sua stessa subalternità, che lo rende invisibile, incastrandosi dentro forme di vita residue da tempi in cui erano modi reali di vita" ["The subaltern world defends itself through its own subalternity, which makes it invisible, and wedges itself into residual forms of life, from the times when they were real"] (72).

The notion of invisibility as an instrument of cultural resistance connects Levi's meditations on language and social order directly to his experience of blindness. For Levi, blindness defines a space of invisibility, as is true for the child who pretends to disappear by closing his eyes (83). Made invisible by the mantle of blind darkness, we are able to penetrate beyond the hedge or wall that separates our consciousness from the rest of reality—thus restoring our primitive unity with the cosmos (45).[7] Outside of the spatio-temporal constraints of physical reality, darkness becomes a space in which everything is contained simultaneously and revealed to the eyes of the blind: "Si possono vedere tutte le cose / nel buio rivelatore" ["We can see all things / in the revealing darkness"] (146). For Levi, then, blindness is no longer an illness but rather a privileged condition in which the subject learns to see more authentically.

The question of vision keeps returning to the fore in *Quaderno a cancelli*, whose writing is aimed at recording, as Levi reminds his readers, "questo guardare chiuso e nero di occhi chiusi o ciechi o aperti e costretti, immobili, in ogni modo tuttavia guardanti: in dentro, alle immobili apparizioni di un mondo probabile, o in fuori, alle ancora cieche apparizioni di un mondo che si afferma reale" ["the dark and closed looking of closed and blind eyes—or eyes that are open and forced to immobility and yet still looking.

It is either a looking inward, at the motionless apparitions of a probable world, or a looking outward, at the still blind apparitions of a world that presents itself as real"] (53). This modality of vision is, for the writer, the only epistemological tool that evades the temptations of ownership and appropriation:

> Ma l'occhio è diverso da ogni altra cosa. Le mani prendono e posseggono. Il sesso prende e possiede. La bocca morde, mastica, gusta e possiede. La lingua la gola la laringe urlano parlano, cantano, intonano lodi e urla, che entrano negli altri e li posseggono. Tutti gli organi interni digeriscono, si nutrono, trasformano, posseggono. Ma l'occhio vede e non possiede. Passa su tutte le cose senza toccarle, né muoverle, né urtarle, né afferrarle, né spostarle. Lontano e vicino, giudica, forma, misura, colora, riconosce, nomina, accomuna, fonde, distingue, scruta, scorge, stupisce, meraviglia, ordina, contempla, ma non possiede. È tutto umano, non divino, e dunque innocente, senza peccato, trasparente, stupito, curioso, entusiasta in felice povertà. (90)

> *But eyes are different from every other thing. Hands take and possess. Sex takes and possesses. The mouth bites, chews, tastes, and possesses. The tongue the throat the larynx scream speak, sing praises and shouts that enter others and possess them. All internal organs digest, feed, transform, possess. But eyes see and do not possess. They pass over all things without touching them or moving them or bumping them or grabbing them or displacing them. Near and far the eyes judge, shape, measure, color, recognize, name, combine, fuse, distinguish, scrutinize, perceive, surprise, amaze, order, contemplate, but do not possess. Eyes are all human, not divine, and therefore innocent, without sin, transparent, surprised, curious, enthusiastic in their happy poverty.*

In its openness, the gaze of the blind does not bear mastery, marking a site of knowledge that is radically opposed to the dimension of the *occhialino*. The *occhialino*, the special optical instrument that Levi is required to use in order to readapt his eyes to normal vision, becomes, in *Quaderno a cancelli*, an allegory of the experience of exile that characterizes modern society and that derives from the individual's alienation from himself and the world (60, 81). As Levi described it in his *Paura della pittura*, the defining factor of modernity is the loss of connection and meaning. This loss empties the world of humanity and fills it with monstrous presences. Man becomes a monster to himself because he is absent to himself (24). Analogously, in *Quaderno a cancelli* the type of vision allowed by the *occhialino* is characterized as one of division and exclusion; as seen through its lens the world appears "divided, dissociated, cracked, broken up, isolated" (60). In its focus on separation, the *occhialino* is tantamount to the visual perspective of the mythical serpent, the tempter that caused humanity's expulsion from the Edenic garden and its subsequent loss of harmonious communion with the rest of creation. Symbolic of the destruction of this unity, the *occhialino* is an instrument of individualization, opposed to an authentic form of vision that allows for the recovery of humanity's primeval wholeness. The *occhialino* is thus a manifestation of the "original sins" that Levi associates with rationalism in contrast with the innocence of subaltern cultures: "La civiltà dell'occhialino è quella dell'Enciclopedia, del Liberalismo classico, dei Lumi" ["The civilization of the *occhialino* is the civilization of the Encyclopedia, of classical Liberalism, of the Enlightenment"] (60). Built upon the Western values of class distinctions and private property, the civilization of the *occhialino* inevitably reifies reality, distancing it from the subject and transforming it into an object of aesthetic enjoyment: "Tutto è nella sua cornice rotonda di quadro: già dentro, fatto per essere bello, felice della propria bellezza, effimera e perfetta. . . . Così, con questo isolamento, si mostra il mondo dell'occhialino" ["Everything fits within its round picture frame: already inside, made to be beautiful, happy of its own ephemeral and perfect beauty . . . It is thus, through this isolation, that the world of the *occhialino* reveals itself"] (59–60).

Levi's reference to forms of artistic representation is, here, not casual, for his meditation on modes of vision as epistemological tools is inextricably linked with his ongoing reflection on art, which constitutes another of the principal thematic threads of *Quaderno a cancelli*. For Levi, the modality of vision fostered by the *occhialino* is the equivalent of a certain artistic aesthetic, which he vehemently criticized in *Paura della pittura* and still sees embodied in the positions of the avant-garde: "L'occhialino è l'Avanguardia . . . Anche l'Occhialino dell'Avanguardia isola i problemi, e i problemi dei problemi, e li rende quindi astratti, ma nello stesso tempo li esalta, li porta all'estremo" ["The *occhialino* is the Avant-garde. The *occhialino* of the Avant-garde, too, isolates problems, and problems in those problems, and makes them abstract, while at the same time it exalts them and pushes them to the extreme"] (*Quaderno* 61). The avant-garde, Levi continues, represents the culminating moment in the process of the isolation of the image that deprives it of meaning and makes it beautiful in absolute and permanent—and therefore abstract—ways (62). Beauty as defined by the avant-garde movements does not depend on the relation between the image and totality but, on the contrary, on its absolute removal from this relationship, within the context of a broader rejection of humanistic values that are perceived as no longer viable after the tragedies of twentieth-century history. Levi himself admits that, after Auschwitz, "perfino le parole di verità, umanità, umanesimo, realtà, realismo, possono, quasi per un riflesso, provocare di per sé una nausea fisica, un moto di repulsione e di fuga" ["even just the words 'truth,' 'humanity,' 'humanism,' 'reality,' 'realism' can, almost as a reflex, cause in and of themselves a physical nausea, an impetus of revulsion and flight"] (103). Traditional aesthetic models are consequently contested and challenged, resulting in the disintegration of form: "Colore versato a secchi, casualmente gocciolato o spruzzato, tele bianche o nere, gesti, lanci, colpi, fori, tagli, confuse mescolanze, o tornate e perdute speranze nella geometria elementare . . . , sfuocamenti, mescolanze, disprezzi, quanti sconforti, dolore, disperazione, quanto amaro, quanto dolente rifiuto!" ["Color is thrown in buckets, or casually dripped or sprayed. Canvases are black or white. Gestures, throws, blows, holes, cuts, confused mixtures, or a recovered and then abandoned hope in elementary geometry, . . . blurrings, mixtures, spite. How much disappointment, grief, desperation! How bitter and painful this rejection is!"] (86). Yet for Levi the subversiveness of the avant-garde movement is thwarted by its easy commercialization. In its rebellion against established norms of artistic expression the avant-garde becomes a desirable commodity, which appeals to the capitalist elites (86).

The most dramatic example of the degeneration of the ideals that motivate avant-garde theory is, in Levi's analysis, the art of Pablo Picasso, whom he considers the origin and symbol of modernist aesthetics. Picasso is both "inventore e vittima dell'arte di massa, . . . di cui Guernica potrebbe diventare un ambivalente archetipo" ["the creator and the victim of the art of the mass, . . . of which Guernica could be seen as the ambivalent archetype"] (199). In his battle against the horrors of history, Picasso becomes, in the end, an accomplice to the very forces that provoked them. In the dream of which he is the protagonist in *Quaderno a cancelli*, in fact, Picasso is no longer able to distinguish between the ideals he fights to defend and their opposite, to recognize clearly whether "la lotta per difendere la sua Grazia non era nello stesso tempo quella che dava forma alla Disgrazia, una . . . mistificatoria psicoanalisi collettiva degli spaventosi idoli della Paura, . . . le vere facce dei campi di concentramento" ["the struggle to defend Grace wasn't at the same time the struggle that shaped Disgrace, . . . a mystifying collective form of psychoanalysis of the frightening idols of Fear, . . . the true face of the concentration camp"] (201). Picasso's rebellion against alienation ultimately coincides with an attempt to transform tragedy into play, to escape the confrontation with the dehumanizing, monstrous gaze of modern human isolation (199). His challenge to realism coincides with a withdrawal from a serious engagement with historical reality and the consequent reduction of art to a form of escape.

Against the emptiness of modern art, Levi decisively reaffirms the humanistic values that had guided his intellectual life since his Turinese years, arguing that art must maintain its fundamental existential and epistemological purpose, which is to make humanity aware of the world's and its own existence. Reiterating in *Quaderno a cancelli* what he had already suggested in *Cristo si è fermato a Eboli*, Levi argues that art fulfills "la funzione certificante del vedere, che è poi il valore esistenziale dell'arte, quella che permette al contadino di vedere per la prima volta, di conoscere il suo campo, il suo volto" ["the certifying function of vision, which is, after all, the existential value of art. This is what allows the peasant to see for the first time, to know his own field, his own face"] (*Quaderno* 205). In order to achieve this aim, art must remain fundamentally realist, affirming the presence of the world of objects and the possibility of engaging in a relationship with it (108). It is, in fact, through this relationship that any form of art can effectively subvert the tainted condition of the world and recover the lost unity between man and the universe: "La parola parlante (o la pittura significante) . . . cambia il mondo, libera il nuovo essere dai propri limiti e dalla propria morte, dal tempo, e lo fa immortale e eterno" ["The speaking word (or the signifying painting) . . . changes the world, frees the new human being from his own limits and his own death, from time, and makes him immortal and eternal"] (188). Levi had already proposed the idea of a salvific function of art in *Paura della libertà*, where he discussed it in universal terms (165). In *Quaderno a cancelli*, though, this notion acquires a more personal and individual aspect. Indeed, as Linuccia Saba testifies in her introduction to the book, *Quaderno a cancelli* is born as an attempt on Levi's part to come to terms, through art, with the sudden realization of his own mortality brought about by his unexpected illness (ix). The intense creative activity that Levi carried on in his hospital room—which soon acquired the same chaotic atmosphere of the artist's own studio—confirms his enduring faith in the redeeming power of art and its capacity to imbue every experience with meaning.

Although Levi forcibly argues for the necessity of realism, he recognizes that the trauma of blindness can lead to a questioning of one's previous understanding of the world, which suddenly appears "contestabile o inesistente, o falso, o, con le sue pretese espressioni, del tutto inespressivo, convenzionale, rituale" ["debatable, or inexistent, or false, or, with its bogus expressions, completely inexpressive, conventional, ritualistic"] (108). The forms through which the experience of reality is usually described are thus questioned as empty of meaning and inadequate to express the disorientation entailed by the loss of the sense of sight. In this respect, blindness is analogous to the avant-garde's position in the face of modern man's tragic alienation (208). But for Levi the rejection of traditional form is tantamount to a rejection of reality itself (209). In fact, he continues, authentic art has the power and duty to imbue the world it engages with the quality of reality: "[Q]uelle sue forme sono quelle della realtà, non perché la imitino, la riproducano, o ne derivino. Sono quelle della realtà perché sono esse che la fanno esistere come tale, che la fanno reale, che creano e danno alle cose la categoria della realtà" ["Those forms are the forms of reality, not because they imitate, reproduce, or derive from it. Indeed they make reality exist as such, they make it real, they create and give things the category of reality"] (108–9). All art entails the discovery of the existence of the other, which comes into being when it is given form for the first time through a word or image. Art, thus, is born in the creative moment in which expression and reality coincide for the first time ("L'invenzione della verità" 52).

The conflict between the perspective of the *occhialino dell'Avanguardia* and the unifying gaze of the true artist is parallel to another fundamental binary opposition of *Quaderno a cancelli*, the one between the diabetic and the allergic.[8] Both categories belong to the sphere of illness, which for Levi constitutes the unadulterated manifestation of humanity's cultural history and offers a much more honest account of its development than the interpretations provided by ideologically motivated historiographies of ideas and institutions (30). Disease, along with art and literature, religion or philosophy, is a cultural construct through which a civilization comes to terms with the moment of its own inception. Reformulating in psychological terms the long-established metaphor of the body politic, Levi proposes that humanity's historical dynamics closely reflect, on a macrolevel, the processes of the human mind. Thus within his understanding of illness as interpretive tool, the images of the allergic and the diabetic also acquire a double valence: while on an individual plane they represent two opposite psychological positions in the face of the traumatic moment of self-identification, on a broader level they assume a profound political and philosophical significance. Branded as illness by the social order, which characteristically rejects that which does not conform to its established norms, diabetes describes, for Levi, a condition of being. The diabetic's desire literally to incorporate everything that surrounds him allows for the restoration of the original communion between man and the rest of reality (140–42). But while the diabetic consumes everything with relish—"i cibi sono considerati amici come tutti gli altri elementi della natura; che è tutta cibo, cioè conoscenza" ["foods are considered as friendly as the other elements of nature, which are all food—that is, knowledge"] (141)—for the allergic "i cibi sono tutti potenziali nemici" ["foods are all potential enemies"] (142). In contrast with the diabetic, then, the allergic emphasizes separation over union, rejecting otherness as dangerous and unhealthy. In a society dominated by the rule of allergy it is only natural for diabetes to be considered "non una costituzione, una condizione, un sistema, un modo di rapporti diversi e complessi, una cultura, una civiltà" ["not a constitution, a condition, a system, a manner of different and complex relationships, a culture, a civilization"] (144) but rather a disease and for the diabetic—"the Fat Man"—to be stigmatized as "a Guilty Monster" (142).

While in minority cultures heaviness coincides with beauty, the stereotypical figure of the overweight diabetic inevitably clashes with ideal of thinness that prevails in contemporary Western aesthetic discourse.

In his discussion of alternative models of beauty in opposition to dominant standards, Levi adopts a language, heavy with allusions to *Cristo si è fermato a Eboli*, where Giulia Venere, his housekeeper in Gagliano, explicitly associated his being desirable as a man with his plumpness: "Quanto sei bello, – diceva, – quanto sei bello grasso –. L'essere grasso è qui il primo segno della bellezza, come nei paesi d'oriente" ["'What a fine fellow you are!' she would say. 'How fine and fat!' In these parts, as in the Orient, fatness is a mark of beauty"] (*Cristo* 134, *154*). If this self-reference confirms the presence of a self-conscious narcissistic strain—unhindered by his illness—in Levi's writing, at the same time it helps situate the antithetic pair of allergic and diabetic in the context of another fundamental binary opposition in his thought, between *Luigini* and *contadini*. This contrast—introduced for the first time in *Cristo si è fermato a Eboli* and developed in more theoretical terms in *L'Orologio*—is openly recuperated in *Quaderno a cancelli*, where the writer associates the *contadini* with the marginality of the diabetic, whose life is confined to institutional places of seclusion, such as jails, hospitals and psychiatric wards, or the modest dwellings of peasants and factory workers (142). Thus opposed to the *Luigini*, the diabetic acquires the additional dimension of a social category, antibourgeois and profoundly revolutionary in its questioning of the hegemonic principles of separation and division. Although ultimately doomed to failure in a society dominated by allergy in its ideologies, superstructures, political economy, and even medicine (144), the diabetic's position incarnates the utopian, humanistic virtues Levi upheld for his entire life and proposed in all his writings.

Levi's reelaboration of concepts that he had introduced in earlier work is typical of his writing in *Quaderno a cancelli*. Indeed, the book is engaged in an ongoing intertextual dialogue that includes Levi's vast literary culture—from Alessandro Manzoni and Giacomo Leopardi to Gabriele D'Annunzio and Cesare Pavese[9]—and especially his own work, which, in this highly memorial account, is reconsidered from a perspective that is charged with the awareness of his own mortality. This is evident in one of the earliest references to his previous writings, which Levi incorporates in the section where he presents the idea of a cultural history constructed as a history of disease: "Di questo avrei parlato a lungo ... quando fossi stato vecchio, che le parole mi cadessero di bocca come pietre. Ahimé, quel momento è venuto, o si avvicina, ed è per questo che ne do qui questo primo accenno" ["I was going to talk about this at length ... when I became old, and the words were falling from my lips like stones. Alas, this moment has come, or is approaching, and thus I begin here to sketch out my argument"] (30). Although the reference to *Le parole sono pietre* is merely an indirect quotation of the poetic phrase that gives it its title, it recasts the meaning of the earlier work in poignant existential terms, connecting it to Levi's new familiarity with his own transience. An equally powerful reminder of the looming presence of death in the pages of *Quaderno a cancelli* is the allusion to his famous reportage on Sardinia, *Tutto il miele è finito*, contained in the poem "Invece di sangue, fiele" ["Instead of blood, venom"], which closes with a moment of elegiac contemplation of finitude: "È finito tutto il miele / e tutto il colore del miele" ["All the honey is gone / and all the color of honey"] (48).

But perhaps the text to which Levi alludes most frequently is the novel *L'Orologio*, which shares with *Quaderno a cancelli* an explicit preoccupation with time. In *L'Orologio*, Levi explored the question of temporality in connection with the political and social issues raised by the historical events surrounding Italy's reconstruction of its political institutions after World War II. He read the failure of the Italian Resistance movement to exercise a positive effect on the country's political landscape—which the able *trasformismo* of the ruling class left substantially unaltered in the aftermath of the war—as proof of the fundamentally illusory nature of a vision of history as progressive temporality. By challenging the consecutive development of the plot through a complex narrative structure based on temporal breaks and ekphrastic digressions, Levi offered an alternative to the positivist idea of time as progress, valorizing circularity over linearity, space over time, and polyphony over monologism, to put it in Bakhtinian terms. While in *L'Orologio* it was the image of the forest that exemplified the all-inclusiveness of this new spatio-temporal dimension, in *Quaderno a cancelli* it is the notion of *futilità* that is charged with the subversion of the laws of Aristotelian logic and the linear succession of events. As we have seen, paradoxically *futilità* becomes accessible to Levi through his blindness, which, while excluding him from normal spatial relationships with the physical world, simultaneously endows him with a *vista di sogno* that expands the temporal boundaries of his existence and creates a privileged mental space in which the distance between past and present, night and day, and dreams and memories is erased.[10] The visionary quality of Levi's writing in *Quaderno a cancelli* imbues its pages with the properties of *futilità*, allowing the narration to develop within the coexistence of contradictory principles and mutually exclusive temporal planes (116). In the memories and dreams that constitute the core of the narrative, events that belong to different eras and places often appear as contemporary, in a unique temporal dimension characterized by a kind of Bergsonian *durée* rather than consequentiality: "I ricordi si accavallano: cose separate da secoli sono in realtà quasi contemporanee: pensieri e opere adulte e originali stanno mescolati a cose informi e non divise da un mondo indistinto di infanzia" ["Memories become confused: things that were separated by centuries are, in fact, almost contemporary: adult and original works and thoughts mix with shapeless and indistinct things that belong to the indistinct world of childhood"] (187).[11] This temporality of *compresenza* is—as Levi's use of the phrase "in realtà" suggests—no less authentic than the world of phenomena, nor does it coincide with its rejection, but it requires him to shape new narrative and linguistic structures that depart from the more conventional realist mode of his earlier literary work.

This search for novel forms of expression that would be more adequate to communicate his *vista di sogno* is apparent also in Levi's art from the period.[12] Especially in the drawings from his first hospitalization, in fact, he paradoxically attempts to give visual expression to his experience of blindness, creating unique works whose highly symbolic style is situated on the verge of nonfigurative art. Moreover, just as in the prose and poetry of *Quaderno a cancelli* he investigates the deep layers of his psyche, so his contemporary painterly production emerges from the landscape of his mind, forcing him to define a new visual language through which the figures that populate his mental universe can be represented. Levi's pictures examine almost obsessively some of the images that recur in *Quaderno a cancelli*, from the owl Graziadio—whose name is actually Levi's own—and the autobiographical projection of the *guerriero birmano*,[13] to the mythical figure of Narcissus and *Gli Amanti*, confirming in this way the existence of an indissoluble link between his painting and writing. His commentary on "I ritratti," on the occasion of its republication in 1968, describes just as aptly the nature of *Quaderno a cancelli*: "Così, questo ritorno nella memoria di tutti gli elementi che hanno accompagnato le pitture, che ne sono stato un materiale necessario o un equivalente, o un fondamento, o un corollario, o una variazione, potrebbe allargarsi all'infinito, e trasformarsi in trattati, in saggi, in romanzi, in poesia" ["Thus this return, in my memory, of all the elements that accompanied my paintings, that were necessary material for them, or their equivalent, or foundation, or corollary, or variation, has the potential to expand infinitely and become treatises, essays, novels, poetry"] ("I ritratti" 15).

Fundamental among the themes that constantly reemerge in Levi's work is the image of Narcissus, to whose myth he openly refers for the first time in *Paura della libertà*,[14] employing it with different connotations in later writings as well, from *Cristo si è fermato a Eboli* to his more theoretical essays. Narcissus represents for Levi the archetype of all other images (Sperduto, *Carlo Levi inedito* plate 28). "Il se stesso è . . . , per ogni artista, la forma assoluta, la forma delle forme" ["For every artist the self is . . . the absolute form, the form of forms"], Levi writes in "I ritratti" (10), specifying at the same time that this form must not be reduced to the aspects of self-love but to the "scoperta prima dell'immagine (nella quale perdersi è mortale), della sua distinzione dalle acque caotiche e dal nero-verde informe della selva" ["the first discovery of the image (in which it is deadly to lose oneself), of its distinction from the chaotic waters and the shapeless dark-green of the forest"] (9). Thus Narcissus is for Levi a symbol of the discovery that, as Rimbaud writes, "I am an other," the foundation of what I have earlier called Levi's poetics of hospitality. On a more universal level, for Levi this discovery grounds the possibility of art and knowledge: "[L]'arte e la conoscenza prima del mondo . . . nascono dalla capacità di comprendere che quell'immagine fondamentale riflessa nel lago e scoperta da Narciso è se stesso come 'altro'" ["Art and the first knowledge of the world . . . are born from the capacity to understand that the fundamental image reflected in the lake and discovered by Narcissus is the self as 'other'"] (Vivarelli, *Temi e luoghi* 12).

In *Narciso dormiente*, dated May 8, 1973, Narcissus's head occupies the left side of the composition, in three-quarter view, resting on a bent arm. His hair is tousled in the abandonment of sleep, his eyes and full-lipped mouth closed, in a face that is marked by a prominent nose. A scarf is just hinted at, rather than represented, by the twisted pencil marks around his neck. Other unruly lines occupy the right side of the drawing, in part overwritten by a few verses that read "se il sonno / ti riprende / il doppio ti rende / semplice" ["if sleep / takes you over / the double will make you / simple"], thus confirming the centrality of the motif of the double to Levi's use of the Narcissus myth in his art. Indeed, both in this and in the other drawing of Narcissus selected by Sperduto, the mythical hero's features closely resemble Levi's in his numerous self-portraits. In this second *Narciso* (Figure 15)—also dated May 8, 1973—the simply sketched human profile that occupies the focal position in the drawing confirms the identification of Narcissus as Levi's double, recognizable in the unique nose line, large eyes, and full mouth. The floral images that surround Levi's face are a further reference to the theme of the garden as the locus of innocence and nonindividualization that precede the discovery of the self and the other signified by Narcissus.

As the artist writes in a brief explanatory note for a 1968 exhibit of paintings of *Alberi e Narciso* in fact, the garden is the subject of what could be considered one great picture, always in the making, in which "i boschi del Narciso, e la fonte, sono quelli dove si ritrova, per la prima volta, l'immagine di una figura" [*"the woods of Narcissus, and the fountain, are those in which, for the first time, we can find a figurative image"*] ("Alberi e Narciso" 35). The recognition of the self as other, made possible by the

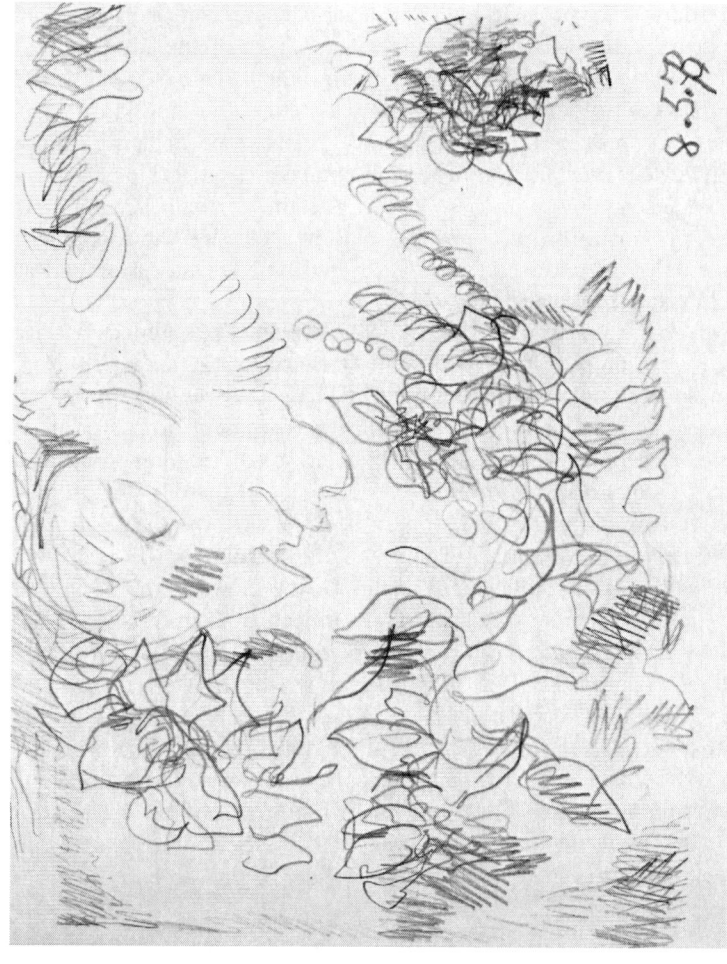

Figure 15. Carlo Levi, *Narciso* (May 8, 1973)
© 2012 Artists Rights Society (ARS), New York / SIAE, Rome

contemplation of one's own figure reflected in the water, then, lies at the origin of all art, which is essentially a search for this primal image.[15] In "I ritratti" Levi confirms this idea, writing that "se la prima immagine è quella di sé come altro, il ritratto è l'immagine dell'altro come se stesso, cioè come quella prima immagine fondamentale che è la capacità e possibilità stessa dell'immagine, che è se stesso come altro" ["if the first image is that of the self as other, the portrait is the image of the other as self—that is, the first fundamental image that coincides with the very capacity and possibility of the image—the self as other"] (9). Thus, he continues, all art consists ultimately of a relationship between the self and the other, which is realized concretely in the portrait but embraces all objects: "Nulla è dunque escluso dal ritratto, neanche le forme cosiddette astratte o pure, o non corrispondenti a oggetto alcuno, purché con esse intervenga o possa intervenire quella relazione vitale" ["Nothing is excluded from the portrait, not even so-called abstract or pure forms, or forms that do not correspond to any object, as long as this vital relationship exists or can be established"] (20).

Levi further explores the relational nature of art in the series of *Amanti*, another theme that he continued to develop throughout his career. His nephew Guido Sacerdoti recounts that in about forty years the painter produced hundreds of images of this subject in an extraordinary variety of media, from charcoal drawings to oil paintings to engravings and monotypes ("Divagazioni" 24). Two are the fundamental iconographic variants of the *Amanti*, both present in Levi's corpus from his blindness: in one version the lovers' faces are juxtaposed, while in the more frequent typology they become one, their two profiles fused by a kiss into one facial image viewed frontally (Figure 16). In this variation, the painter explores visually "il motivo della Persona e dell'Altro; dell'Uno e del Due; della doppiezza unita che è nelle cose" ["the motif of the Person and the Other; of the One and the Two; of the united duality that exists in things"] (Levi, qtd. in *Levi inedito* plate 23), which remains a constant theme in his lifelong artistic and philosophical search, beginning with his first notes on portraiture written during the 1935 imprisonment at Regina Coeli. After arguing that the self constitutes the ultimate model that the artist is constantly seeking to reproduce, Levi explains that this model never asserts itself in explicit form but is paradoxically revealed in the existence of the world of objects. In recognizing the presence of the world as other, in fact, the self becomes aware of its own being, while the surrounding reality acquires, in turn, actuality only when the conscious subject acknowledges it ("I ritratti" 10–11). Thus what Levi calls reality exists as the absolute unity of self and other, of which *Amanti* represents the perfect icon.

The assimilation of the two lovers' faces into one expresses concretely the theme of love as relationship and love as freedom (*Levi inedito*, plate

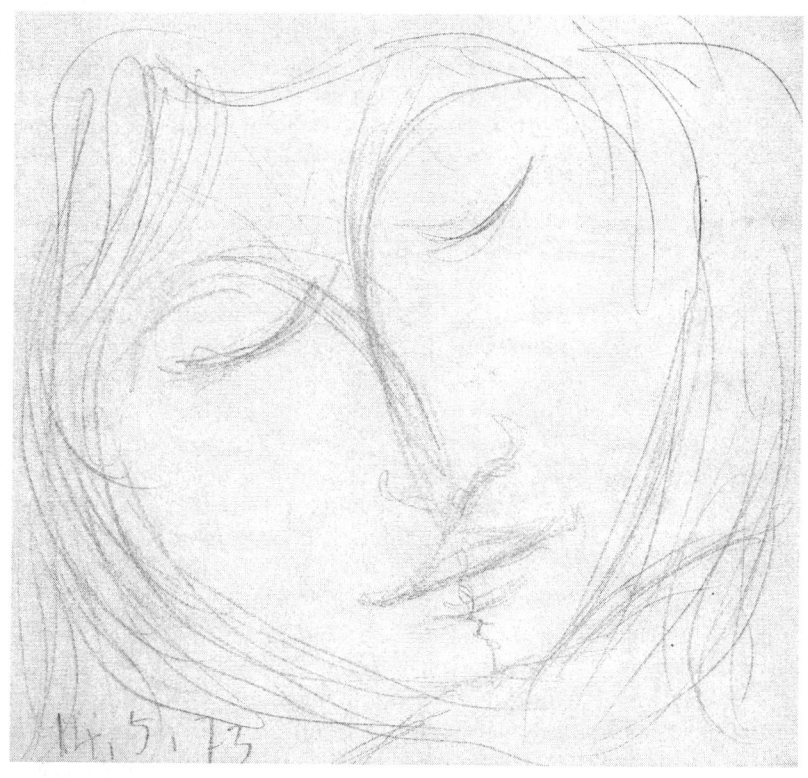

Figure 16. Carlo Levi, *Gli Amanti* (1973)
© 2012 Artists Rights Society (ARS), New York / SIAE, Rome

23), which is for Levi the foundation of all art. Vivarelli points out that the idea of painting as an epistemic moment, based on a loving relationship between self and other (*Lo specchio* xiv), returns insistently in Levi's theoretical writings. In a brief reflection on children's drawings dated 1958, for instance, he distinguishes between painting proper and the child's tentative use of symbolic forms in defining his own I as separate from the world: "La pittura, l'arte, il linguaggio poetico e personale sono un'altra cosa, perché presuppongono l'individuo formato e il rapporto di libertà con quello che è altro da sé" ["Painting, art, poetic and personal language are something different, as they presuppose a mature individual and a free relationship with the other"] ("Il disegno infantile" 32). For Levi, then, authentic art is based on a relationship that involves consciousness and freedom, and is, in this sense, the opposite of power as possession and authoritative control over the other ("I ritratti" 19). In *Quaderno a cancelli*, Levi recasts this opposition in new terms, by contrasting the notion of power with *futilità* and suggesting thus that both art and love belong to this privileged space of renewed unity between the self and the other. An earlier poem, created as a commentary to the *Amanti* series, offers a lyric reelaboration of this theme, confirming, once again, the existence of a perfect correspondence among the different artistic media that Levi employs to explore his longstanding philosophical concerns: "Amore, di due cose ne fai una / doppia ed ambigua, completa ed incerta" ["Love, you make of two things one / Double and ambiguous, complete and uncertain"] (*Levi inedito*, plate 24). Although in this poem the lovers' union is a way to restore humanity's "paradise lost," Levi concludes these verses with a powerful reminder of the death that awaits the *solitudine* of the individual, whose final destiny cannot be shared.

That love is ultimately unable to heal the tragic wound inflicted by death is proven in Levi's drawings of the *Madre*, which relate very closely to his meditations in *Quaderno a cancelli*. The detachment of his retina, according to Linuccia Saba, was for Levi the ineludible sign of the inexorable march of time and the loss of his immortality: "Quella che io chiamo l'immortalità, quel vivere di Carlo così naturale dentro il cerchio fermo della sua totale armonia con il mondo, era già stato vicino a rompersi una volta, quando, nel '52, aveva perso sua madre. Ma allora si era salvato per amore" ["That which I call immortality, Carlo's natural living within the steady circle of his total harmony with the world, had already been close to breaking once, when, in 1952, he had lost his mother. But then he saved himself through love"] (ix). While earlier Levi had been able to mend the tear in the texture of his existence through love—as the *Amanti* testify—in his old age the specter of defeat seems to loom too close to be ignored.

The *guerriero birmano* in *Quaderno a cancelli* laments his failure to prevent his mother's passing: "Se la corazza è stata perforata, se la freccia mi ha colpito, è perché mi hai lasciato, e non ho potuto saputo trattenerti" ["If the armor has been perforated, if the arrow has wounded me, it is because you left me, and I was not able to keep you"] (27). The *guerriero birmano* is at the same time an autobiographical projection of Levi and a universal figure, representing the individual, wounded by the loss of the original symbiotic unity with the Mother. Drawing from the ancient semiotic tradition that associates the circle with perfection, totality, and eternity, Levi characterizes this primal relationship as a circular structure, thus attributing to it metahistorical, archetypal value:

> Quello che è sferico in ogni parte, nella sua totale natura, nel suo tutto e in ogni minima cella e corpuscolo e struttura la più nascosta nel suo tutto: nel suo fuori e nel suo dentro, e in ogni sua direzione e impalcatura e struttura e forza: nello sferico del seno, e del latte che è dentro il seno e delle forze che lo succhiano da ogni parte, quello sferico dell'occhio che vede ed è visto, quella curva che è sempre due forze che lo determinano . . . , quella identità amorosa di concavo e convesso, generante e generato, amante e amato, intoccabile, senza rotture, perfetta. Perfetto, eterno, senza fine, immortale, oh! (27)

> *That which is spherical in each part, in its entire nature, in its totality and in each cell and corpuscle and most hidden structure of its totality: in its outside and in its inside, and in every direction and scaffolding and structure and force; in the sphere of the breast, and of the milk inside the breast and the forces that suck on it from every side; in the sphere of the eye that sees and is seen, the curve that depends on the two forces that determine it . . . , that amorous identity of the concave and the convex, generating and generated, loving and loved, untouchable, with no break, perfect. Perfect, eternal, infinite, immortal, oh!*

Here, Levi constructs the description of the bond with the mother as yet another variation on the motif of the unity between self and other that—as we have seen—constitutes one of his lifelong obsessions. The preservation of this unity, signified by the uninterrupted circumference, is, according to the Turinese intellectual, the essence of life. The self's discovery of its own separate existence, by breaking the circle of the symbiotic relationship with the mother, ultimately represents a form of submission to the death instinct: "Ma che cosa è quella forza che lo tira e lo infrange, quel tentativo di individuazione, di separazione, di proprietà, di possesso, di separazione, di esilio, di nascita: che cosa è dunque quell'istinto di morte . . . ?" ["But what is that force that pulls and breaks him, that attempt to achieve individualization, separation, property, possession, separation, exile, birth: what is it, then, this death instinct . . . ?"] (28). As Adam's expulsion from the Garden of Eden marked humanity's loss of its original immortality, so the abandonment of the *indistinto originario* in the process of individualization results from a death drive, mistaken for the drive to live (28). In the moment of the self's separation from the mother, "rotta la naturale unità della sfera materno-filiale, dell'uovo, della curva perfetta e senza paura, comincia il tempo, l'individuo, la paura, la storia, gli avvenimenti, il terrore del buio, l'insonnia, la malattia, cioè la civiltà e la cultura" ["once broken the natural unity of the mother-child sphere, of the egg, the perfect and fearless curve, there begins time and the individual, fear, history, event, the fear of darkness, insomnia, disease—that is, civilization and culture"] (29).

As these passages show, the image of the circle or sphere takes different forms in Levi's work, assimilating the contour of the mother's breasts, for instance, or the convex surface of the human eye, or the curvilinear shape of the egg—a traditional signifier of feminine fertility. Levi had begun to explore the symbolic function of the egg in a series of etchings, directly inspired by the verses of Umberto Saba's poem "Fratellanza": "e siamo tutti / nati da un uovo" ["and we all / come from an egg"] (626).[16] In them, the egg is clearly cast as a symbol of the archetypal Mother from whom all human beings are born. In the drawings that follow his hospitalization in 1973, though, Levi's emphasis is on the notion of birth as trauma, as the irreparable rupture of the eggshell that enclosed in a symbiotic unity mother and son. In *Perdita della madre*, dated February 21, 1973 (Figure 17), Levi visualizes the moment in which the two are no longer one, and the wholeness of the circle is broken in the process of individualization. Adopting a style that, in its focus on the symbolic value of form, appears closer to abstraction than any other image in his visual corpus, Levi places against a background of black and dark-brown doodling lines two green round shapes, touching each other, yet clearly distinct one from the other. By tracing each circle in thick overlying marks, which suggest spatial depth and movement, the artist conveys the dynamic of separation that is taking place as the smaller circle on the right pulls away from the matrix on the left, thus breaking its circumference. Dotted lines replace the originally continuous curves that defined the larger shape, creating a visual parallel to the *guerriero birmano*'s refrain in *Quaderno a cancelli*: "La Madre è morta, la sfera è rotta o incrinata" ["The Mother is dead, the sphere is broken, or cracked"] (qtd. in *Carlo Levi inedito* 31).

The image of the shattered sphere returns in several other drawings, among which the most significant is perhaps *Perdita dell'immortalità*, from March 19, 1973 (Figure 18). In this work in pencil, Levi presents a mirror image of *Perdita della Madre*, inverting the relative positions of the circles against the same abstract background of indistinct signs. But here, each of the circles contains an image of the artist's face, thus rendering strikingly concrete the notion of the "due in uno," or two-in-one, in the process of splitting. In its duplication of Levi's visage, *Perdita dell'immortalità*

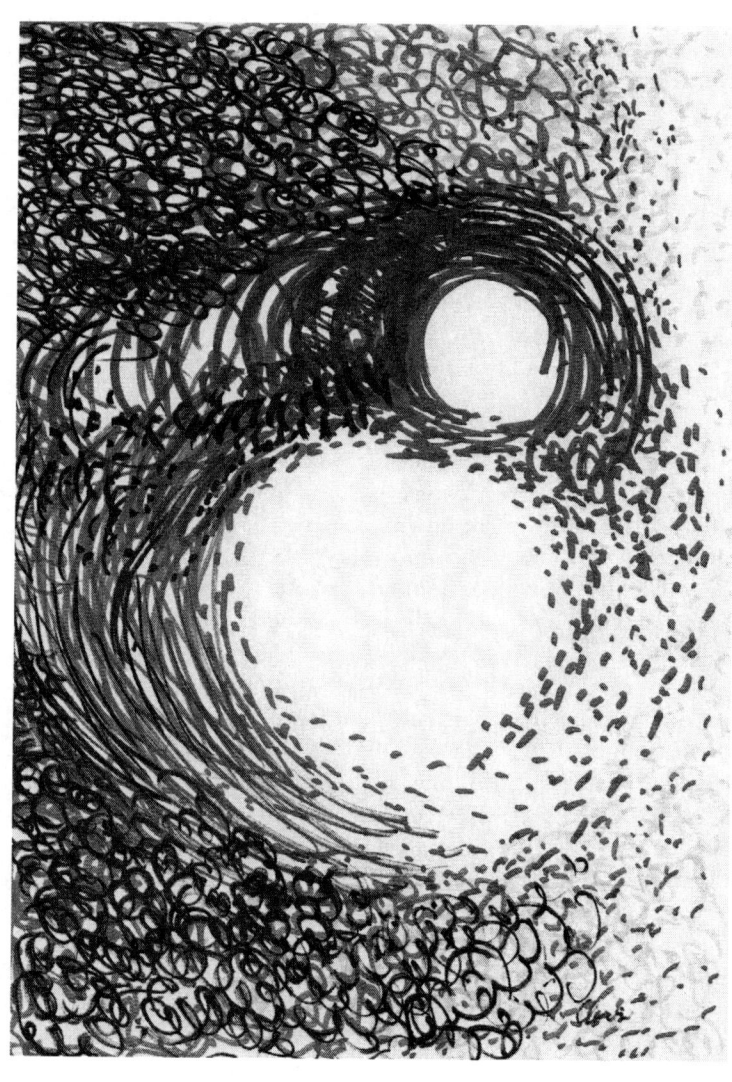

Figure 17. Carlo Levi, *Perdita della madre* (February 21, 1973)
© 2012 Artists Rights Society (ARS), New York / SIAE, Rome

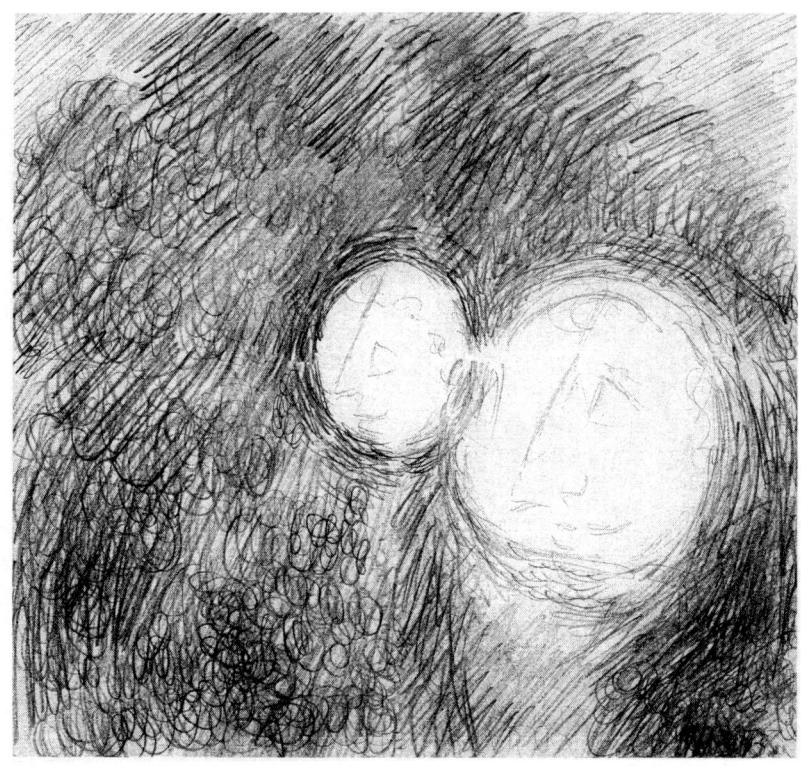

Figure 18. Carlo Levi, *Perdita dell'immortalità* (March 19, 1973)
© 2012 Artists Rights Society (ARS), New York / SIAE, Rome

represents also the exact opposite of the series *Amanti*, where the lovers absorbed one another, becoming one in their embrace. As Levi writes in *Quaderno a cancelli*, indeed love and death are opposites that can be coupled only in the distorted sensibility of bourgeois romanticism (28). While the series *Amanti* represented the individual's capacity to restore, through Eros, the primal unity with the other, in fact, the drawings centered on the theme of the loss of the Mother seem to invite the viewer, on the contrary, to admit the inevitable defeat in the face of death. These images seem to visualize the *guerriero birmano*'s tragic downfall as Levi describes it in *Quaderno a cancelli*:

> Il guerriero ... con qualcosa almeno di curvo, di rotondo nei tratti, come un geroglifico di una sua lingua ad archi, un arco delle sue case e chiese, una pennellata delle sue miniature; sta del tutto dimenticato, sotto uno degli spalti più remoti di un castello sconosciuto che non si sa se egli dovesse difendere o conquistare. E neppure egli lo sa, e non gli importa saperlo. È là, ferito da una freccia che non si sa da che parte gli sia venuta, che qualcuno ha tirato, come qualcuno gli ha tratto dal petto, e se ne è andato ... Il guerriero (perché?) riverso sull'erba trascolorante della controscarpa remota pensa e grida al cielo, al suo avvoltoio di morte: Madre, perché sei morta? Madre, come non ti ho saputo difendere? (26–29)

> *The warrior ... with at least something curved, round in its features, like the hieroglyph of his own language, drawn as an arch, the arch of his houses and churches, a brushstroke from a manuscript illumination. He stays, completely forgotten, under one of the most remote battlements of an unknown castle, which nobody knows whether he was expected to defend or conquer. And he does not know either, and he does not care to know. He is there, wounded by an arrow that nobody knows where it arrived from, an arrow that someone threw and that someone pulled out from his chest and left ... The warrior (why?), lying on the translucent grass of the remote battlement, thinks and shouts to the sky, to his deadly vulture: Oh Mother, why have you died? Mother, why wasn't I able to defend you?*

As the motif of the Mother occupies a fundamental position in Levi's production during his blindness, equally important is an image derived from his childhood memories and linked to his father: Il Naufragio del Piloro. The motif appears in various paintings from the artist's last years, as Levi explains, as a result of the discovery of the "senso riposto, e inconsapevole, di un disegno eseguito da mio Padre per divertire i figli, quando avevo forse 4–5 anni" ["hidden and unconscious meaning of a drawing my Father made to amuse his children when I was perhaps four or five years old"] (*Carlo Levi si ferma a Firenze* 118). Levi recounts how his father, whose frustrated ambition was to become a painter, used to entertain his children by sketching wonderful ink drawings, stories that were being written and drawn as the words illustrated them ("Il naufragio del Piloro" 38). One in particular remained always present in Levi's memory, perhaps the unconscious origin of all his art:

> Un oceano artico, con balene, iceberg, gabbiani, pesci, foche, e poi onde nascenti, fino alla tempesta; e una nave, prima dolcemente navigante nella calma del mare, con tutte le sue vele gonfie; e poi il vento, il fulmine, l'albero maestro spezzato, le barche di salvataggio inutili, gli uomini vanamente cercanti scampo nel mare terribile, la poppa che si solleva mentre la nave precipita nell'abisso. Questo disegno mi parve, allora, sublime...
>
> Quel disegno fu l'origine della mia pittura: mi accorsi della sua infinita possibilità di creazione del reale, vidi, con estasi e rapimento, la realtà farsi, sotto le mani, forma e figura. ("Il naufragio del Piloro" 38)
>
> *An arctic ocean, with whales, icebergs, seagulls, fish, seals, and then waves that rise to become a storm; and a ship, which at the beginning was gently navigating the quiet sea in full sail; and then wind, lightning, the broken mast, the useless lifeboats, the men uselessly seeking safety in the terrible sea, the stern rising while the ship falls into the abyss. This drawing seemed to me, at the time, sublime...*
>
> *That drawing was the origin of my painting: I realized its infinite potential to create reality; I saw, in a moment of ecstatic rupture, reality becoming shape and figure under human hands.*

His fascination with the drawing, however, was at the same time accompanied by a sense of revulsion for the name that his father had jokingly given the sinking ship, "Il Piloro" ("Sphincter"), which the child Levi associated—without fully understanding the meaning of the term—with something undignified and vulgar. Only several decades after his father's death did the artist decode the message hidden in the drawing: "Mio padre morì, 30 anni dopo quel disegno, per una improvvisa emorragia da ulcera al piloro, il giorno dello scoppio della guerra mondiale. *Il Piloro era la sua morte*: la sua morte per orgoglio di uomo libero e autosufficiente, per rifiuto di ogni condizione servile. La tempesta aveva spezzato l'albero maestro, non vi era scampo nel mare glaciale popolato di mostri" ["My father died, thirty years after that drawing, for a sudden pyloric hemorrhage, the day that World War II was declared. The Pylorus was his death: his death by pride, the pride of a free and independent man, the rejection of any condition of servitude. The storm had broken the mast, there was no rescue from the icy sea inhabited by monsters"] (38–39).

Ercole Levi died, that is to say, of his own choice, in an act of rejection of the monstrosity of fascist racial laws and Italy's shameful alliance with

Germany (37). Thus Ercole's body becomes the incarnation of the metaphor of the political body, ceasing to function in the moment in which his country's politics appear to be too severely diseased to foresee any recovery. But even understanding his father's position, the son cannot and will not accept his suicidal will to shipwreck (41). In prophetically depicting his own death as fascinating and desirable, Levi's father betrayed his vocation as "creatore della divina pittura, che non ammette la morte" ["creator of divine painting, which rejects death"] (39). Thus Levi's own revisiting of the "Naufragio del Piloro" aims to offer a correction to his father's defeat, ultimately reaffirming art as a salvific force, even in the face of illness and death. Art cannot, that is to say, be a form of withdrawal from life, for it implies a responsibility toward humanity. And thus, Levi's *Quaderno a cancelli* ultimately does not end as an intimist exploration of the life of the artist's unconscious mind, nor as a self-referential revisitation of his work's themes and motifs. On the contrary, the book's final words—"mi risveglio," "I wake up"—leave behind the dimension of dreams and open up the world of the text to engage, once again, with contemporary social, political, and cultural reality, in a renewed affirmation of art's power to inspire *futilità*, as the capacity to embrace the entirety of human experience in all its richness and inconsistencies, without pretending to reduce it to a formula or ideology.

Indeed, as I hope to have shown in my readings of his major works, Levi's cultural project created a new form of humanism, which expressed itself first of all as a unity of purpose in all aspects of his multifarious activity—a coherence that he had first encountered in Piero Gobetti's intellectual model. Painting, social activism, literature, all belonged to the same uninterrupted discourse among the various forms of creativity that Levi pursued throughout his life, engaging in a rich intertextual and interartistic dialogue, whose voices I have followed in this book. Painting and writing, in particular, participate in an intensely dialogic exchange in all Levi's literary works and are the foundation of what I have proposed to call Levi's "visual poetics." This visual poetics expresses itself at times as a direct correspondence between word and image, as in the case of *Quaderno a cancelli*, in which the figures of Narcissus or the Burmese warrior that he explores in the book are also illustrated in his drawing portfolio. In other instances, as in *Cristo si è fermato a Eboli* or in *Le parole sono pietre*, the word evokes verbally a specific painting of Levi's. In *L'Orologio*, the relationship between visual and verbal modes of representation expresses itself through a descriptive impulse that, by giving prominence to the visual image, challenges the temporal dynamics of traditional storytelling and contributes to the highly innovative and original narrative technique of the novel.

But the dialogism of Levi's visual poetics is not simply a matter of style, because it expresses in formal terms his constant dialogue with other human experiences, a dialogue that he began in *Cristo si è fermato a Eboli* and sustained throughout his life. Levi's work, whether in words or images, is the expression of his exploration of otherness, whether it be in southern Italy, India, or China. As I conclude these observations, I would like to propose that this openness and ethical commitment to the other, which Levi theorized in the essay "I ritratti" and pursued in his writings and in the portraits he painted, makes his intellectual contribution particularly relevant to contemporary culture. In a moment in which Italy is facing unprecedented pressure from migrants from the global South and a political discourse of terror and suspicion toward otherness imposes itself more and more explicitly in Italian society, Levi's work offers a much-needed lesson in civic and artistic courage. In an increasingly polarized world, in which we are witnessing the nationalistic reemergence of Ur-fascism (to borrow Umberto Eco's phrase), Levi's summons to fellow intellectuals and citizens not to fear freedom but to embrace the responsibility that such freedom entails seems as important and urgent as it was in 1939.

Notes

Preface

1. A note on translations. Whenever a published English-language translation of an Italian quotation was available, I inserted it in square brackets after the Italian quote, and the translation for a block quote is italicized. The corresponding page numbers for all English translations are in italics. Where no italicized page reference is given, the translation is mine.

Introduction

1. All translations without an italicized page reference are mine.
2. It needs to be observed, however, that no univocal definition of *humanism* really exists in intellectual history but that the meaning of the term has always been object of debate. See Tom Rockmore (60–69) for a very synthetic but useful historical survey of the uses of the term, especially in the French context, which, as we shall see, was particularly influential on Levi.
3. I use the term *conversation* here in the sense that Michael Oakeshott gives the word in his classic essay, *The Voice of Poetry in the Conversation of Mankind*. Richard Rorty reelaborates the notion of "conversation of mankind" in *Philosophy and the Mirror of Nature*, casting philosophy—in a postmodern turn—as participating in a conversation that constitutes the context for knowledge (389).
4. In addition to Levi, the group included Enrico Paulucci, Francesco Menzio, the British Jessie Boswell, Nicola Galante, and Gigi Chessa.
5. Levi and his friends considered the "Novecento" movement as being too closely connected to the Fascist regime. The Novecento was a creation of Margherita Sarfatti, art editor of the national newspaper *Il popolo d'Italia*, who organized an art exhibit at the Galleria Pesaro in Milan, inviting a number of painters (Anselmo Bucci, Lonardi Dudreville, Achille Funi, Gian Emilio Malerba, Piero Marussig, Ubaldo Oppi, Mario Sironi) whom she considered representative of Italian twentieth-century art. They had very little in common, except for a shared interest in the restoration of the values of the Italian art historical tradition. Mussolini participated in the inauguration, thus demonstrating the party's approval of the aesthetics of the group, which came to be known as the "Novecento italiano." In the following years, the "Novecento" attracted more and more artists—including Carlo Carrà and Giorgio Morandi, Giorgio de Chirico and Giacomo Balla, among others—who were defined as "artisti

giovani—pattuglia di arditi all'avanguardia in ogni campo di attività spirituali, e fascisti, cioè rivoluzionari della moderna restaurazione, nell'arte come nella vita sociale e politica" ["young artists—a brave patrol at the avant-garde of every field of spiritual activity—and Fascists, that is, activists of modern restoration, in art as in social and political life"] (qtd. in Bertelli, Briganti, Giuliano 386). Although by the 1930s the "Novecento" had lost Fascist favor due to its lenience toward foreign artistic influences, the movement was still perceived by Levi and his friends as compromised with fascist ideology. Their group's name itself, "Sei pittori di Torino," constitutes an evident reaction to the "Sette pittori del Novecento" who presented their work at the Venice Biennale in 1924. Unlike the "Novecento," these young artists proposed the French impressionist and postimpressionist tradition as a model, experimenting with the expressive potentialities of color in the manner of both the *fauves* and the expressionists (Bertelli, Briganti, Giuliano 380–414). For a more complete discussion of fascist cultural and artistic politics, see Mabel Berezin as well as Marla Susan Stone.

6. Excellent documentation of Levi's activity among the Italian political émigrés in Paris can be found in Levi, *Gli anni di Parigi: Carlo Levi e i fuorusciti, 1926–1933*.
7. Vincenzo Napolillo disagrees with Gigliola De Donato on the European dimension of Levi's intellectual history, preferring to associate him with a tradition of southern Italian writers (104–5).
8. Born in Turin in 1901, after brilliantly concluding his studies at the Liceo Gioberti, Piero Gobetti rapidly became a protagonist of the city's political and cultural life. During his first year as a law student, in 1918, he founded and directed the journal *Energie Nove*, inspired by the thought of Gaetano Salvemini and Benedetto Croce. He then became closer to the communist wing of the Socialist Party and engaged in a friendship with Antonio Gramsci. In this period he began collaborating with the Communist newspaper *Ordine Nuovo*, for which he wrote theater reviews. In 1922 he brought together his previous experiences and created the weekly *Rivoluzione Liberale*. The aim of the journal was to propound a radical renewal of Italian national politics through the fruitful collaboration of the intellectual élites and the proletariat, which only would make possible an authentic revolution. Its "liberalismo rivoluzionario," or revolutionary liberalism—to borrow the phrase with which Carlo Levi defines it in an essay on Gobetti's work—caused the journal to be shut down, while its founder and director was brutally beaten by Fascist thugs. Not succumbing to such intimidations, he maintained his relentless opposition to Mussolini's dictatorial regime and created a publishing house that printed, among other controversial works, Eugenio Montale's *Ossi di seppia*. Gobetti's publishing project was meant to encourage forms of resistance against fascism in literature and culture, once open political opposition became impossible. For this reason, in 1926 he was made the target of another violent attack by the *camicie nere*, which caused him irreparable physical damage. Gobetti left for France, where he died in exile shortly after, at the age

of 25. For a comprehensive consideration of Gobetti's impact on antifascist circles in Turin and beyond, see David Ward's excellent book, *Piero Gobetti's New World*, as well as Nino Borsellino. Ward's work includes other studies that consider Levi's antifascist activitiy, such as *Antifascisms: Cultural Politics in Italy, 1943–46* and *Carlo Levi. Gli italiani e la paura della libertà*.

9. The friendship between Gramsci and Gobetti began when the latter wrote as a theater critic for Gramsci's *Ordine Nuovo*. Gobetti recognized the value of class struggle, which would result in a unifying myth inspiring creative action (Martin 59). On the role of myth in Gobetti's thought, see also Ward (*Piero Gobetti* 101–6), and Marco Gervasoni (232ff).
10. For details on their friendship, see Gigliola De Donato and Sergio D'Amaro's biography of Carlo Levi.
11. On the two different approaches to humanism see Joseph Fell.
12. See, for example, Tom Rockmore (119ff.) and Anson Rabinbach (97ff).
13. In *Vico and Humanism*, Ernesto Grassi criticizes Martin Heidegger's rejection of humanism as fundamentally uninformed and highlights the similarity between Heidegger's philosophy and the humanist tradition's interest in language, particularly in poetic language (see, for instance, the chapter titled "Italian Humanism and Heidegger's Thesis of the End of Philosophy").
14. Partly in response to Heidegger's (at best) ambiguous relation with German National Socialism, Emmanuel Levinas entered the polemic surrounding the German philosopher, who had been his teacher, by condemning his phenomenology in no uncertain terms and declaring that "contemporary philosophy takes satisfaction [*se complaît*] in the multiplicity of cultural significations ... Philosophy is produced as a form that manifests the refusal of engagement in the Other, a preference for waiting over action, indifference toward others—the universal allergy of the first childhood of philosophers" (*Humanism* 25–26). Levinas's critique of the infinite multiplication of "cultural significations" as ultimately leading to ethical indifference is, as we shall see, startlingly close to Levi's own analysis of modernist relativism in "Paura della pittura."
15. The term *poema filosofico* itself is suggestive of Levi's intellectual indebtedness to Giambattista Vico and his "poetic philosophy"—to adopt a phrase used by Vichian scholars from Antonio Sarno to Giuseppe Mazzotta. But many others are the analogies and influences recognizable in the text. Vittorio Giacopini and Nicola Carducci mention, for example, Johan Huizinga, José Ortega y Gasset, Oswald Spengler, Carl Jung, Sigmund Freud, Henri Bergson, Rudolf Otto, and Friedrich Nietzsche. Stanislao Pugliese analyses *Paura della libertà* in connection to Levi's contemporary Eric Fromm but draws parallels with Terry Eagleton and Umberto Eco, as well.
16. See Conni-Kay Jørgensen for a thorough philological study of the correspondences between *Paura della libertà* and the 1744 edition of *La Scienza Nuova*.
17. René Girard's classic study of violence and religion, *Violence and the Sacred*, presents many analogies with Levi's account.
18. Chiara Bauzulli examines this shift in her dissertation, "*Carlo Levi filosofo*" (see especially 45–46 and 101). Although I do agree that Levi's approach becomes,

after his encounter with southern Italy, more organic and less rationalistic, my understanding of his humanism is in contradiction with Bauzulli's reading of Levi as an early proponent of "weak thought."

19. In Levi's eminently Vichian text, this critique of Western rationalism is an echo of Vico's own challenge to the Cartesian notion of the stability of the knowing subject. As Mazzotta has pointed out, Vico is aware of the instability of the human mind, of its "indefinite nature," against Descartes's model of the rational mind as nondialectic (Mazzotta 105). Sandra Luft also discusses "the nihilistic tendencies of theoretic knowledge and the reduction of theory to technique" (197) that Vico feared at the beginning of modernity and that both Levi and Heidegger recognize at the end of it.

20. Levi explains, "Questa mia affermazione, la poesia è l'invenzione della verità, non pretende di essere una rigorosa enunciazione filosofica, non ho nessuna intenzione, qui oggi, di inquadrarla in un sistema" ["This statement, that poetry is the invention of truth, does not pretend to be a rigorous philosophical enunciation. Today, here, I have no intention to fit it into a system"] ("L'invenzione" 51).

21. Levi's anthropological view of southern peasantry—partly informed by the work of Ernesto De Martino—is, from our contemporary perspective, outdated and utterly problematic. *Cristo si è fermato a Eboli* was, in fact, criticized by Mario Alicata in *Il meridionalismo non si può fermare a Eboli* for Levi's failure to analyze the historical causes of the southern question and for representing the peasantry in unrealistic, romanticized terms. For a discussion of the issues raised by De Martino's ethnographic approach, see George Saunders's article, in which he highlights the conflict between De Martino's "critical ethnocentrism" and his underlying belief that Western rationalism was actually superior to other cultural forms.

22. Levi anticipates here the contemporary reconsideration of mimesis as an effective instrument of *reconnaissance*, as Antoine Compagnon defines it: "a cognitive activity taking form from the experience of time, configuration, synthesis, dynamic *praxis*, which, instead of imitating, produces what it represents, augments common meaning, and issues in recognition" (96).

23. Similarly, Heidegger theorizes that the moment in which a people begins to produce art coincides with the beginning of its historical being ("On the Origin of the Work of Art" 149). As Levi makes clear in *Paura della libertà*, however, there is a radical difference between Heidegger's and his notions of a people's role in history, for Heidegger embraces the notion of a historical destiny, which for Levi is a negation of freedom (*Paura della libertà* 197).

24. For a more thorough discussion of Jungian influences in Levi's theory, see De Donato (*Saggio* 55ff), and Lawrence Baldassaro. Levi acknowledges these influences explicitly, as in a note dated January 17, 1933, in a desk calendar: "Con gli archetipi di Jung si spiega il carattere . . . delle forme più indeterminate, e il significato di quanto c'è di *caos indifferenziato* nella mia pittura" ["Jungian archetypes explain the character . . . of the most indeterminate forms and the meaning of the indifferentiated chaos of my painting"] (Manuscript, 17 January).

25. Again, Levi's thought parallels here Heidegger's notion of the work of art as setting forth truth, rather than representation ("On the Origin of the Work of Art" 140–41).
26. For a more detailed discussion of Levi's paintings of Lucania, see Pia Vivarelli, "Diario pittorico del confino," as well as Chapter 1.
27. Italo Calvino confirms the strict relation between the rediscovery of a realist poetics by Italian writers and artists after World War II and their reevaluation of expressionism. In his introduction to *Il sentiero dei nidi di ragno*, he observes that writers of their generation often represented the individual as a grotesque and excessive figure, exhibiting contorted grimaces that expressed the visceral dramas of postwar Italian collectivity. If Italian intellectuals had missed the encounter with expressionist aesthetics in the first half of the century, the post-Fascist period allowed them to absorb it fully. For this reason, Calvino concludes, perhaps the correct denomination for that season of Italian literature should not be "neorealism" as much as "neo-expressionism" (xi).
28. For a full examination of Vico's notions of mimesis and historical memory, see Mazzotta (140–61).
29. See Luft for a discussion of the *New Science* as an examination of "the diverse expressions of *poiesis*, the interpretive sense-making of beings-in-the-world that takes place in language, a hermeneutic process *ontologically* creative of a real, though artifactual, human world" (xv).
30. Levi's critique of modern art, as well as his positive emphasis on realism, incorporates Marxist elements, in many ways anticipating the arguments later put forth by Georgy Lukács in his analysis of literary modernism. Like Levi, Lukács criticizes the antirealist art of modernism as a form of irresponsible escapism, whose origins he traces back to Heidegger's aestheticization of philosophy, as a means to isolate it from social and historical reality. Levi's personal philosophical commitment to realism reflects the same conviction in the need for an engaged art. In his personal elaboration of humanism Levi is also influenced by Antonio Gramsci's Marxist *umanismo*. Gramsci saw Marxism as a humanist philosophy of history that repudiated determinism and its view of human history as an extension of natural history. Although Levi embraced the Gramscian notion of *umanismo*, Levi perceived Marxist dialectical materialism as a limitation that he transcended through a profoundly ethical concern for the Other.
31. The inconsistent capitalization of "other" in this passage reflects the original.
32. It is important, of course, to recognize also the differences between Levi and Levinas. Levi resisted the idea of visual representation as a necessarily totalizing tool that forces the Other into the subject's own categories of thought—as Levinas suggested—emphasizing instead the need for an amorous and creative relationship with the Other. Whereas Levinas underlines the passivity of the subject in relation to the Other, Levi—like Martin Buber—identifies in reciprocity a fundamental element of the self's relation to otherness. Levinas explicitly questions the authenticity of Buber's notion of reciprocity (*Totality* 68). For Levinas, responsibility is total and defenseless exposure to the Other,

which precedes any response from the Other; reciprocity, in contrast, implies the expectation to be treated by the Other as an equal Thou (see Bauman 49). In affirming reciprocity in the relationship, the self thus seems to retain a position of primacy. Levi's conceptualization of subjectivity reflects Buber's notion of reciprocity and parallels Sartre's reluctance completely to efface the subject, in a defense of individual freedom and historical responsibility (Fox 52).

33. On the question of power in the specific case of the artist/model relationship, see Wendy Steiner's *The Real Real Thing*.
34. I use the term *dialogic* in a Bakthinian sense. In "Discourse in the Novel," Mikhail Bakhtin treats free indirect discourse as a manifestation of *heteroglossia*, the fundamental plurilingualism that he attributes to the novel—seen as a tendency in literature that affects other genres beyond prose fiction. Free indirect speech is, for Bakhtin, "an utterance that belongs, by its grammatical (syntactic) and compositional markers, to a single speaker, but that actually contains mixed within it two utterances, two speech manners, two styles, two 'languages,' two semantic and axiological belief systems," and is, therefore, highly dialogic (304).
35. Jean Mitry calls the free indirect point-of-view shot "semisubjective," as the camera constantly shifts between a subjective and an objective position: "Retaining all the attributes of the descriptive image, [it] *adopts* the viewpoint of a particular character who, objectively described, occupies a special position in the frame . . . The camera follows him wherever he goes, acts like him, sees with him and him at the same time" (218).
36. On the political implications of Pasolini's idea, see Ward (*A Poetics of Resistance* 117, 136–37). Gilles Deleuze renders fully explicit the subversive potential of Pasolini's poetic notion of cinema in both *Cinéma I: L'Image-Mouvement* and *Cinéma II: L'Image-Temps*.

Chapter 1

1. All translations without an italicized page reference are mine.
2. Levi writes, "Uscirò dunque da questa valle: per andarmene, pare, su un colle. Me lo figuro altissimo, come quei luoghi che i santi sceglievano per appartarsi dal mondo, dal secolo mortale, e dove sulle loro ossa si fondavano i monasteri, la cui fama andava per tutta la terra" ["I will, then, leave this valley, apparently to go to a hill top. I imagine it being very tall, as one of those places that saints used to choose to be detached from the world, from the secular world, and where, above their remains, they used to found monasteries, whose fame traveled the world"] (*È questo il carcer tetro?* 141).
3. Although Levi had never been to the rural South (he had visited Naples once with his brother Riccardo in the 1920s), being involved in the circle of Pietro Gobetti meant that he was engaged in reflecting on the *questione meridionale*. As Manlio Rossi Doria explained, "effettivamente tutta la formazione di almeno dieci anni precedenti di Carlo Levi era stata una formazione

tipicamente gobettiana e la formazione gobettiana è assolutamente permeata della importanza e della centralità della questione meridionale" ["in effect Carlo Levi's education during at least the preceding ten years had been a typical Gobettian education, and this education is absolutely infused with the importance and centrality of the southern question"] ("La crisi" 68). Well before traveling to Lucania, he had written an article against the former prime minister and minister of agriculture, Antonio Salandra, criticizing his attempts to solve the problems of the South by trusting it to the classes that had the strongest interests in safeguarding its backwardness ("Antonio Salandra" 3–16). His characterization of the South as a completely new discovery thus proves to be not entirely accurate.

4. Levi was transferred from Grassano to Aliano after a visit from his lover Paola Olivetti, at the time married to Adriano Olivetti. The *podestà*, considering Levi's behavior as profoundly opposed to fascist moral and social values, requested that he be assigned a more remote location, where such visits would be more difficult (cf. D'Amaro and De Donato, *Un torinese del sud* 120). In *Cristo si è fermato a Eboli*, Levi hides the real name of Aliano, the village where he spent the greater part of his exile, distorting it in "Gagliano."
5. Levi reelaborates here a thesis proposed by Giustino Fortunato and embraced by Piero Gobetti in an article in *Rivoluzione Liberale*, "La nostra cultura politica" (26).
6. For a recent discussion of the relationship between *Cristo si è fermato a Eboli* and D'Annunzio's work, see Donato Sperduto, "Tra azione e inazione."
7. On the self-reflectivity of ekphrasis see, among others, W. J. T. Mitchell, *Iconology* (155).
8. On this point, see in particular Julia Kristeva's seminal essay on Mikhail Bakhtin, "Word, Dialogue, and Novel," which introduced the Russian thinker's work to Western European literary circles.
9. David Ward reads Pier Paolo Pasolini's work as fundamentally an expression of the writer's resistance to bourgeois society in his book *A Poetics of Resistance*.
10. Alessia Ricciardi's notion is, in turn, influenced by Jacques Derrida's concept of "impossible" hospitality—total openness to the other—as the French philosopher develops it in *Of Hospitality*.
11. For a more detailed discussion of Pasolini's "cinema of poetry" in relation to *Cristo si è fermato a Eboli*, see my "Francesco Rosi's *Cristo si è fermato a Eboli*: Toward a Cinema of Painting," *Italica* 86.2 (2009): 272–92.
12. Only in 1974, a few months before his death, would Levi create illustrations for *Cristo si è fermato a Eboli*, with a series of lithographs that were published in portfolio form by the editor Esposito of Turin.
13. For a thorough philological study of *Cristo si è fermato a Eboli* and the history of its manuscript and typescript redactions, see Maria Antonietta Grignani.
14. The picture was exhibited for the first time in 1948 at the Venice Biennale, which hosted it again in 1954. Considered lost for several years, it was shown to the public again in 2008.

15. Levi's choice of subjects during the first months of his exile is clearly connected to his existential condition—for example, the first place that inspires him to paint is the cemetery, which, with its barren solitude, reflects the loneliness of the exiled artist (cf. Arouimi 58).
16. In this letter, Levi mentions both Dante and Virgil as illustrious precedents in calling Lucania *umile*. There also exists a linguistic connection between the dark wood of Dante's poem and Lucania, as the Latin name of this southern region means "land of woods." The link could escape neither Levi's classical formation nor his humanistic belief in the all-encompassing relationality of the world.
17. I am indebted to Victoria Kirkham, who suggested that I look at illustrations of the *Divine Comedy* to support my point.
18. See Giuseppe Lupo and Giovanni Battista Bronzini, *Viaggio antropologico*, for good discussions of the Dantean presences in *Cristo si è fermato a Eboli* as well as Levi's other literary works.
19. Michel Arouimi interprets the expression "chiave magica" as referring to the magic of literary constructs and of narrative writing in particular—while at the same time emphasizing the parallels between literature and the arts (22).
20. Levi's words, in describing his discovery of the Other as separate, manifest the strong influence that Freudian and Jungian theory exercised upon his thought, as shown in his more philosophical works, *Paura della libertà* and *Paura della pittura*. For another discussion of Levi's "pittura del confino" see Maria Mimita Lamberti.
21. Cf. Daniela Bini's excellent gendered discussion of Levi's relationship with the women in his books.
22. The question of the role of the intellectual in political and social life is central to Gramsci's thought. See, for example, *Selections from Cultural Writings* (167–71, 211, 245–47).
23. Arouimi sees Father Trajella's naïve pictorial mimetism as a reflex of his presumed homosexuality (59).
24. Levi's views on autonomy as a political principle reflect closely Gobetti's own political thought (Ward, *Piero Gobetti* 111). I will return to an in-depth consideration of Gobetti's influence on Levi's *meridionalismo* in Chapter 3.

Chapter 2

1. Other scholars, too, recognize a continuity between *Cristo si è fermato a Eboli* and *L'Orologio*; Michel Arouimi, for example, describes *L'Orologio* as the urbanistic equivalent of *Cristo si è fermato a Eboli* (26).
2. All translations without an italicized page reference are mine.
3. For an account of Levi's political activity and frequentations in the years immediately following World War II, see also Leonardo Sacco. Helpful in reconstructing the political context of Levi's novel are the essays edited by Gigliola De Donato and collected in *L'"Orologio" di Carlo Levi e la crisi della Repubblica*.

4. In the catalogue of a 2008 exhibit, *Carlo Levi e Roma. Il respiro della città*, Fonti writes that in *L'Orologio*, there is a unique exchange between painting and the written word. Only few paintings of tranquil Roman landscapes correspond to the busy scenes of the novel. Fonti identifies only one direct correlation between the novel and a painting, *Scena allegorica*, where Rome becomes an older prostitute who must sell contraband goods in order to survive (25).
5. The Garbatella, a run-down *borgata* at the southeastern outskirts of the capital, is the only peripheral area visited by Levi's character in *L'Orologio*. Unlike Pier Paolo Pasolini, whose explorations of Rome focus especially on its most destitute areas and underprivileged citizens, Levi's fascination with the historically layered structure of the city confines him, as we shall see, to its central quarters. But his Rome is not the Rome of privilege and wealth. On the contrary, in drawing a map of the capital in the immediate postwar years, he conveys the extreme diversity of its population, made up of civil servants, American soldiers, prostitutes, priests, black marketeers, and so on. Levi's own story is presented as part of this same adventure, without any character of exceptionality.
6. Particularly infamous is Carlo Muscetta's review of the book, in which he recognizes Levi's tendencies to *superomismo* and to represent himself as a life-bestowing divinity (see "Leggenda e verità di Carlo Levi" 52–67). Muscetta appears in the novel as the protagonist's friend Moneta.
7. For Benjamin, Baudelaire's poetry has always in the background the "metropolitan" mass of Paris, by which he is fascinated, in terms very similar to the *flâneur*'s captivation with the crowd ("On Some Motifs" 165ff.)
8. In addition to the essay on Baudelaire, Benjamin explores the urban space in *One Way Street and Other Writings* and the unfinished *Arcades Project*.
9. On linear narrative as a form of representation linked to a progressive notion of history, see Hayden White.
10. According to Vanna Gazzola Stacchini, all of Levi's characters in the novel either are mouthpieces for his own ideas or are represented parodically through free indirect discourse (cf. Gazzola Stacchini, "Personaggi" 144, as well as Ward, *Antifascisms* 175). A brilliant example of Levi's ironic use of language can be found in the pages devoted to his conversations with Iolanda, the housekeeper he has inherited with his new apartment, and her *fidanzato*. Inspired by the aristocratic origins of Palazzo Altieri and by the bohemian life of the artists that occupied the apartment before Levi, the two constantly try to imitate their manners and way of speaking, with amusing results (*L'Orologio* 220–32).
11. Carl Gustav Jung, whose theories of myth and the archetype are extremely influential on Levi's thought, describes the image of the forest in connection to the Mother archetype, which represents, in turn, a symbol of preindividualization. See in particular Jung, "The Archetypes and the Collective Unconscious."
12. In his classic study, *The Sense of an Ending*, Frank Kermode distinguishes between *chronos*—the linear time of history and the novel—and *kairos*, the cyclical, ahistorical time of myth, in a manner parallel to Levi's own distinction between two temporalities.

13. The construction of Palazzo Altieri began in 1600, under the auspices of Cardinal Giovan Battista Altieri, whose family had owned property in the area since the 1300s. Under the direction of the architect Giovanni Antonio de Rossi, the building was brought to conclusion in 1675, when the original design was considerably expanded thanks to the lavish support of Emilio Altieri, elected to the papacy with the name of Clement X. The complex was originally divided into a number of separate princely apartments and developed around two courtyards, the *corte d'onore* and a larger *corte di servizio*. The northern side and the stables were added in 1734.

14. After moving into the Palazzo, Levi accidentally meets an old man, who is familiar with the history of the building and some of its legendary occupiers: "Questo palazzo ... è come una città. C'è dentro di tutto: una banca, una scuola, dei negozi, un cinematografo, dei magazzini. C'era anche un'ambasciata, e la sede della Massoneria, e tante altre cose; e, una volta c'era qui anche il tribunale di Roma" ["This palace ... is like a city. It has everything inside it: a bank, a school, shops, a moving picture theater, and storerooms. Once there was an embassy, too, and Masonic Headquarters, and many other things. Also, once the city court of Rome"] (136, *149*).

15. In *Atlas of the European Novel 1800–1900* Moretti explains how the mythical notion of the Court of Miracles was born around the time of the Great Internment of all beggars of Paris in the 1650s, making its first appearance on a map of the city in 1652. For Moretti, the Court of Miracles was a way for society to negotiate the presence in its midst of disorder and anarchy, confining it to a specific and enclosed space.

16. The uncomfortable and adventurous journey and the randomness of the people encountered during the trip are for Levi powerful reminders of another journey toward the South he undertook in France to escape the Nazis. In one of the long digressive flashbacks typical of the novel, the desolate landscape where the ruins of the war are still visible triggers in Levi memories of his flight southward from Paris, then from Bordeaux toward the Garonne, and finally to southern France, where he found refuge during the Occupation (256–60). This is one of the rare moments of *L'Orologio* in which Levi explicitly refers to his experience of the war. Another such moment occurs toward the beginning of the book, when he recalls the murder of a Fascist collaborator by a Florentine *gappista*, which occurred under the windows of his hiding place (34–36). In both cases, memories are provoked by a visual experience that, as in Marcel Proust's *mémoire involontaire*, allows the reappropriation of the lost past by reproducing a feeling associated with it.

17. The title itself of "King of Poggioreale" suggests a deliberate subversion of conventional linguistic connotations. The peripheric quarter of Poggioreale was especially known for the prison and the Central Station, spaces traditionally associated with the *malavita* and certainly not with the royal family. However improbable a figure, the king was a real *camorrista*, Giuseppe Navarra, who helped the Neapolitan people survive the deprivations of the war, providing with his ingenuity and generosity what the local government failed to offer. By

the end of the war, he will have become a mythical figure, soon to be forgotten after order is restored. The adventurous events of his life inspired the 1961 film by the director Duilio Coletti, *Il Re di Poggioreale*.
18. In *Il ventre di Napoli*, Matilde Serao denounced the subhuman conditions in which the poor of the city lived.
19. In his memoir Levi writes, "Parlavo con i contadini, e ne guardavo i visi, e le forme: piccoli, neri, con le teste rotonde, i grandi occhi e le labbra sottili, nel loro aspetto arcaico essi non avevano nulla dei romani, né dei greci, né degli etruschi, né dei normanni, né degli altri popoli conquistatori passati sulla loro terra, ma mi ricordavano le figure italiche antichissime. Pensavo che la loro vita, nelle identiche forme di oggi, si svolgeva uguale nei tempi più remoti, e che tutta la storia era passata su di loro senza toccarli" ["I was struck by the peasants' build: they are short and swarthy with round heads, large eyes, and thin lips; their archaic faces do not stem from the Romans, Greeks, Etruscans, Normans, or any of the other invaders who have passed through their land, but recall the most ancient Italic types. They have led exactly the same life since the beginning of time, and History has swept over them without effect"] (*Cristo* 123, *140*).

Chapter 3

1. See, among others, Vanna Zaccaro, "Reportages dai sud del mondo" (xxv) and Sergio Pautasso (181).
2. For an account of the trip, see Levi's biography by Gigliola De Donato and Sergio D'Amaro (181–86). After his visit, *Life* published an essay titled "The Myth of America," which appears in Italian in *Le mille patrie*.
3. Levi himself issued in volume form his travel journals from the Soviet Union, Germany, Sicily, and Sardinia, which were published by Einaudi. Levi's travel journals from the Soviet Union appeared with the title *Il futuro ha il cuore antico* in 1956. His somewhat naïve enthusiasm for the USSR during the height of the Cold War was probably the reason that his book was never translated into English. *Tutto il miele è finito*, recounting the writer's trips to Sardinia, came out in 1964 and was never translated into English. The reportage from Germany, *La doppia notte dei tigli*, appeared in 1959 and was translated into English by Joseph M. Bernstein, as *The Linden Tree*, for the New York publisher Albert Knopf in 1962. *Le parole sono pietre* (1955) was translated by Antony Shugaar as *Words Are Stones: Impressions of Sicily* for the London publisher Hesperus Press in 2005. Some other texts were posthumously collected in *Il pianeta senza confini*, edited by Guido Ferroni and Vanna Zaccaro for the publisher Donzelli (2003). Others have appeared in *Le mille patrie*, also issued by Donzelli (2000). Shugaar translated the texts on India as *Proses on India* for the independent London publisher, Hesperus Press, in 2007. Shugaar also translated a series of essays on Rome, published in Italian as *Roma fuggitiva* (Roma: Donzelli, 2002) in the 2004 volume, *Fleeting Rome* (Chichester, UK and Hoboken, NJ: Wiley).

4. All translations without an italicized page number are mine.
5. Levi's friend and agronomist Manlio Rossi Doria was a strong proponent of a radical reform of Italian agricultural economy. With his book *La riforma agraria e azione meridionalista* (1948), as well as the Centro di Specializzazione e Ricerche Economico-agrarie per il Mezzogiorno, he shaped Italian policies for the South. For recent studies on the goals and results of the 1950 riforma agraria in Italy see Emanuele Bernardi, Antonino Bacarella, Maurizio De Vitis. Vincenzo Napolillo is very critical of Levi's failure to recognize the limits of the state-promoted rural reform in the South: Levi, he writes, "non intende gli effetti della riforma agraria che, dal punto di vista sociale, rafforza il ceto dei piccoli proprietari ... e, dal punto di vista politico, organizza la 'clientela' sotto il controllo non più del latifondista, ma della Cassa e degli Enti di riforma" ["does not understand the effects of the agrarian reform that, from a social point of view, strengthens the small landowners ... and, from a political point of view, organizes the 'clientele' no longer under the large landowner, but under the Cassa and the Reform organizations"] (72–73).
6. Despite the direct parallels existing between Levi's travel journals of southern Italy and his painting, the first editions of both *Tutto il miele è finito* and *Le parole sono pietre* do not include any of his works. Only later will the publisher Einaudi include cover images chosen from Levi's paintings. For example, the 2010 edition of *Le parole sono pietre* displays, as a cover image, the Lucanian painting *I due amici* (1936); in 2003 the Sardinian publisher Ilisso reissued *Tutto il miele è finito* with an image of *Il miele di Orune* (undated).
7. Millicent Marcus sees this notion as the crux of Francesco Rosi's adaptation of *Cristo si è fermato a Eboli* (see the chapter devoted to Rosi in her *Italian Film in the Light of Neorealism*).
8. For a further examination of the notion of creativity in Levi's *Paura della libertà*, see David Ward's *Antifascisms* (160–63), as well as Lawrence Baldassaro.
9. While Levi is in Lucania, he witnesses a moment of autonomous creativity on the peasants' part, when they put up a theatrical performance—modeled on the passion play of the holy week—to protest against the interdiction for Levi to practice the medical profession. Levi speaks of it as displaying an artistic passion and a certain tragic talent in the actors, who, after all, were staging the tragic reality of their lives (*Cristo* 203–5). Another episode that manifests the newly acquired desire, on the villagers' part, to acquire the instruments to tell their own stories is the one in which a group of children asks Levi to teach them how to read and write (190). In Francesco Rosi's film adaptation of *Cristo si è fermato a Eboli*, the director makes an important modification to the original text and has the children demand that Levi teach them how to paint (see Lerner 289–90).
10. Levi's view of southern culture as an alternative to the alienation of modernity is particularly relevant to today's discussions of Mediterranean thinking. Levi's encounter with the South led him to a reconsideration of Enlightenment values and the limits of modernity. He struggled to let "a thinking of southern Europe thinking itself as a subject" happen (Dainotto 381). Franco

Cassano examines the connection between southern thinking and Levi's work in a brief article, "Cinquantasei anni dopo «Cristo»."
11. See Giovanni Battista Bronzini, *L'universo contadino*, for an exhaustive analysis of Scotellaro's political and literary work. Also useful is Anna Maria Torriglia's brief discussion. Scotellaro's poems and short stories were all published after he died prematurely at the age of thirty. As Bronzini mentions, his work was reviewed poorly by the same leftist critics who had berated Carlo Levi for his lyricism and a-historicism in representing the South (see, for example, Muscetta), but was reevaluated during the 1970s and 1980s, especially thanks to *meridionalisti* such as Luigi Sacco or Rossi Doria (Bronzini, *L'universo* 11).
12. Levi uses the phrase "non si ferma a Eboli" in direct response to Mario Alicata's criticism of his *Cristo si è fermato a Eboli* in the famous *Il meridionalismo non si può fermare a Eboli* (1954).
13. Here, Levi expresses a belief in the agrarian proletariat to appropriate and manage its own historical role that surpasses Gramsci's own confidence in the southern workers' movement. Brian Moloney has identified specifically in this faith in the self-determination of the rural underclasses the novelty of Levi's *meridionalismo* ("*Cristo si è fermato a Eboli*" 112). For Russo, this trust in the possibility of autonomous action distinguishes Levi not only from traditional *meridionalismo* but also from postwar Marxist positions, incarnated by Carlo Muscetta in particular (39).
14. The somewhat vague ideal of autonomy generated, in the immediate postwar period, a variety of social experiments. Scotellaro, for one, created a democratic and locally based committee to help finance and manage the Civic Hospital in Tricarico; Adriano Olivetti's Comunità movement developed a housing project in Matera with funds from the United Nations Relief and Rehabilitation Administration, which aimed to a "compenetrazione tra valori urbani e civiltà contadina" ["compenetration between urban values and peasant civilization"], as Giuseppe Berta has described it (571). As Berta explains, Olivetti's social venture was based on a precise choice of *regionalità*, which derived from the awareness of the limits of centralized power and embraced a vision of power that could only be local and based on a grassroots movement (571). For Berta, it is impossible to understand Comunità without Levi and Scotellaro's own ideas of autonomy for the South.
15. The privileging of dark tonalities and the emphasis on the hardness of the lines is characteristic, as Alberto Moravia once observed, of Levi's painting of the 1950s and 1960s, a period that for some critics can be associated with socialist realism and a more explicit thematization of social and political concerns (26).
16. Gramsci's preoccupation with the failures of Risorgimento to constitute a united nation exercised an enormous influence on Gobetti, whom he knew and respected as "an organizer of culture" (qtd. in Cammett 129).
17. Levi, of course, disagreed with Gramsci that political leadership should remain with the northern industrial workers, as he believed in the capacity of the southern peasant classes for autonomy, as he discusses, for example, in *Cristo si è fermato a Eboli*.

18. I thank Antonella Lavorgna of the Fondazione Carlo Levi in Rome for assisting me in finding an electronic copy of this painting, a 6.5' by 9.8' canvas that was exposed in the 1974 retrospective exhibition in Mantua, whose owner is unknown.
19. For a contemporary account of the trial, see the article "The Sting of Conscience," which appeared in the foreign news section of *Time* magazine on April 9, 1956 http://www.time.com/time/magazine/article/0,9171,866866,00.html (accessed November 8, 2010).
20. See Levi's letter to his family dated September 7, 1935 (qtd. in Romani 33).
21. The evangelical subtext is also present through the mediation of Iacopone da Todi, the influence of whose lauda, "Donna de Paradiso," has been recognized by Napolillo (77).
22. Another influence on Levi's positions on language is certainly Gobetti. Although Gobetti did not write as extensively as Gramsci on questions of language, he reflected on its political role both in his writings on Vittorio Alfieri and in short articles, such as a brief essay, "Le parole," which he published in *La Rivoluzione Liberale* in 1922. In "Le parole," Gobetti criticizes the meaninglessness of the language of politics, which privileges rhetoric over substance (cf. Ward, *Piero Gobetti* 134).
23. Levi visits, for example, the Capuchin catacombs in Palermo, lingering on the mummification process and describing in vivid detail some of the most striking mummies preserved there: the young girl whose body was added to the cemetery in 1920, the general of Garibaldi's army murdered in 1863, the American consul, the famous surgeon (85ff.). He also describes the traditions linked to the cult of Saint Agatha in Catania. In the iconographical convention, she is often shown contemplating her own excised breasts, and Levi is quick to trace the origin of this folkloric practice to the presence of Mount Etna in the local landscape (102). In Catania, Levi attends another traditional event: a *pupi* (or marionette) show, narrating the glorious adventures of the Paladins. In relating the spectacle, Levi emphasizes the overlap between art and life that the stories of the Paladins generate: the public is so completely invested in the events on stage that they mourn the death of its heroes and celebrate the joy of their victories outside the theater as well as in it (103–5). Levi's prose in describing these parts of his visit is tight and synthetic, rather than lyrical and descriptive, as though to underscore that he is not there as a tourist or a folklorist but rather a visitor whose attention focuses on the present lives of local Sicilians and not on local "color." In this respect, his writings on Sicily are very different from his Lucanian memoirs, where he recorded his discovery of a world where folklore was fully integrated into daily life.
24. See in particular "Il contadino e l'orologio."
25. Levi's notion is not entirely original, for his friend Carlo Rosselli had written, in the 1930 *Socialismo liberale*, that "[c]i sono due Italie . . . : un'Italia moderna, cittadina, industriale e un'Italia antica rurale ancora estranea alla civiltà occidentale, paese di masse ancora vergini e serve, mantenute ostinatamente

fuori delle condizioni di esistenza che rappresentano la premessa indispensabile per la nascita e l'affermazione di un movimento socialista a carattere marxista" ["there are two Italies . . . : a modern Italy, urban, industrialized, and an ancient Italy, rural, still alien to Western civilization, a land of masses that are still untouched and enslaved, systematically kept outside the conditions that represent the indispensable premise for the birth and affirmation of a socialist marxist movement"] (qtd. in Battaglia 125).

26. Luca Clerici's anthology of Italian travel narratives from the eighteenth to the twentieth century, *Il viaggiatore meravigliato*, underscores the importance of the feeling of wonder as a common characteristic of any travel writer. But Levi's response to the encounter with the novelty of different cultures comprises the additional dimension of love, as Italo Calvino explains: "Questa dell'amore per le cose di cui parla è una caratteristica che bisogna tener presente se si vuole riuscire a definire la singolarità dell'operazione letteraria di Levi . . . Il suo metodo è di descrivere con rispetto e devozione ciò che vede, con uno scrupolo di fedeltà che gli fa moltiplicare particolari e aggettivi. La sua scrittura è un puro strumento di questo suo rapporto amoroso col mondo, di questa fedeltà agli oggetti della sua rappresentazione" ["It is necessary to keep in mind this love for things, about which he speaks, as a characteristic that defines the originality of Levi's literary project . . . His method is the respectful and devoted description of what he sees, with a preoccupation for fidelity that causes him to multiply details and adjectives. His writing is a pure instrument of his loving relationship with the world, of his faithfulness to the objects of his representation"] ("La compresenza dei tempi" xii).

27. Mario Soldati explained the painting thus: "[È] divisa in tre grandi parti, in tre cantiche: un inferno, un purgatorio e un paradiso, ovvero potremmo dire l'epoca geologica, la vita delle caverne, la vita dell'uomo; e poi la vita agricola, le opere, l'agricoltura, e poi la terza parte, invece, la vita civile, l'organizzazione politica, sulle piazze, degli uomini; oppure possiamo dire più semplicemente, forse ancora più giustamente, il passato magico, il presente, con tutti i suoi problemi del lavoro, della terra, e l'avvenire, l'organizzazione politica dell'uomo verso l'avvenire" ["It is divided into three parts, three *cantiche*: an inferno, a purgatory, and a paradise; or we could say the geological era, life in the caves, human life; and then rural life, labor, agriculture; and then the third part, civic life, political organization, in the squares, of men. Or we could more simply say, and perhaps more correctly, the magical past, the present with all its labor and land problems, and the future, man's political organization toward the future"] (*Carlo Levi e Lucania '61* 9).

28. See Capalbo. Of the four hundred pictures Carbone took, many were later published in the volume *Viaggio in Lucania con Levi*. Levi also collaborated with the photographer Janos Reismann for *Un volto che ci somiglia. Ritratto dell'Italia*, which offered a sort of elegy of the agrarian Italy that was being rapidly being replaced by the landscape of industrial development and capitalistic growth.

29. The real last representation of the South on which Levi worked was, in fact, a series of lithographs illustrating *Cristo si è fermato a Eboli*, which he printed in 1974 with the publisher Esposito in Turin and were later reproduced in *L'altro mondo è il mezzogiorno* 41–72.

Chapter 4

1. The actual *quaderno a cancelli* is now preserved at the Central National Archives in Rome, Fondo Carlo Levi, b. 61 f. 1899.
2. All translations without an italicized page reference are mine.
3. The vagueness of Levi's own definition of *futilità* has left ample space for interpretive hypotheses on its origin and meaning. Thus, for instance, Augusto Placanica recognizes an analogy between *futilità* and the Biblical idea of *vanitas* (164). Donato Sperduto instead draws a link between Levi's notion of *futilità* and the philosophy of Emanuele Severino, defining both as exponents of *pensiero futile* ("Carlo Levi pensatore" 123–27). However suggestive these hypotheses may be, it is important to acknowledge and accept the openendedness that characterizes Levi's thought.
4. Levi coins the verb *baalizzare*, "to turn into Baal," in an allusion to the practice of idolatry condemned by Mosaic monotheism. For Levi, hegemonic culture is authoritarian in imposing its own idols to the masses. Idolatry, whether of religious ideals or political ideologies, turns men into slaves.
5. Levi has been harshly criticized for his Romanticized vision of preindustrial societies. However, as the poet Andrea Zanzotto remarks in regard to Pier Paolo Pasolini—who was also perceived as a reactionary nostalgic for an imaginary blissful past—for Levi, too, the past is the symbol of a new beginning, charged with possibilities to transform the present. David Ward persuasively sides with Zanzotto in *A Poetics of Resistance* (127).
6. The power of poetic language to unveil the hidden connections among things is also explored in Elsa Morante's *La Storia*. In the novel, Useppe's linguistic imagination "serves to heighten similarities by ignoring basic differences and by interchanging essences and attributes"—creating, in other words, metaphors (see Lucente 251). Useppe's poetic gaze upon the world, although full of loving wonder at the things that it contains, lacks the desire to exercise power on them that Levi, as well, attributes to poetry. Gregory Lucente describes Useppe's position as a "lack of possessiveness, his open, unfearful, and in that sense non-Freudian (because nonconflictual) affective relationships with the contents of the world around him" (254), which corresponds to Levi's characterization of the Ronga people. If the innocence of Useppe's gaze on the world cannot resist the crushing power of history and condemns him to death, Levi seems, on the contrary, to assert his enduring faith in poetic discourse as a form of resistance, however marginalized by institutional authority.
7. The image of the hedge, *la siepe*, is a reference to Giacomo Leopardi's poem "L'infinito," in which the poet describes the experience of envisioning through

his imagination the landscape hidden by a hill and hedge, a space that he figures as an infinite expansion reflecting the quiet and peace he is seeking in his own soul. As we shall see, this allusion is just one example of the thick web of intertextual references that crosses *Quaderno a cancelli*, including first and foremost those to Levi's own texts.
8. The choice of diabetes is not casual: Levi himself suffered from this condition, which was the ultimate cause of his vision problems.
9. *Quaderno a cancelli* is crowded with literary allusions. Alessandro Manzoni's *I Promessi Sposi*, for instance, is recognizable in an ironic remark on "la peste, i grandi avvenimenti provvidenziali dei romanzieri" ["the plague, the novelists' great providential events"] as impossible forms of resolution in real life (159). The famous page from the same novel in which Lucia bids farewell to the familiar landscape of her village, "Addio ai monti" ["Goodbye to the mountains"], is parodied in a passage in which Levi, arising from sleep, abandons the realm of dreams and returns to a state of consciousness (117). Levi's parodic approach to Manzoni's fiction, moreover, contains a self-referential allusion to his own 1950 novel *L'Orologio*, where the writer challenged the viability of traditional forms of narration after the tragedies of the twentieth century caused the questioning of the meaningfulness of history (cf. *L'Orologio* 57).
10. The first two dreams that Levi records in his diary, for instance, are presented in continuity with other observations and reflections. Only the grammatical switch from the present tense to the imperfect, which is the verbal mode typically adopted in Italian when reporting a dream, suggests the passage from conscious thought to the oneiric process (cf. *Quaderno* 11–12, 19).
11. In Levi's dreams important characters—from his ancient lover Paola Olivetti to his friend and fellow painter Francesco Menzio, from the head of the *Partito d'Azione*, Ferruccio Parri, to the archenemy Pablo Picasso—and sites of his past—from the Soviet Union to Israel, to Florence during the Nazi occupation, to Rome in the immediate postwar years—appear to overlap freely, often subverting the order of events in the writer's biography.
12. According to Donato Sperduto—who edited a selection of these works under the title *Carlo Levi inedito*—between his first hospitalization in February 1973 and his second surgery in April of the same year the artist produced a total of 146 drawings—more than half of which can be dated after his second operation. The first drawings are in blue ink, but later Levi used also pencil and colored crayons (Sperduto, "Ogni rosa" 12–13).
13. It is not clear what inspired the image of the *guerriero birmano*—perhaps a trip to Burma that Dr. Mario Stirpe, Levi's surgeon, took while the writer was under his care. Levi himself wonders explicitly, "[C]hissà perché guerriero" ["Who knows why a warrior?"] and a few lines below he admits that the warrior could be perhaps Burmese, or else Circassian or Turkman or Kazak (26).
14. In *Paura della libertà*, Narcissus is presented as the object of desire of a subject, whose immature erotic impulse pushes her to turn inward the arms of desire (149).

15. Levi recasts in his own terms the argument that Leon Battista Alberti presents in his treatise *On painting*, where Alberti discusses Narcissus as the mythical inventor of painting (64).
16. Saba and Levi met for the first time in 1924 in Turin and renewed their acquaintance in Nazi-occupied Florence in 1944, where both found shelter in the home of Anna Maria Ichino. In this occasion Levi met also Saba's daughter, Linuccia, who would become his life companion. For a detailed account of the friendship between the two writers, see Ghiazza.

Works Cited

Alberti, Leon Battista. *On Painting*. Ed. and trans. John R. Spencer. New Haven, CT: Yale UP, 1967.
Alicata, Mario. "Il meridionalismo non si può fermare a Eboli." *Cronache meridionali* 9 (1954): 585–603. Rpt. in *Intellettuali e azione politica*. Eds. Renzo Martinelli and Roberto Maini. Rome: Editori Riuniti, 1976, 153–72.
Arouimi, Michel. *Magies de Levi: L'expérience picturale et littéraire de Carlo Levi confrontée aux leçons de Rimbaud, Melville, Tolstoï, Jean de Patmos et Xue Xiake*. Fasano: Schena, 2006.
Bacarella, Antonino. *Le politiche agricole nello sviluppo economico in Italia: Dalla riforma agraria alle riforme della politica agricola comunitaria*. Palermo: L'Epos, 1999.
Bachelard, Gaston. *The Poetics of Space*. Trans. Maria Jolas. Boston: Beacon Press, 1969.
Bakhtin, Mikhail. "Discourse in the Novel." Bakhtin, *Dialogic Imagination* 259–422.
———. "Forms of Time and the Chronotope in the Novel." Bakhtin, *The Dialogic Imagination: Four Essays*. Ed. Michael Holquist. Trans. Caryl Emerson and Michael Holquist. Austin: Texas UP, 1984. 84–258.
———. *Problems of Dostoevsky's Poetics*. Ed. and trans. Caryl Emerson. Minneapolis: U of Minnesota P, 1984.
Baldassaro, Lawrence. "*Paura della libertà*: Carlo Levi's Unfinished Preface." *Italica* 72 (1995): 143–54.
Battaglia, Achille, Piero Calamandrei, Gabriele De Rosa, Emilio Lussu, et al. *Dieci anni dopo. 1945–1955, saggi sulla vita democratica italiana*. Bari: Laterza, 1955.
Baudelaire, Charles. *The Painter of Modern Life and Other Essays*. Ed. and trans. Jonathan Mayne. London: Phaidon Press, 1974. 1–40.
Baudrillard, Jean. *Simulacra and Simulations*. Trans. Sheila Faria Glaser. Ann Arbor: U of Michigan P, 1994.
———. *Simulations*. Trans. Paul Foss, Paul Patton, and Philip Beitchman. New York: Semiotext(e) Inc., 1983.
Bauman, Zygmunt. *Postmodern Ethics*. Oxford, UK: Blackwell, 1993.
Bauzulli, Chiara. "Carlo Levi filosofo. Evoluzione del pensiero leviano dagli anni venti agli anni quaranta." Diss., City University of New York, 2007.
Beauvoir, Simone de. "Un uomo d'oggi." Trans. Aldo Marcovecchio. *Galleria* 17 (1967): 275–76.
Benjamin, Walter. *The Arcades Project*. Trans. Howard Eiland and Kevin McLaughlin. Cambridge, MA: Harvard UP, 1999.

———. *The Correspondence of Walter Benjamin*. Theodor Adorno and G. Scholem, eds. Chicago: U of Chicago P, 1994.

———. "On Some Motifs in Baudelaire." Benjamin, *Illuminations*. Ed. Hannah Arendt. Trans. Harry Zohn. New York: Shocken Books, 1969. 155–200.

———. *One Way Street and Other Writings*. Trans. Edmund Jephcott and Kingsley Shorter. London: NLB, 1979.

Berezin, Mabel. *Making the Fascist Self: The Political Culture of Interwar Italy*. Ithaca, NY: Cornell UP, 1997.

Bernardi, Emanuele. *La riforma agraria in Italia e gli Stati Uniti: Guerra fredda, Piano Marshall e interventi per il Mezzogiorno negli anni del centrismo degasperiano*. Bologna: Il Mulino, 2006.

Berta, Giuseppe. "Fra centrismo e centro sinistra: Olivetti e il Movimento di Comunità." *Studi Storici* 19.3 (1978): 545–87.

Bertelli, Carlo, Giuliano Briganti, and Antonio Giuliano, eds. *Storia dell'arte italiana*. Vol. 4. Milan: Electa/Bruno Mondadori, 1988.

Bini, Daniela. "Women of the South and the Art of Carlo Levi." *Forum Italicum* 37 (2003): 103–20.

Borsellino, Nino. "Una giovinezza a Torino: Levi, Gobetti e Sapegno." *Belfagor* 63.4 (2008): 460–66.

Bronzini, Giovanni Battista. *L'universo contadino e l'immaginario poetico di Rocco Scotellaro*. Bari: Dedalo, 1987.

———. *Il viaggio antropologico di Carlo Levi: Da eroe stendhaliano a guerriero birmano*. Bari: Dedalo, 1996.

Buber, Martin. *I and Thou*. Ed. and trans. Walter Kaufmann. New York: Charles Scribner's Sons, 1970.

Calvino, Italo. Presentazione. 1964. *Il sentiero dei nidi di ragno*. Milan: Mondadori, 1993. v–xxv.

———. "La compresenza dei tempi." *Galleria* 17 (1967): 237–41. Rpt. in Levi, *Cristo si è fermato a Eboli* ix–xii.

———. "Visibilità." Calvino, *Lezioni Americane: Sei proposte per il prossimo millennio*. Milan: Mondadori, 1993. 89–111.

Cammett, John McKay. *Antonio Gramsci and the Origins of Italian Communism*. Stanford, CA: Stanford UP, 1967.

Cancogni, Manlio. "Testimonianza." Levi, *Carlo Levi e la Lucania* 9–10.

Capalbo, Francesco. "Il documentarista calabrese amico di Carlo Levi e di Vasco Pratolini." *Giornale interattivo di San Sosti e dintorni*. 30 June 2008.

Carbone, Mario. *Viaggio in Lucania con Levi*. Lerici: Edistampa Ed., 1980.

Carducci, Nicola. *Il viaggio intellettuale di Carlo Levi*. Lecce: Ed. Pensa/MultiMedia, 1999.

Cassano, Franco. "Cinquantasei anni dopo «Cristo»." De Donato and D'Amaro, "Carlo Levi e il Mezzogiorno" 9–16.

———. *Il pensiero meridiano*. Bari: Laterza, 1996.

Certeau, Michel de. *The Practice of Everyday Life*. Trans. Steven Rendall. Berkeley: U of California P, 1984.

Chambers, Iain. *Mediterranean Crossings: The Politics of an Interrupted Modernity*. Durham, NC: Duke UP, 2008.

Clerici, Luca. *Il viaggiatore meravigliato*. Milan: Il Saggiatore, 1999.

Clüver, Claus. "Quotation, Enargeia, and the Functions of Ekphrasis." *Pictures into Words: Theoretical and Descriptive Approaches to Ekphrasis*. Eds. Valerie Robillard and Else Jongeneel. Amsterdam: VU UP, 1998. 35–52.

Cohen, Richard. "Introduction: Humanism and Anti-humanism. Levinas, Cassirer, and Heidegger." Levinas, *Humanism of the Other* vii–xlvi.

Compagnon, Antoine. *Literature, Theory, and Common Sense*. Trans. Carol Cosman. Princeton, NJ: Princeton UP, 2004.

Consolo, Vincenzo. Prefazione. *Le parole sono pietre*. By Carlo Levi. 2nd ed. Turin: Einaudi, 1979. v–xiii.

Crang, Mike, and Nigel Thrift, eds. *Thinking Space*. London: Routledge, 2000.

Critchley, Simon. Introduction. *The Cambridge Companion to Levinas*. Eds. Simon Critchley and Robert Bernasconi. Cambridge, UK: Cambridge UP, 2002. 1–32.

Cristo si è fermato a Eboli. Dir. Francesco Rosi. Perf. Gian Maria Volontè, Paolo Bonacelli, Alain Cuny, Lea Massari, and Irene Papas. Franco Cristaldi and Nicola Carraro for RAI-TV2/Vides Cinematografica, Rome; Action Film, Paris, 1979.

Dainotto, Roberto. "A South with a View: Europe and Its Other." *Nepantla: Views from South* 1.2 (2000): 375–90.

D'Annunzio, Gabriele. *Nocturne and Five Tales of Love and Death*. Trans. Raymond Rosenthal. Marlboro, VT: Marlboro P, 1988.

———. *Notturno*. Milan: Treves, 1917.

D'Amaro, Sergio. *Le parole di Carlo Levi. Guida e dizionario tematico*. Bari: Stilo editrice, 2010.

———, and Salvatore Ritrovato, eds. "Carlo Levi e la letteratura di viaggio nel Novecento: Tra memoria, saggio e narrativa." *Proceedings of the international conference, San Marco in Lamis, 1 June 2002*. Foggia: Claudio Grenzi, 2003.

De Donato, Gigliola, ed. "Carlo Levi, il 'tempo' e la 'durata' in *Cristo si è fermato a Eboli* (1945–1995)." *Proceedings of the International Conference, Rome 15–16 March 1996*. Rome: Fahrenheit 451, 1999.

———, ed. "Carlo Levi nella storia e nella cultura italiana." *Conference Proceedings, Rome: May–June 1984*. Manduria: Lacaita, 1993.

———. "Carlo Levi e la narrativa del dopoguerra." Vitelli, *Il germoglio sotto la scorza* 205–20.

———. "Il viaggio in Carlo Levi tra mito e storia." D'Amaro and Ritrovato 9–17.

———. *Le parole del reale. Ricerche sulla prosa di Carlo Levi*. Bari: Dedalo, 1998.

———, ed. "L' 'Orologio' di Carlo Levi e la crisi della Repubblica." *Conference Proceedings, Rome, 9–10 June 1993*. Rome: Lacaita, 1997.

———. *Saggio su Carlo Levi*. Bari: De Donato, 1974.

———, and Sergio D'Amaro. *Un torinese del Sud: Carlo Levi*. Milan: Baldini and Castoldi, 2001.

———, and Sergio D'Amaro, eds. "Carlo Levi e il Mezzogiorno tra passato e presente." *Proceedings of the International Conference, Torremaggiore, 5 November 2001*. Foggia: Claudio Grenzi, 2003.

———, and Luisa Orioli, eds. "Carlo Levi nella storia e nella cultura italiana." *Seminar proceedings, Roma 1984*. Manduria: Lacaita, 1993.
Deleuze, Gilles. *Cinéma I: L'image-mouvement*. Paris: Les Éditions de Minuit, 1983.
———. *Cinéma II: L'image-temps*. Paris: Les Éditions de Minuit, 1985.
Del Guercio, Antonio. "Per Carlo Levi pittore." Levi, *Carlo Levi. Autoritratto* 61–78.
Derrida, Jacques. *Memoirs of the Blind: The Self-Portrait and Other Ruins*. Trans. Pascale-Anne Brault and Michael Naas. Chicago: Chicago UP, 1993.
———, and Anne Dufourmantelle. *Of Hospitality*. Trans. Rachel Bowlby. Stanford, CA: Stanford UP, 2000.
De Vitis, Maurizio. *Riforme agrarie e movimento contadino nel Mezzogiorno d'Italia. (1944–1950)*. Lecce: Piero Nanni, 1996.
Eco, Umberto. *Six Walks in the Fictional Woods*. Cambridge, MA: Harvard UP, 1994.
Falaschi, Giovanni. *Carlo Levi*. 1972. Firenze: La Nuova Italia, 1978.
Farrell, Joseph, ed. *The Voices of Carlo Levi*. New York: Peter Lang, 2007.
———. "Introduction: Carlo Levi and the Reconstruction of Civilization." Farrell 11–25.
———. "Conversations in Sicily." Farrell 127–146.
Fell, Joseph P. *Heidegger and Sartre: An Essay on Being and Place*. New York: Columbia UP, 1979.
Fonti, Daniela. "Carlo Levi pittore a Roma negli anni Trenta." *Carlo Levi e Roma. Il respiro della città: Catalogue of the Exhibit. Musei di Villa Torlonia, Casino dei Principi, 27 February–15 June 2008, Rome*. Ed. and cur. Daniela Fonti. Rome: Palombi editori, 2008. 13–27.
Fox, Nik Farrell. *The New Sartre: Explorations in Postmodernism*. New York: Continuum, 2003.
Freud, Sigmund. *Civilization and Its Discontents*. Ed. and trans. James Strachey. New York: Norton, 1961.
Gervasoni, Marco. *L'intellettuale come eroe*. Milan: La Nuova Italia, 2000.
Giacopini, Vittorio. "Paura della libertà." Vitelli, *Il germoglio sotto la scorza* 59–66.
Ghiazza, Silvana. *Carlo Levi e Umberto Saba. Storia di un'amicizia*. Bari: Dedalo, 2002.
Ginzburg, Natalia. "Testimonianza." Levi, *Carlo Levi e la Lucania* 12–14.
Girard, René. *La violence et le sacré*. Paris: Pluriel, 1972.
Gobetti, Piero. "La nostra cultura politica. 2." *La Rivoluzione Liberale* 2.6 (15 March 1923): 25–26.
———. "Manifesto." *La Rivoluzione Liberale* 1.1 (12 December 1922): 1–2. http://www.erasmo.it/liberale/ricerca.asp.
———. "Our Liberalism." *On Liberal Revolution*. By Gobetti. Ed. Nadia Urbinati. Trans. William McCuaig. New Haven, CT: Yale UP, 2000. 63–140.
Gramsci, Antonio. *The Gramsci Reader: Selected Writings, 1916–1935*. Ed. David Forgacs. Rev. ed. New York: New York UP, 2000.
———. *La questione meridionale*. Ed. Stefania Calledda. Cagliari: Davide Zedda, 2008.
———. *Selections from Cultural Writings*. Eds. David Forgacs and Geoffey Nowell-Smith. Trans. William Boelhower. Cambridge, MA: Harvard UP, 1985.

———. *The Southern Question.* Trans. Pasquale Verdicchio. Toronto: Guernica, 2006.
Grassi, Ernesto. *Vico and Humanism: Essays on Vico, Heidegger, and Rhetoric.* New York: Peter Lang, 1990.
Gregory, Derek. *Geographical Imaginations.* Cambridge, MA: Blackwell, 1994.
Grignani, Maria Antonietta, ed. *L'invenzione della verità: Testi e intertesti per* Cristo si è fermato a Eboli. Alessandria: Edizioni dell'Orso, 1998.
Harding, Desmond. *Writing the City: Urban Visions and Literary Modernism.* New York: Routledge, 2003.
Heidegger, Martin. "Letter on Humanism." Trans. William Barrett and Henry D. Aiken. *The Existentialist Tradition.* Ed. Nino Langiulli. Garden City, NY: Doubleday, 1971. 204–45.
———. "On the Origin of the Work of Art." *The Heidegger Reader.* Ed. Günter Figal. Trans. Jerome Veith. Bloomington: Indiana UP, 2009. 130–150.
Jørgensen, Conni-Kay. *L'eredità vichiana nel novecento letterario. Pavese, Savinio, Levi, Gadda.* Naples: Alfredo Guida, 2008.
Jung, Carl Gustav. "The Archetypes and the Collective Unconscious." *Collected Works of Carl Gustav Jung.* Vol. 9. 2nd ed. Princeton, NJ: Princeton UP, 1987.
Kermode, Frank. *The Sense of an Ending: Studies in the Theory of Fiction.* New York: Oxford UP, 1967.
Krieger, Murray. *Ekphrasis: The Illusion of the Natural Sign.* Baltimore, MD: Johns Hopkins UP, 1992.
Kristeva, Julia. *Revolution in Poetic Language.* Ed. Leon S. Roudiez. Trans. Margaret Waller. New York: Columbia UP, 1984.
———. "Word, Dialogue, and Novel." *Desire in Language: A Semiotic Approach to Literature and Art.* ed. Leon S. Roudiez. Trans. Thomas Gora, Alice Jardine, and Leon S. Roudiez. New York: Columbia UP, 1980. 64–91.
Lamberti, Maria Mimita. "La pittura del confino." De Donato, "Carlo Levi, il 'tempo' e la 'durata'" 231–40.
Lerner, Giovanna Faleschini. "Toward a Cinema of Painting: Francesco Rosi's *Cristo si è fermato a Eboli.*" *Italica* 86.2 (2009): 272–92.
Levi, Carlo. "Alberi e Narciso." Levi, *Lo specchio* 35–38.
———. "Antonio Salandra." *La Rivoluzione liberale* 1.25 (27 August 27). Rpt. in Levi, *Scritti politici* 3–16.
———. *Carlo Levi. Autoritratto.* Ed. Domenico Javarone. Rome: Carte Segrete, 1970.
———. *Carlo Levi. Con testo critico di Carlo Ludovico Ragghianti e testo inedito di Carlo Levi.* Firenze: Edizioni U, 1948.
———. *Carlo Levi e Lucania '61. Opere dal 1935 al 1961: Catalogue of the Exhibit, Centro d'arte e cultura, 12 November–12 December 1989, Benevento.* Ed. and cur. Giuseppe Appella. Rome: De Luca, 1989.
———. *Carlo Levi e la Lucania. Dipinti del confino 1935–1936: Catalogue of the Exhibit, Centro Carlo Levi in Palazzo Lanfranchi, Matera, 16 June–21 October 1990.* Ed. Pia Vivarelli. Rome: De Luca, 1990.

———. *Carlo Levi e Roma. Il respiro della città: Catalogue of the Exhibit.* Musei di Villa Torlonia, Casino dei Principi, 27 February–15 June 2008, Rome. Ed. and cur. Daniela Fonti. Rome: Palombi editori, 2008.

———. *Carlo Levi. Galleria di ritratti 1926–1960: Catalogue of the Exhibit,* Fondazione Carlo Levi, Roma, 8 March–26 November 2000. Ed. and cur. Pia Vivarelli. Rome: Donzelli, 2000.

———. *Carlo Levi. Gli anni fiorentini 1941–1945: Catalogue of the Exhibit.* Sala Esposizioni dell'Accademia del Disegno, Firenze, 4 July–29 August 2003. Ed. and cur. Piero Brunello and Pia Vivarelli. Rome: Donzelli, 2003.

———. *Carlo Levi. Mostra antologica: Catalogue of the Exhibit,* Mantova, Palazzo Te, 21 September–20 October 1974. Milan: Electa, 1974.

———. *Carlo Levi. Opere dal 1926 al 1973: Catalogue of the Exhibit,* Chiostro di S. Francesco, 16 Aprile–28 August 2005, Serra de' Conti. Ed. and cur. Fabio Benzi and Héloïse Romani. Serra de' Conti (AN): Comune di Serra de Conti, 2005.

———. *Carlo Levi. Opere grafiche: Catalogue of the Exhibit,* Sala Levi, Palazzo Lanfranchi, Matera 21 October 1997–10 January 1998. Eds. F. Fiorano and P. P. Tarasco. Matera: Centro Carlo Levi, 1997.

———. *Carlo Levi. Paesaggi 1926–1974. Lirismo e metamorfosi della natura: Catalogue of the Exhibit.* Fondazione Carlo Levi, Roma, 21 November 2001–27 April 2002. Ed. Pia Vivarelli. Rome: Donzelli, 2002.

———. *Carlo Levi si ferma a Firenze: Catalogue of the Exhibit,* Orsanmichele, May–July 1977. Ed. Carlo Ludovico Ragghianti. Firenze: Fratelli Alinari, 1977.

———. *Christ Stopped at Eboli.* Trans. Frances Frenaye. 1947. New York: Farrar, Straus and Giroux, 2006.

———. "Consiglio a un fotografo." Levi, *Lo specchio* 71–74.

———. "Crisi di civiltà." Levi, *Il dovere dei tempi* 60–62.

———. *Cristo si è fermato a Eboli.* 2nd ed. Turin: Einaudi, 1963.

———. *È questo il carcer tetro? Lettere dal carcere 1934–1935.* Ed. Daniela Ferraro. Genoa: Il melangolo, 1991.

———. *Essays on India.* Trans. Antony Shugaar. London: Hesperus, 2007.

———. *Fear of Freedom.* Ed. Stanislao Pugliese. Trans. Adolphe Gourevitch. New York: Columbia UP, 2008.

———. *Figure prima della storia 1935–1936: Catalogue of the Exhibit.* Museo Civico d'arte Palazzo Ricchieri, Pordenone, 11 March–14 March 2006. Ed. and cur. Giancarlo Pauletto. Pordenone: Comune di Pordenone, 2006.

———. *Fleeting Rome: In Search of La Dolce Vita.* Trans. Antony Shugaar. Hoboken, NJ: Wiley, 2004.

———. *Gli acquerelli di Carlo Levi per il film "Pietro Micca": Catalogue of the Exhibit.* Ed. Paolo Bertetto. Milan, Electa 1997.

———. *Gli anni di Parigi. Carlo Levi e i fuoriusciti 1926–1933: Catalogue of the Exhibit.* Archivio di Stato, Torino, 5 May–15 June 2003. Ed. Maria Cristina Maiocchi. Turin: Ministero per i Beni e le Attivita Culturali, 2003.

———. "Gramsci e il Mezzogiorno." Levi, *Il dovere dei tempi* 284–98.

———. "I ritratti." Levi, *Lo specchio* 9–21.

———. "I Sei di Torino." Levi, *Lo specchio* 99–104.

———. *I Sei di Torino 1929–1932: Catalogue of the Exhibit*. Ed. and cur. V. Viale. Turin: Galleria Civica d'Arte Moderna, 1965.

———. "Il contadino e l'orologio." Levi, *Prima e dopo le parole* 17–36.

———. *Il coraggio dei miti: Scritti contemporanei 1922–1974*. Ed. Gigliola De Donato. Bari: De Donato, 1975.

———. "Il disegno infantile." Levi, *Lo specchio* 31–34.

———. *Il dovere dei tempi. Prose politiche e civili*. Ed. Luisa Montevecchi. Rome: Donzelli, 2004.

———. "Il naufragio del Piloro." Levi, *Le tracce della memoria* 37–41.

———. *Il pianeta senza confini. Prose di viaggio*. Ed. Vanna Zaccaro. Rome: Donzelli, 2003.

———. "Il Tristram Shandy di Sterne." Levi, *Prima e dopo le parole* 147–54.

———. *L'altro mondo è il mezzogiorno. Contadini e luigini. Testi e disegni di Carlo Levi*. Ed. Leonardo Sacco. Rome: Basilicata ed., 1975. 2nd ed. Reggio Calabria: Casa del Libro, 1980.

———. "L'arte luigina e l'arte contadina." Levi, *Prima e dopo le parole* 37–50.

———. *La doppia notte dei tigli*. Turin: Einaudi, 1959.

———. *La strana idea di battersi per la libertà. Dai giornali della Liberazione (1944–1946)*. Ed. Filippo Benfante. Santa Maria Capua Vetere (CE): Edizioni Spartaco, 2005.

———. *Le mille patrie. Uomini, fatti, paesi d'Italia*. Ed. Gigliola De Donato. Rome: Donzelli, 2000.

———. *Le parole sono pietre (Tre giornate in Sicilia)*. Turin: Einaudi, 1955.

———. "Le ragioni di Danilo Dolci." *Racconti siciliani*. By Danilo Dolci. Palermo: Sellerio, 2008. 7–12.

———. *Le tracce della memoria*. Ed. Maria Pagliara. Rome: Donzelli, 2002.

———. "L'invenzione della verità." Levi, *Prima e dopo le parole* 51–54.

———. *L'Orologio*. 1950. Turin: Einaudi, 1989.

———. *Lo specchio: Scritti di critica d'arte*. Ed. Pia Vivarelli. Rome: Donzelli, 2001.

———. Manuscript, 6 April 1955. Università of Pavia, Fondo Manoscritti di Autori Moderni e Contemporanei, Fondo Carlo Levi, Diari e riflessioni, Cartella I.

———. Manuscript, 28 April 1957. Università of Pavia, Fondo Manoscritti, Cartella I.

———. Manuscript, 17 January 1933. Biblioteca Civica di Alassio, Fondo Carlo Levi, T4.

———. *Paura della libertà*. 1946. Rpt. in Levi, *Scritti politici* 132–204.

———. "Paura della pittura." Levi, *Lo specchio* 23–26.

———. "Piero Gobetti e 'La Rivoluzione Liberale.'" Levi, *Scritti politici* 85–108.

———. "Prefazione a *L'uva puttanella* e a *Contadini del sud*." Levi, *Prima e dopo le parole* 227–33.

———. *Prima e dopo le parole: Scritti e discorsi sulla letteratura*. Eds. Gigliola De Donato and Rosalba Galvagno. Rome: Donzelli, 2001.

———. *Quaderno a cancelli*. Turin: Einaudi, 1979.

———. "Riflessioni su 'Paura della pittura.'" Levi, *Lo specchio* 27–29.

———. *Ritratti, monotipi e disegni dal carcere: Catalogue of the Exhibit, Comune di Asiago*. Ed. Pia Vivarelli. Ferrara-Roma: Gabriele Corbo, 1995.

———. *Roma fuggitiva: Una città e i suoi dintorni*. Ed. Gigliola De Donato. Rome: Donzelli, 2002.

———. *Scritti politici*. Ed. David Bidussa. Turin: Einaudi, 2001.

———. "Seconda lettera dall'Italia." *Quaderni di Giustizia e Libertà*. 1.2 (1932): 10–16. Rpt. in Levi, *Scritti politici* 52–61.

———. "Sul nuovo umanesimo." Levi, *Prima e dopo le parole* 79–82.

———. *Temi e luoghi della pittura di Carlo Levi. Catalogue of the Exhibit, Matera: Palazzo Lanfranchi*. Ed. and cur. Pia Vivarelli. Naples: Paparo Edizioni, 1999.

———. *Tutto il miele è finito*. Turin: Einaudi, 1964.

———. *The Watch*. Trans. John Farrar. New York: Farrar, Straus & Young, 1951. Rpt. South Royalton, VT: Steerforth P, 1999.

———. *Words are Stones: Impressions of Sicily*. Trans. Antony Shugaar. London: Hesperus, 2005.

———, and Linuccia Saba. *Carissimo Puck. Lettere d'amore e di vita (1945–1969)*. Ed. Sergio D'Amaro. Rome: C. Mancosu, 1994.

Levinas, Emmanuel. *Humanism of the Other*. Trans. Nidra Poller. Urbana: U of Illinois P, 2003.

———. *Otherwise Than Being: Or Beyond Essence*. Trans. Alphonso Lingis. Boston: Kluwer, 1981.

———. *Totality and Infinity: An Essay on Exteriority*. Trans. Alphonso Lingis. Pittsburgh, PA: Duquesne UP, 1969.

Lucente, Gregory. *Beautiful Fables*. Baltimore, MD: Johns Hopkins UP, 1986. 246–65.

Luft, Sandra Rudnick. *Vico's Uncanny Humanism: Reading the New Science between Modern and Postmodern*. Ithaca, NY: Cornell UP, 2003.

Lukács, Georgy. "The Ideology of Modernism." Lukács, *Meaning of Contemporary Realism*. Trans. John and Necke Mander. London: Merlin P, 1963. 17–46.

Lupo, Giuseppe. "Tra inferno contadino e paradiso americano: Carlo Levi, Dante e la Bibbia." *Otto/Novecento* 18.1 (2004): 69–86.

Marcovecchio, Aldo, ed. *Carlo Levi*. Spec. issue of *Galleria* 17 (1967).

Marcus, Millicent. "Rosi's *Christ Stopped at Eboli*: A Tale of Two Italies." Marcus, *Italian Film in the Light of Neorealism*. Princeton, NJ: Princeton UP, 1986. 338–59.

Martin, James. *Piero Gobetti and the Politics of Liberal Revolution*. New York: Palgrave MacMillan, 2008.

Mazzotta, Giuseppe. *The New Map of the World: The Poetic Philosophy of Giambattista Vico*. Princeton, NJ: Princeton UP, 1999.

Meltzer, Françoise. *Salomé and the Dance of Writing: Portraits of Mimesis in Literature*. Chicago: Chicago UP, 1987.

Mitchell, W. J. T. *Iconology: Image, Text, Ideology*. Chicago: Chicago UP, 1986.

———. *Picture Theory: Essays on Verbal and Visual Representation*. Chicago: Chicago UP, 1994.

Mitry, Jean. *Aesthetics and Psychology in the Cinema.* Trans. Christopher King. Bloomington: Indiana UP, 1997.
Moloney, Brian. "*Cristo si è fermato a Eboli* and the Problem of the North." Farrell 99–118.
———. *Italian Novels of Peasant Crisis, 1930–1950: Bonfires in the Night.* Dublin: Four Courts P, 2005.
Morante, Elsa. *La Storia: Romanzo.* Turin: Einaudi, 1974.
Moravia, Alberto. "Carlo Levi." Levi, *Carlo Levi. Autoritratto.* 23–27.
Moretti, Franco. *Atlas of the European Novel 1800–1900.* London: Verso, 1998.
Muscetta, Carlo. "Leggenda e verità di Carlo Levi." Muscetta, *Realismo neorealismo controrealismo.* Milan: Garzanti 1976. 52–67.
Napolillo, Vincenzo. *Carlo Levi. Dall'antifascismo al mito contadino.* Cosenza: Ed. Brenner, 1984.
Nealon, Jeffrey. "The Ethics of Dialogue: Bakhtin and Levinas." *College English* 59 (1997): 129–48.
Oakeshott, Michael. *The Voice of Poetry in the Conversation of Mankind.* Cambridge, UK: Bowes and Bowes, 1959.
Pasolini, Pier Paolo. "Battute sul cinema." Pasolini, *Empirismo eretico* 227–36.
———. *Empirismo eretico.* Milan: Garzanti, 1972 (1991).
———. *Heretical Empiricism.* Trans. Ben Lawton and Louise K. Barnett. Bloomington: Indiana UP, 1988.
Patrizi, Giorgio. *Narrare l'immagine. La tradizione degli scrittori d'arte.* Rome: Donzelli, 2000.
Pauletto, Giancarlo. "Figure prima della storia 1935–1936." Levi, *Figure prima della storia.* 13–17.
Pautasso, Sergio. "Carlo Levi in Sardegna: Viaggiare da scrittore." *Carlo Levi: Le parole sono pietre. Proceedings of the International Conference. San Salvatore Monferrato, 28–30 April 1995.* Ed. Giovanna Ioli. San Salvatore Monferrato: Editrice Biennale Piemonte e Letteratura, 1977. 177–187.
Placanica, Augusto. "*Quaderno a cancelli.*" Vitelli, *Il germoglio sotto la scorza* 161–68.
Pugliese, Stanislao. "Introduction: Fear of Freedom and the Eternal Tendency Toward Fascism." Levi, *Fear of Freedom.* xxi–lvi.
Quintilian, Marcus Fabius. *Institutio Oratoria.* Trans. H. E. Butler. 4 vols. London: G. P. Putnam, 1921.
Rabinbach, Anson. "Heidegger's Letter on Humanism as Text and Event." *New German Critique* 62 (1994): 3–38.
Ricciardi, Alessia. *The Ends of Mourning: Psychoanalysis, Literature, and Film.* Stanford, CA: Stanford UP, 2003.
Rockmore, Tom. *Heidegger and French philosophy: Humanism, Antihumanism, and Being.* New York: Routledge, 1995.
Romani, Heloïse. "Carlo Levi: Breve diario di un percorso pittorico." Levi, *Opere dal 1926 al 1973* 23–40.
Rorty, Richard. *Philosophy and the Mirror of Nature.* Princeton, NJ: Princeton UP, 2009.
Rosenthal, Raymond. Preface. D'Annunzio, *Nocturne* 1–6.

Rossi Doria, Manlio. "La crisi del governo Parri nel racconto di Carlo Levi." De Donato, "Carlo Levi nella storia e nella cultura italiana" 181–192.

———. *La riforma agraria e azione meridionalista*. Bologna: Ed. Agricole, 1948.

Russo, Giovanni. *Lettera a Carlo Levi*. Rome: Ed Riuniti, 2001.

Russo, John Paul. "Freud and Italy," *Literature and Psychology* 36.1–2 (1990): 1-25.

Saba, Linuccia. "Testimonianza." Levi, *Quaderno a cancelli* ix–xi.

Saba, Umberto. "Fratellanza." Saba, *Tutte le Poesie*. Ed. Arrigo Stara. Milan: Mondadori, 1988. 626.

Sacco, Leonardo. *L'Orologio della Repubblica. Carlo Levi e il caso Italia*. Rev. ed. Rome: Basilicata Ed., 1999.

Sacerdoti, Guido. "Divagazioni sugli *Amanti* di Carlo Levi." Levi, *Carlo Levi. Opere grafiche*. 23-35.

Sartre, Jean-Paul. *The Humanism of Existentialism*. Trans. Bernard Frechtman. New York: Philosophical Library, 1947.

———. "L'universale singolare." Trans. Aldo Marcovecchio. *Galleria* 17 (1967): 259–60.

Saunders, George R. "Critical ethnocentrism and the Ethnology of Ernesto De Martino." *The American Anthropologist* 95 (1993): 875–93.

Scotellaro, Rocco. *Contadini del sud*. Rome: Laterza, 1954.

———. *L'uva puttanella*. Rome: Laterza, 1956.

Serao, Matilde. *Il ventre di Napoli*. Milan: Treves, 1884.

Sholz, Bernhard F. "'Sub Oculos Subiecto' Quintilian on *Ekphrasis* and *Enargeia*." *Pictures into Words: Theoretical and Descriptive Approaches to Ekphrasis*. Eds. Valerie Robillard and Else Jongeneel. Amsterdam: VU UP, 1998. 73–99.

Sperduto, Donato. "Carlo Levi e l'invenzione della verità." *Critica letteraria* 125 (2004): 789–95.

———, ed. *Carlo Levi inedito con 40 disegni della cecità*. Milazzo: Spes, 2002.

———. "Carlo Levi pensatore." Sperduto, *Carlo Levi inedito* 123–27.

———. *Maestri futili? Gabriele D'Annunzio, Carlo Levi, Cesare Pavese, Emanuele Severino*. Rome: Aracne, 2009.

———. "Carlo Levi: Un vero 'poeta.'" *Forum Italicum* 43. 1 (2009): 247–55.

———. "Ogni rosa è nera quando è sera." Sperduto, *Carlo Levi inedito* 11–15.

———. "'Tempus Fugit.' Sul *Quaderno a cancelli* di Carlo Levi." *Levia Gravia* 10 (2008): 147–57.

———. "Tra azione e inazione: Il *Cristo si è fermato a Eboli* di Levi e *La fiaccola sotto il moggio* di D'Annunzio." *Critica letteraria* 135 (2007): 319–36.

Stacchini, Vanna Gazzola. "Forme di coscienza ebraica in Carlo Levi." De Donato, "Carlo Levi, il 'tempo' e la 'durata.'" 115–24.

———. "Personaggi nella storia-non storia." De Donato, "L' 'Orologio' di Carlo Levi e la crisi della Repubblica." 139–46.

Steiner, Wendy. *The Real Real Thing*. Chicago: U of Chicago P, 2010.

Stone, Marla Susan. *The Patron State: Culture and Politics in Fascist Italy*. Princeton, NJ: Princeton UP, 1998.

Torriglia, Anna Maria. *Broken Time, Fragmented Space: A Cultural Map for Postwar Italy*. Toronto: Toronto UP, 2002.

Trombadori, Antonello. "Rosi nell'occhio dell'attore." *Francesco Rosi.* Ed. Sebastiano Gesù. Acicatena: Incontri con il cinema, 1991. 75-77.
Visconti, Luchino. "Anthropomorphic Cinema." *Springtime in Italy: A Reader on Neo-Realism.* Ed. and trans. David Overbey. London: Talisman Books, 1978. 83–85.
———. "Il cinema antropomorfico." Luchino Visconti. http://www.luchinovisconti.net/visconti_al/cinema_antropomorfico.htm.
Vitelli, Franco, ed. "Il germoglio sotto la scorza. Carlo Levi vent'anni dopo." *Proceedings of the "Giornate leviane," Matera, 1995.* Cava de' Tirreni: Avagliano, 1998.
Vivarelli, Pia. "Carlo Levi pittore negli anni della Guerra." Levi, *Carlo Levi. Gli anni fiorentini* 217–22.
———. "Carlo Levi tra impegno politico e pittura." Levi, *Ritratti, monotipi e disegni dal carcere.* N.p.
———. "Diario pittorico del confino." Levi, *Carlo Levi e la Lucania* 23–29.
———. Introduction. Levi, *Temi e luoghi della pittura di Carlo Levi* 7–15.
———. Introduction. Levi, *Lo specchio* xi–xix.
Ward, David. *A Poetics of Resistance: Narrative and the Writings of Pier Paolo Pasolini.* Madison, NJ: Fairleigh Dickinson Press, 1995.
———. *Antifascisms: Cultural Politics in Italy, 1943–46: Benedetto Croce and the Liberals, Carlo Levi and the "Actionists."* Madison, NJ: Farleigh Dickinson UP, 1996.
———. *Carlo Levi: Gli italiani e la paura della libertà.* Milan: Rizzoli/Nuova Italia, 2002.
———. "From North to South. Resistance and Creativity in Carlo Levi's *L'orologio.*" *Italy and America, 1943–1944: Italian, American, and Italian American Experiences of the Liberation of the Italian Mezzogiorno.* Ed. John Davis. Naples: La città del sole, 1997. 391–410.
———. *Piero Gobetti's New World: Antifascism, Liberalism, Writing.* Toronto: Toronto UP, 2010.
Wells, Maria Xenia. "Carlo Levi e la Lucania: La parola e l'immagine." Grignani 167–79.
———. "La parola e l'immagine. Un'esame dei quadri di Lucania e del manoscritto di *Cristo si è fermato a Eboli.*" De Donato, "Carlo Levi, il 'tempo' e la 'durata'" 241–49.
White, Hayden. *The Content of the Form: Narrative Discourse and Historical Representation.* Baltimore, MD: Johns Hopkins UP, 1987.
Zaccaro, Vanna. "Il viaggio di Carlo Levi in India. Carlo Levi e la letteratura di viaggio nel Novecento." D'Amaro and Ritrovato 103–16.
———. "Reportages dai sud del mondo." Levi, *Il pianeta senza confini* xxv–xlviii.

Index

In this index, numbers in italics refer to illustrations.

Aci Trezza, 109–10
Action Party, 55, 57–58, 60, 82, 169n11
Adorno, Theodor, 54, 65
Africa. *See* colonialism
Alberti, Leon Battista, 170n15
Aliano. *See* Gagliano
Alicata, Mario, 156n21, 165n12
Alighieri, Dante, 10, 28, 81, 112, 160n16, 160n18
animality, 34–39, 109–10, 116
animals
   and Giulia Venere, 34–35, 38–39
   and peasant mentality, 36–37, 109–10, 116
   as artistic subjects, 10, 11, 64
   as part of multiplicity of reality, 67, 111, 113, 116
   See also animality
antifascism, 2–3, 88, 154–55n8
   See also fascism, totalitarianism
Arouimi, Michel, 160n19, 160n23
art
   abstract, 8–9, 11–12, 14, 126, 141, 145
   as epistemological tool, xviii, 35–36, 46–49, 83, 87–88, 90, 143
   as freedom, 2, 5–8, 12, 143
   as invention of truth, 9–12, 17, 19, 46–49, 61, 90–91, 135, 159n20
   as salvation, 67, 134
   as totality, 7, 67
   modern, 2, 7–12, 132–33, 157n30
   realist, 9–12, 17, 30, 46, 126–28, 132, 133–35, 138, 157n30
   theory of, 7–12

   See also avant-garde, painting, portraiture, realism
   See also under Levi, *paintings*
autonomy, 3, 15, 49, 50, 88–92, 96, 160n24, 165n14, 165n17
   See also Gobetti
avant-garde, 132–34

Bacarella, Antonino, 164n5
Bakhtin, Mikhail, 1, 24, 67, 137, 158n34
Baldassaro, Lawrence, 5, 156n24, 164n8
Balla, Giacomo, 153n5
Baudelaire, Charles, 54, 62–65, 79, 161n7
Bauzulli, Chiara, 155n18
Benjamin, Walter, 65–66, 161n7, 161n8
Berezin, Mabel, 154n5
Bergson, Henri, 53, 137–38, 155n15
Bernardi, Emanuele, 164n5
Berta, Giuseppe, 165n14
Berto, Gian Paolo, 126
Bible, 5, 80, 97
blindness, 85, 125–48
   and invisibility, 130–31
   as illness, 126, 130–31, 134–35
Borsellino, Nino, 155n8
Boswell, Jessie, 153n4
Bronzini, Giovanni Battista, 160n18, 165n11
Buber, Martin, 14, 157–58n32
Bucci, Anselmo, 153n5
Burmese warrior, 126, 138, 143–48, 169n13

Calvino, Italo, 64, 157n27, 167n26
Camus, Albert, 5
Cancogni, Manlio, xv, 25–26
Carbone, Mario, 119–23, *121*, *122*
Carbonia, 115–16
Carnevale, Salvatore, 101, 104–7
Carrà, Mario, 153n5
Cassano, Franco, 50–51, 165n10
Catania, 166n23
Cézanne, Paul, 7
Chessa, Gigi, 153n4
Christ
 and Lucanian peasants (*see under* peasants)
 Carnevale as, 104, 106–7
 Dolci as, 104
 Impellitteri as, 97–98
Christian Democratic Party, 56, 57
Clerici, Luca, 167n26
Cola Pesce, 81
Coletti, Duilio, 163n17
colonialism
 in southern Italy, 86, 116
 Italian, in Africa, 50–51
 Portuguese, in Madagascar, 129
Compagnon, Antoine, 156n22
Consolo, Vincenzo, 86
contadini. *See* peasants
contemporaneità
 in *L'Orologio*, 66–73, 76–77, 82
 in *Quaderno a cancelli*, 137–38
 in *Tutto il miele è finito*, 111–18
Court of Miracles
 as space of resistance, 76, 162n14
Croce, Benedetto, 3, 71, 81, 154n8

D'Amaro, Sergio, 155n10, 163n2
D'Annunzio, Gabriele, 22, 125, 136, 159n6
death, 17, 30, 50, 109–10, 136, 137, 149–50, 166n20
 and love, 143–45, 148
 and poetry, 134, 168n6
 and religion, 5
 and time, 53, 81–82

Carnevale's, 104, 106–7
 mother's, 143, 145, 148
 of Lercara miner, 98
 of Levi's father, 81, 149–50
 of Levi's uncle, 81–82
 Scotellaro's, 94
De Chirico, Giorgio, 153n5
De Donato, Gigliola, 85, 154n7, 155n10, 156n24, 160n2, 163n2
De Martino, Ernesto, 156n21
Democrazia Cristiana (DC). *See* Christian Democratic Party
Del Guercio, Antonio, 101
Deleuze, Gilles, 158n36
Derrida, Jacques, 159n16
De Vitis, Maurizio, 164n5
dialogism, 1, 16, 18–19, 24–25, 36–37, 53, 150–51, 158n34, 159n8
 See also interart dialogue
Dolci, Danilo, 87, 101–4, *102*, *103*, 119, *120*
Dorso, Guido, 92, 119, *120*
dreams, xx, 53–54, 71, 125, 127, 133, 137, 169n9, 169n10, 169n11
Dudreville, Lonardi, 153n5
durée, 53, 137

Eagleton, Terry, 155n15
Eco, Umberto, 151, 155n15
Einaudi, Giulio, 25
Einaudi, Luigi, 3
ekphrasis, xvi–xvii, xix, 18, 23–28, 37–38, 41–44, 46, 61–65, 73–76, 82–83, 86, 137, 159n7
Energie Nove, 154n8
engagement, political, xvii, xviii, xx, 2, 24, 86, 90, 123, 133, 150
Enlightenment, xviii, 18, 24, 88, 132, 164–65n10
exile
 from Eden, 71, 131–33, 144–45
 in Lucania, 5, 11, 21–23, 25, 28, 30, 90, 123, 160n15
Expressionism, 11, 30, 154n5, 157n27

Fanelli, Giovanni, 46–47
Farrell, Joseph, 97–98
fascism, 2–3, 5–7, 44–46, 69, 81, 88–90, 153n5, 154–55n8
  See also totalitarianism
father, 70–71, 81–82
  and *Il Naufragio del Piloro*, 148–50
  uncle as, 76
fear
  of freedom, 3, 5–6, 8, 89–90, 118, 133, 144–45, 151
  of representation, 34–35, 90
Fell, Joseph, 155n11
FILEF, xix
flâneur. *See* Baudelaire
folklore, 24, 35–36, 86, 108, 166n23
Fortunato, Giustino, 92, 119, *120*, 159n5
freedom
  and adulthood, 71, 81
  and art, 2, 5, 7, 10, 30
  and creativity, 90, 91, 104
  and love, 12, 30, 141–43
  and the Other, 13, 15, 30
  as opposed to religion, 5–7
  political, 3, 54, 60, 64, 88, 96, 115, 151
  Compare fear, totalitarianism
Freud, Sigmund, 68, 155n15, 160n20,
Fromm, Eric, 155n15
Funi, Achille, 153n5
futility, 128–30, 137–38, 143, 150, 168n3

Gagliano, Rita, 21, 33, 35–36, 44, 46–48, 159n4
Galante, Nicola, 153n4
galantuomini. *See* Luigini
Gallura, 113–14
Garosci, Aldo, 30
Gazzola Stacchini, Vanna, 161n10
gender, 14–15, 158n33, 160n21
  and power, 30–41
Gervasoni, Marco, 155n9
Ginzburg, Leone, 2

Ginzburg, Natalia, 25
Girard, René, 155n17
Giustizia e Libertà, 2, 87
Gobetti, Piero
  and Gramsci, 3, 88, 89, 154n8, 155n9, 165n16
  autonomy, 3, 15, 88–89
  biography, 154–55n8
  fascism, 3, 81
  southern question, 87–89, 158–59n3, 159n5
  influence on Levi, xvii, 2–3, 6, 15, 87–89, 111, 150, 158–59n3, 160n24, 166n22
  "Manifesto della Rivoluzione Liberale," 88–89
Gramsci, Antonio, 3, 89, 157n30
  folklore, 24
  language, 22, 60, 107
  organic intellectual, 46, 90, 160n22
  Risorgimento, 60, 88, 165n16
  southern question, 94, 96, 165n13, 165n17
Grassano, 10, 21, 26–28, *29*, 123
Grassi, Ernesto, 4, 10, 11, 155n13
Grignani, Maria Antonietta, 159n13

Heidegger, Martin, xvii-xvii, 156n19, 157n30
  Letter on Humanism, 4, 155n13
  "On the Origin of the Work of Art," 9, 156n23, 157n25
  relativism, 9, 155n
history
  and narrative, 54, 66–67, 161n9, 161n12, 169n9
  and the South, xviii, 10–12, 15, 21, 23–24, 37, 38, 49, 78, 86–87, 92, 94, 96–99, 107–11, 114–19, 163n19
  as opposed to futility, 108–9, 168n6
  as progress, xviii, xix, 3–4, 6, 23, 50–53, 65–66, 68, 69–71, 82, 132–33, 137, 145
  cultural, 135–36

history (*continued*)
   Levi's theory of, 5–8, 89–90, 156n23
   See also narrative, progress, time, Vico
Homer, 109
Huizinga, Johan, 155n15
humanism, xvii-xviii, 1–19, 136, 150, 153n2, 155n11, 155n13, 156–57n18, 160n16
   and modern art, 132–33, 157n30
   of existentialism, 3–4
   of the Other, xvii-xviii, 12–19

Iacopone da Todi, 166n21
Ichino, Anna Maria, 170n16
illness, 33, 78, 125–26, 130, 145
   as cultural construct 135–36, 145
   as political metaphor, 3, 81, 150
   malaria, 44, 46
   See also blindness
image
   abstract, 132
   and consciousness, 9–14, 47, 135, 139, 141
   and gender, 19, 33, 38
   and power, 14–15, 33, 37–38, 99
   and religion, 6
   as irrational, 24, 38
   as subversive, 17, 24, 37–38, 41, 49
   cinematic, 17, 25, 110, 158n35, 158n36
   in tension with time, xviii, 49, 53
   in word-image relations (*see* interart dialogue; *see also under* word)
   See also art
impegno. *See* engagement
Impellitteri, Vincent, 97–98
Impressionism, 82–83, 154n5
India, 85, 151, 163n3
indistinction, 5, 10–11, 15, 18, 85, 90–91, 94, 116, 144–45
indistinto originario. *See* indistinction
interart dialogue, xv-xx, 18–19, 23–26, 37–38, 61–62, 111, 126, 136, 150–51

intellectual project
   Levi's, 1–19, 21, 81, 87, 133, 151
intellectuals
   and the subaltern, 21–22, 24, 46–47, 90–91
   as *contadini*, 59–60, 119
   See also under Gramsci
Isnello, 97–98, 110
Italia Libera, 55
Italian Communist Party (PCI), 55, 82
Italy
   postwar, 55–56, 77, 82, 137
   theory of the two Italies, 15, 21, 22, 50, 59, 88, 115, 117–18, 166–67n25

Jonah, 80–81
Joyce, James, 53
Jung, Carl Gustav, 10, 155n15, 156n24, 160n20, 161n11

Kermode, Frank, 161n12
Kristeva, Julia, 159n8

labor movement
   in prewar Turin, 3, 89
   in Sardinia, 85, 87, 115
   in Sicily, 85, 87, 98–99, 108–9
Lamberti, Maria Mimita, 160n20
language, 166n22
   and religion (*see under* religion)
   and the peasants (*see under* peasants)
   dialogic, xvii, 15–19, 25, 83, 158n34
   distrust of, 57
   Italian, 16, 22, 57, 107–8
   Latin, 47, 57
   of *contemporaneità* (see *contemporaneità*)
   of politics, 45–46, 58–62, 106–8, 116
   nonreferential, 127–28
   poetic (*see* poetic language)
   visual, xvi, xix, 26, 46, 73, 138 (*see also* ekphrasis)
Lavorgna, Antonella, 166n18

Leopardi, Giacomo, 136, 168–9n7
Lercara. *See* labor movement in Sicily
Levi, Carlo
　drawings: *Gli Amanti*, 12, 138, 141, 143, *142*, 148; *Narcissus*, 138–39, *140*; *Perdita della madre*, 145, *146*; *Perdita dell'immortalità*, 145, *147*, 148
　literary works: *Cristo si è fermato a Eboli* xvii-xix, 10, 12, 14–16, 18–19, 25–51, 59, 61, 69–70, 78, 86–90, 97, 99, 106–7, 109–10, 116–17, 136, 151, 156n21, 159n6, 159n11, 159n13, 160n18, 160n1; *Le parole sono pietre*, xix, 85–111, 116, 136–37, 163n3, 164n6; *L'Orologio*, xvii, xviii-xix, 18–19, 53–83, 85, 107, 111, 117, 136–37, 150, 160n1, 161n4, 161n5, 161n10, 162n16; *Paura della libertà*, xvii, 5–7, 14–15, 17–18, 37, 67, 69, 89, 118, 134, 155n15, 155n16, 156n23, 160n20, 164n8, 169n14; "Paura della pittura," xvii, 7–9, 11, 126, 131–32, 155n14, 160n20; *Quaderno a cancelli*, xvii, xix, xx, 12, 125–51; *Tutto il miele è finito*, xix, 86–87, 111–18, 123, 137, 164n6
　other writings: "Alberi e Narciso," 139; "Antonio Salandra," 45, 159n3; "Consiglio a un fotografo," 123; "Crisi di civiltà," 6–7, 69; *È questo il carcer tetro?*, 126, 158n2; "Gramsci e il Mezzogiorno," 94, 96; "Il contadino e l'orologio," 10–11, 15, 30, 46, 83, 90–91, 115, 117, 166n24; "Il disegno infantile," 143; "Il naufragio del Piloro," 148–50; "Il Tristram Shandy di Sterne," 53; "I ritratti," 13–14, 28, 36, 87, 138, 139, 141, 143, 151; "I Sei di Torino," 2; "L'arte luigina e l'arte contadina," 61–62; "L'invenzione della verità," 19, 48–49, 135; "Le ragioni di Danilo Dolci," 104; "Piero Gobetti e 'La Rivoluzione Liberale,'" 2–3; "Prefazione a *L'uva puttanella* e a *Contadini del sud*," 90–91; "Riflessioni su 'Paura della pittura,'" 9; "Seconda lettera dall'Italia," 3; "Sul nuovo umanesimo," 1, 11–12
　paintings: *Grassano come Gerusalemme*, 26–28, *29*, 123; *Lamento per Rocco Scotellaro*, 94, *95*, 119, 123; *La porta del sud*, 104, *105*; *La Santarcangelese*, 41, *42*; *Le parole sono pietre*, 101, *102*; *L'eroe cinese*, 30, *32*; *Lucania '61*, 119, *120*, 123, 167n27; *Ritratto del dottore*, 41, *43*; *Ritratto della madre*, 30, *31*; *Ritratto di Danilo Dolci*, 87, 101, *103*; *Ritratto di Giulia Venere*, 37–41, *40*; *Ritratto di Rocco Scotellaro*, 87, 92, *93*
Levinas, Emmanuel, xviii, 4, 13–14, 19, 155n14, 157n32
　See also humanism of the Other
Liberal Party, 45, 55
liberalism, 45, 81
　and Gobetti (*see under* Gobetti)
Libya. *See* colonialism
Longhi, Roberto, 74
Lucania, xviii, 10–11, 19, 21–51, 85, 98, 115, 116, 117, 123, 129, 160n16
　See also under peasants
Lucente, Gregory, 168n6
Luft, Sandra, 156n19, 157n29
Luigini, 57–61, 82, 107, 136
　Compare to peasants

Lukács, Georgy, 157n30
Lupo, Giuseppe, 160n18

Magalone, Luigi, 44–46
　See also *Luigini*
magic
　and death, 33
　and Giulia Venere (*see* Venere, Giulia)
　as illusory power, 8, 129
　in peasant mentality (*see under* peasants)
　painting as (*see under* painting)
　poetry as (*see* poetry)
Malerba, Gian Emilio, 153n5
Manzoni, Alessandro, 136, 169n9
Marcus, Millicent, 164n7
Marussig, Piero, 153n5
mass, concept of the, 6, 8, 50, 54, 65, 133, 161n7, 168n4
Matera, 49, 115, 117–18, 169n14
Mazzarone, Rocco, 119, *120*
Mazzotta, Giuseppe, 155n15, 156n19, 157n28
memory, xix, 54, 68, 73, 91, 111–13, 125–52, 162n16
　See also *contemporaneità*, time
Menzio, Francesco, 153n4, 165n11
meridionalismo
　classic, 92, 119,
　Levi's, 90–92, 94–96, 156n21, 160n24, 165n13
　See also Gobetti, Gramsci
Mitchell, W. J. T., xvi, 24, 38, 159n7
Mitry, Jean, 158n35
modernism. *See* art
modernity, xviii, 8, 21, 24, 49–51, 65–69, 90–91, 115–16, 131–34, 156n19, 164n10
Moloney, Brian, 165n13
Montale, Eugenio, 154n8
Morandi, Giorgio, 153n5
Morante, Elsa, 168n6
Moravia, Alberto, 104, 165n15
Moretti, Franco, 162n15
mortality. *See* death

mother
　as archetype, 143–48, 161n11
　in peasant civilization, 35
　Levi's, correspondence with, 27–28
　　(*see also* portraits)
Mostra delle regioni, 119
Muscetta, Carlo, 98, 119, *120*, 161n6, 165n11, 165n13
Mussolini, Benito, 45, 50–51, 115, 153n5, 154n8
myth, 155n9, 161n11,
　and memory, 126–27
　as opposed to religion, 5, 7
mythical imagination, xviii, 24, 36, 38, 70
mythical time. *See under* time
mythopoiesis. *See* poetry

Naples, 55, 68, 76–82, 158n3
Napolillo, Vincenzo, 154n7, 164n5, 166n1
Narcissus, xx, 12, 126, 138–39, *140*, 150, 169n14, 170n15
Navarra, Giuseppe
　king of Poggioreale, 162n17
Nazione del popolo, La, 6, 69
Nazism, 5–6, 69, 162n16, 54, 66, 132
Nietzsche, Friedrich, 155n15
Nitti, Vincenzo, 119, *120*
Novecento, 2, 153–54n5

Oakeshott, Michael, 153n3
occhialino, 131–35
Olivetti, Adriano
　and Comunità, 165n14
Olivetti, Paola, 159n4, 169n11
Oppi, Ubaldo, 153n5
Ordine Nuovo, 154n8, 155n9
Ortega y Gasset, José, 155n15
Orune, 111
Other, 4, 24, 30, 36, 49, 67, 135, 139–43, 151, 155n14, 157–58n32, 159n10, 160n20
　See also humanism of the Other
Otto, Rudolf, 155n15

painting
    and magic, xviii, 29, 33–34, 46–47, 48
    and power, xviii, xix, 12–16, 33–36 (*see also* gender, image)
    and writing, xv-xx, 25–26, 28, 61–62, 86–77, 111 (*see also* ekphrasis, interart dialogue, visual)
    oetics, word
    as epistemological tool (*see under* art)
    as source for *Cristo si è fermato a Eboli*, 25, 86–87
    before Lucania, 2, 30
    landscape, 26–28
    Lucanian, 11–12, 25–51, 160n20 (*see also under* Levi, *individual paintings*)
    portraiture: and photography, 123; theory of, 12–14, 36, 44, 87, 99, 141; verbal, xvii, 26, 38–39, 41, 44–45, 101
    See also art, image
Palazzo Altieri, 73–76, 161n10, 162n13, 162n14
Paris, 2, 3, 54, 76, 154n6, 161n7, 162n15, 162n16
Parrella, Michele, 119, *120*
Parri, Ferruccio, 55–56, 58, 60, 169n11
Partito d'Azione. *See* Action Party
Pasolini, Pier Paolo
    cinema of poetry, 17–18, 25, 158n36, 159n11
    free indirect discourse 15–17, 24, 159n9
    language, 107–8, 168n5
Patrizi, Giorgio, 74
Paulucci, Enrico, 153n4
Pavese, Cesare, 136
peasant movement, 85–86, 96–97, 104, 115, 118–19, 123
peasant poetry, 11–13, 61–62, 86, 90–91, 129–30
peasant revolution, 49, 60, 82

peasants
    and language, 58–61, 86
    culture of, 70, 78, 90–91
    Lucanian xviii, 21–51: and art, 9–12, 14–16, 18–19, 35–36, 46–49, 61, 86–87; and Christ, 21–23, 97, 129; and death, 107; and language, 21–23, 45–46, 48; in Levi's painting, 12, 28–30, 41; mentality, xviii, 18, 21–24, 25, 35–37
    See also art, autonomy, portraits, realism
philosophy. *See* theory
photography, 99–100, 119, 123, 167n28
Piano di rinascita, 118
Picasso, Pablo, 7–8, 133, 169n11
Placanica, Augusto, 168n3
poetic language, 4, 5, 10–11, 90–91, 106, 129–30, 143, 155n13, 168n6
poetry, 9, 83
    and painting (*see* interart dialogue; *see also under* image)
    as invention of truth (*see under* art)
    as metonymy for art, 9–12, 19, 25, 90
    as opposed to religion, 5–7
    cinema of (*see under* Pasolini)
    Levi's, 7, 25, 30, 86–87, 126, 127, 128, 137, 143
    Lucania '61 as pictorial poem, 119
    Paura della libertà as philosophical poem, xvi, 5, 89, 155n15
    Scotellaro's, 90–92, 94, 108, 119, 165n11
politics. *See* engagement, labor movement, resistance; *See also* language
portraits, discussion of 11, 63–64, 87
    of Lucanian peasants, 41, 99, 104
    See also portraiture, self-portrait
    See also under Levi, *individual paintings*
portraiture. *See under* painting

positivism, xvii, 3, 4, 65, 81, 137
　See also rationalism
power
　as opposed to futility, 129, 143
　of art, 67, 86–87, 89–90, 99, 134, 143, 150 (*see also under* painting)
　of language, 18, 107–9, 114, 129
　of sexual desire, 35
　of the image (*see under* image)
　of the individual, 67
　of the party, 106
　of the state, 6, 9–10, 59–61, 22, 167n14 (*compare* autonomy)
　subversive, 76, 77–78
primordial chaos. *See* indistinction
progress. *See under* history, time
Proust, Marcel, 162n16
psychoanalysis, 6, 9, 68, 133, 155n15, 156n24, 160n20
psychology, 5, 28, 85, 117, 135, 138
Pugliese, Stanislao, 155n15

questione meridionale. *See* southern question; *See also* Gobetti, Gramsci
Quintilian, 23, 27, 61

Rabinbach, Anson, 155n12
rationalism, xviii, 5–7, 65, 70, 82, 132, 156n19, 156n21
　See also positivism, reason
realism, 126, 132, 134, 157n30, 165n15
　as *realismo contadino*, 11–12, 30, 46
　See also under art
reason, 6, 21–22, 36–37, 66–67, 69, 90, 98, 113, 118
Reismann, Janos, 167n28
religion, 15, 36–37, 129, 135, 155n17, 168n4
　and art, 6–7, 41
　and language, 5–6
　as sacrifice, 5–6
　of the state, 49, 88
　Compare to sacred

religious. *See* religion
representation. *See* art, gender, image, painting, poetry
resistance
　cultural, xviii, 2, 24, 33, 35, 49–50, 101, 130, 154n8, 168n6
　antifascist Resistance: as *rivoluzione contadina*, 60, 82; failure of, xvii, xix, 54, 55–56, 60, 82–83, 137
Ricciardi, Alessia, 24, 159n10
Rimbaud, Arthur, 13, 139
Rivoluzione liberale, 2, 87, 88, 154n8, 159n5, 166n22
Rockmore, Tom, 153n2, 155n12
Rome, 53–76, 161n5, 162n14
　and painting, 161n4
　as opposed to Matera, 49
　as opposed to Turin, 68–69
　See also contemporaneità
Ronga people, 129–30, 168n6
Rorty, Richard, 153n3
Rosi, Francesco, 159n11, 164n7
Rosselli, Carlo, 2, 87, 166–7n25
Rossi Doria, Manlio, 58, 90, 119, *120*, 158n3, 164n5, 165n11
Russo, Giovanni, 165n13

Saba, Linuccia, 127, 134, 143, 170n16
Saba, Umberto, 119, *120*, 145, 170n16
Sacco, Leonardo, 160n3
Sacco, Luigi, 165n11
Sacerdoti, Guido, 141
sacred
　as opposed to religion, 5–6, 15, 36–37
Salandra, Antonio, 45, 159n3
Salvemini, Gaetano, 3, 154n8
Santarcangelese, la. *See* Venere, Giulia
Sapegno, Natalino, 3
Sardinia, xix, 85, 86, 87, 137, 163n3, 164n6
　in *Tutto il miele è finito*, 111–19
　See also contemporaneità

Sarfatti, Margherita, 153n5
Sarno, Antonio, 155n15
Sartre, Jean-Paul, xvii, 3–4
Saunders, George, 156n21
Scotellaro, Rocco, 11, 86, 87, 90–94, 93, 95, 108, 119, *120*, 123, 165n11, 165n14
Sei di Torino, i, 2
self-portrait, 99, 138–39
Serao, Matilde, 163n18
Serio, Francesca, 101, *102*, *103*, 104–8, 111, 116
Severino, Emanuele, 168n3
sexuality, 34–35, 131
  See also gender
Sicily, xix, 85, 86, 87
  in *Le parole sono pietre*, 96–111
  See also Carnevale, labor movement, Serio
Simonides of Ceos. See interart dialogue
Sironi, Mario, 153n5
Soldati, Mario, 119, 167n27
South. See Lucania, peasants, Sardinia, Sicily, southern question, southern thought
southern question, 87–88, 94, 96, 156n21, 158–9n3
  See also autonomy, Gobetti, Gramsci
southern thought, 49–51, 163n3, 169n11
Soviet Union, 85
Spengler, Oswald, 155n15
Sperduto, Donato, 138, 139, 159n6, 168n3, 169n12
Stampa, La, xix, 85
Steiner, Wendy, 158n33
Sterne, Laurence, 53
Stirpe, Mario, 169n13
Stone, Marla, 154n5

theory
  of art (*see under* art)
  of creativity, 86, 89–91, 164n8
  of history (*see under* history)
  of narrative, 54, 66–67, 82–83
time
  as *contemporaneità* (see *contemporaneità*)
  as progress, xvii-xix, 21, 50–53, 65–68, 69–70, 73, 76, 78, 82–83, 117, 137
  cyclical, xvii, xix, 21
  in tension with space, xvi, xviii, 23, 66, 83
  mythical, xvii, 71, 78–81, 97–98, 110–11, 115–18, 123, 161n12
  See also history
Tolstoy, Leo, 82–83
Torriglia, Anna Maria, 165n11
Trajella, don Antonio, 47–48, 160n23
trasformismo, 137
  See also resistance, Rome
travel writing, xvii, xix, 10, 85–123, 163n3, 164n6, 167n26
Treves, Claudio, 2
Turin, xviii, 69
  as opposed to Matera 115, 117–18, 119
  Compare to Rome

undifferentiation. See indistinction

Valiani, Leo, 58
Venere, Giulia, 14–15, 19, 30–41, *40*, *42*, 136
  See also animals, gender, portraits, sexuality
Verga, Giovanni, 109–10
Vico, Giambattista, xvii-xviii, 4, 9–11, 81, 155n13, 155n15, 156n19, 157n28
Virgin Mary, 37, 41
Visconti, Luchino, 109–10
vision, xvi, 62, 87, 110, 114, 127, 130–34, 137
visuality, xvi, 83, 110
visual poetics, xv-xix, 16–19, 24–25, 150–51
Vivarelli, Pia, 143, 157n26

Ward, David, 24, 89, 155n8, 159n9, 164n8, 168n5
White, Hayden, 161n9
word
   and image, 23–26, 28, 37–38, 46, 61–62, 83, 119, 126, 150–51

See also interart dialogue, painting
See also language, poetry

Zaccaro, Vanna, 85, 163n1
Zanardelli, Giuseppe, 119, *120*
Zanzotto, Andrea, 168n5